Kenji Mizoguchi and the
Art of Japanese Cinema

Kenji Mizoguchi and the Art of Japanese Cinema

Tadao Sato

Translated by
Brij Tankha

Edited by
Aruna Vasudev & Latika Padgaonkar

Oxford • New York

The publisher gratefully acknowledges the support of Japan Foundation
and NETPAC in the publication of this book.

English Edition
First published in 2008 by
Berg
Editorial offices:
1st Floor, Angel Court, 81 St Clements Street, Oxford, OX4 1AW, UK
175 Fifth Avenue, New York, NY 10010, USA

English language translation © NETPAC (Network for the Promotion
of Asian Cinema) 2008
Original work © Tadao Sato, 1982. Originally published in Japanese
as *The World of Kenji Mizoguchi* by Chikuma Shobo Publishing Co. Ltd., Tokyo

Berg is the imprint of Oxford International Publishers Ltd.

Library of Congress Cataloguing-in-Publication Data
Sato, Tadao, 1930-
    [Mizoguchi Kenji no sekai. English]
    Kenji Mizoguchi and the art of Japanese cinema / Tadao Sato ;
translated by Brij Tankha ; edited by Aruna Vasudev & Latika
Padgaonkar.
       p. cm.
    Includes bibliographical references and index.
    ISBN 978-1-84788-231-8 (cloth) — ISBN 978-1-84788-230-1
(pbk.) 1. Mizoguchi, Kenji, 1898-1956. 2. Motion picture pro-
ducers and directors—Japan—Biography. I. Vasudev, Aruna. II.
Padgaonkar, Latika. III. Title.

    PN1998.3.M58S2813 2008
    791.43023'3092—dc22   2008010839

British Library Cataloguing-in-Publication Data
A catalogue record for this book is available from the British Library.

ISBN 978 1 84788 231 8 (Cloth)
ISBN 978 1 84788 230 1 (Paper)

Typeset by Avocet Typeset, Chilton, Aylesbury, Bucks
Printed in the United Kingdom by Biddles Ltd, King's Lynn

www.bergpublishers.com

Contents

Author's Note   vii

Editors' Note   ix

1   An Original Spirit   1

2   Encountering the New School Theatre   15

3   From New School Theatre to Naturalism-Realism   31

4   Social Realism   41

5   The Fate of Matinee Idols   55

6   Art Imitates Life   69

7   Three Traditional Art Films (*Geidomono*)   77

8   A Difficult Woman   85

9   Recreating the Classics   97

10 The Last Works   131

11 The Dialectic of Camera and Performance   143

12 Looking Up, Looking Down   163

List of Illustrations   181

Mizoguchi's Filmography   183

List of English and Original Titles of Films of Other Directors Cited
    in the Book   187

Index   189

Author's Note

Between 1922 and 1956 Mizoguchi Kenji made eighty-six films. Among them, *Life of Oharu* (1952), *Ugetsu* (1953), *Sansho the Bailiff* (1954) are masterpieces, widely recognized as the finest expressions of the Asian aesthetic tradition. However, there are many other powerful works as well that deal with the painful experience of people caught in the process of modernization of Japanese society.

This book is an examination of Mizoguchi Kenji's films, but my main interest was to evaluate the position of his work within Japan's social and cultural history.

I have often been asked by foreigners interested in Japanese cinema: who among the great directors, Mizoguchi Kenji, Ozu Yasujiro and Kurosawa Akira, is the most faithful to Japanese tradition, and who has been most influenced by Western culture?

To this question my answer has always been that there has never been a single, pure Japanese culture. Because of the existence of a feudal hierarchy until the middle of the nineteenth century, Japanese culture and its ethical and aesthetic sensibilities were very different from what they are today. It was around this time that the class system was abolished and Westernization and modernization began. The two processes were integrated then and they remain fused even today. However, when it comes to subtle artistic expression, the continuing influence of the earlier class culture on the artist is sharply revealed. Kurosawa Akira, who came from a samurai family, expressed the samurai ethical and aesthetic tradition with skill; Ozu Yasujiro, who belonged to a well-off merchant family, though he himself was not particularly rich, made films that are the finest expression of the petit bourgeois culture created during Japan's modernization; Mizoguchi Kenji's brilliance lay in transferring to the screen the style of kabuki and the tradition of Japanese dance, both products of the merchant culture of feudal Japan. Finally, the name of Imamura Shohei, the film-maker who learnt the most from the largest social class – the farmers – must be mentioned. This is how these directors were linked to tradition in their own special way, but each in his own way struggled, under the influence of Westernization, to create a modern sense of self and transform the individual.

I wrote a series of biographies of these directors from the perspective of this relationship between Japanese films and Japanese culture. This book is one of the series. Therefore, more than the usual sort of study of film, this is a social and cultural history. This is my critical method.

Tadao Sato

Editors' Note

Mizoguchi Kenji, recognized as one of the world's masters of cinema, has invited high praise from film-makers and critics from different parts of the world. But the critical commentary has come principally from Western writers. We have not so far had the good fortune of reading an insider's view, relating his work to Japanese history, thought, customs and traditions that found expression in Mizoguchi's films. Tadao Sato's book on Mizoguchi was first published in Japan in 1982 but has only now been translated into English. It enables us to 'feel' the films, to 'see' how the Japanese viewed him, to understand the subtleties of the Japanese way of thinking, looking, being.

The Japan Foundation gave us at NETPAC-India a grant to get the book translated into English, and we were fortunate enough to be able to draw upon the competence of Brij Tankha for this. Having launched and edited *Cinemaya* (now called *Osian's-Cinemaya*) *The Asian Film Quarterly* for twenty years, for which Tadao Sato was a regular contributor and Brij Tankha our valued translator, made the task somewhat easier. All the same, the names, the spellings, the subtleties of the language presented certain difficulties. We have tried to overcome them, with constant cross-checking by Tadao Sato and his wife Hisako. Jahanara Wasi did a helpful first reading of the manuscript. For Tristan Palmer and Berg Publishers, considerable rewriting and editing had to be carried out. Aparajita B was tireless in the corrections and re-corrections that were required in the preparation of the final manuscript.

We are proud to be associated with this work of Tadao Sato, which is only the second book of the 130 he has written, to be translated into English. We would like to express our gratitude to Tadao Sato for his trust in us, and to NETPAC for its indefatigable promotion of Asian cinema that provided the impetus to embark on this project.

Aruna Vasudev and Latika Padgaonkar

–1–

An Original Spirit

Mizoguchi Kenji, the eldest son of Mizoguchi Zentaro and Masa, was born on 16 May 1898 at No. 11 Shin Hanamachi Yushima in Tokyo's Hongo district. His sister Suzu, was three years older than him and his brother Yoshio seven years younger. Only one brother and one sister are recorded in the family register (*koseki*) and it is not clear whether he had other siblings. The Mizoguchi family had been contractors living in Kaga-cho, Shimbashi, for generations. Zentaro was so striking to look at that a kabuki family had been keen to adopt him. A believer in Nichiren (a thirteenth-century Japanese monk; Nichiren Buddhism is a branch of Buddhism based on his teachings), he seemed to have been a serious and reserved person. His grandchildren were told how, when he was young, he was once taken to a geisha house where he was so frightened that he spent the night curled up in the *tokonoma* (alcove).

Mizoguchi Zentaro carried on the family business, but during the war with Russia saw a new business opportunity in making raincoats. It did not turn out well, and by the end of the war he lost heavily. His two or three other business ventures also failed and, receiving no help from his relatives, his house was auctioned to settle his debts. The family of Kenji's mother, Masa, had been palace doctors for generations. She had been used to a more comfortable life and tried to handle her difficulties as best she could, but her husband's failure in business eventually led to her becoming paralysed. The family then moved to Asakusa and Suzu the daughter, who was just ten, was put into service with Mikawaya, one of the three famous geisha houses in Nihonbashi. Suzu became an apprentice geisha to Ohama, the woman who ran Mikawaya, and who was the lover of Kanagaki Robun.

Born into an impoverished family, Mizoguchi managed to study only up to primary school. He was admitted to Asakusa Tagawa Primary School, a sort of 'temple school' or *terakoya*, and later shifted to Ishihama Primary, a newly established public school in the neighbourhood. Here he studied with Kawaguchi Matsutaro who would later become a novelist. Kawaguchi, too, did not go beyond the primary school level. They were to meet again many years later when Mizoguchi was a director and Kawaguchi an executive at Daiei (he would be directly involved in many of Mizoguchi's films in the 1950s), and became close friends and colleagues. In a conversation in the weekly magazine *Sankei* (25 December 1955) they look back on their early life:

Mizoguchi: It's only now that I have finally stopped going to the pawnshop.

Kawaguchi: Well, if you stop going then the kids will go, won't they? The elder kid probably takes the father's camera or something. It's amazing isn't it? (*laughs*)

Mizoguchi: Hey, you know, I made my wife go to the pawnshop when I got married.

Kawaguchi: Well, I was what you might call an errand boy for the pawnshop. And you... (*laughs*) After graduating from Sanyabori (Tokyo Asakusa) primary school I went to the Fukushimaya pawnshop as an errand boy. It was right in front of the shop selling *kabayaki* boxes.

Mizoguchi: There was a beautiful girl at Fukushimaya.

Kawaguchi: Yes, but she was older then me.

Mizoguchi: That's right.

Kawaguchi: My life in the pawnshop didn't last more than half a year. I was thrown out.

Mizoguchi: You know, in those days ... girls in pawnshops were usually beautiful. This guy has some connection with pawnshop girls. (*Laughs*) There was another one, wasn't there. Takeda's ...? Met her behind the Keio temple.

Mizoguchi: Do you still remember the last time we met when we were young?

Kawaguchi: No, I don't.

Mizoguchi: Well it was on my return. Okabe of Sakanya or Kuko, the *geta* [wooden sandals] seller was with me. We were hanging around. On the street next to Danzaimon there is a large ditch. We were planning to do something when you turned up looking really jaunty in a Tozan kimono, *nomeri geta* and some strange cap.

Kawaguchi: That really happened.

Mizoguchi: There was this beautiful woman in Danzaimon's house.

Kawaguchi: She was there, yeah that's for sure.

Mizoguchi: Then there was Tsumakawa's daughter, Wakabayashi.

Kawaguchi: Yeah, she was also a beauty. She was really close to your house. She went and committed double suicide with a young man named Mizuno.

Mizoguchi: You wrote about that later in *Bungeikurabu*. It really stirred things up. People said: 'He should really be taken apart for writing about friends.' Kuko and Okabe were really angry.

Kawaguchi: It is exactly as in 'Takekurabe'. [*Translator's note*: ref. to a story by Higuchi Ichiyo.]

Their reminiscences bring alive the lives of streetwise kids in the downtown area of a large metropolis, and perhaps it was this cheekiness that shaped them.

As soon as Mizoguchi's sister Suzu, was presented as a *hangyoku* (not as yet a full geisha), she became the lover of Viscount Matsudaira Tadamasa, who was nine years older than her. The Matsudaira family were originally *daimyo* (powerful feudal rulers) from Ueda in Shinshu. Although deeply in love with her he was, nonetheless, a thoroughly indecisive man. Suzu soon became pregnant but had an abortion, probably to protect the honour of the Viscount's family. It was a time when the marriage of an aristocrat had to be approved by the Imperial Household Ministry and marrying a geisha was absolutely prohibited. Suzu continued to live in the house the Viscount had given her in Asakusa where she bore him four children. Soon after her first child was born, the bachelor Matsudaira was married off to a 'proper' wife from another aristocratic family. From his family residence in Eiihara, Shinagawa, he would occasionally go to Akasuka to visit his concubine. Suzu, like her father, was a follower of Nichiren.

When she was eighteen, Suzu's sick mother and her brother Kenji came to live with her. Kenji, who had just finished primary school, spent his time hanging around the neighbourhood. With her youngest brother, the seven-year-old Yoshio, also in her care, Suzu carried the burden of looking after the whole family, including her father who lived nearby. In 1915 her mother's condition deteriorated. She was admitted to Fuji Hospital in Asakusa where she died in October. Suzu paid for everything.

At the age of eighteen Mizoguchi did not have a fixed job. Suzu took him to learn a profession from Watanabe, a designer and draughtsman, in Imatogawa. The following year she moved to Nihonbashi while Mizoguchi moved to a draughtsman's place in Hamacho. However, he did not hold on to his job. He then joined Kuroda Kiyoteru's's Aoibashi Western Painting Research Institute at

FIGURE 1 Mizoguchi Kenji

Akasaka Tameike City to learn oil painting. The head of the school was Wada Sanzo. This one year was the only time Mizoguchi spent as a regular student. Around that time a comic opera was staged by the Rossi couple – a husband-and-wife team – at the Akasaka Royal Hall nearby and the Institute was asked to design the backdrop. As he worked on this project, Mizoguchi became an opera fan and began frequenting the Asakusa Opera. He loved the professional storytellers and *rakugo* (Japanese verbal entertainment) of the vaudeville, and devoured the novels of Tolstoy, Maupassant, Soseki, Ozaki, Izumi and Kafu. The year was 1917.

The same year he obtained a post in the advertising department of the *Kobe Yuishin* Journal. But this, too, he quit within a year and returned to Tokyo, although why he stopped working at the newspaper is not clear. He was just twenty and getting to the age when he needed to have a proper job, but had not come across one that he felt he could do for the rest of his life. Those times were different from today when a successful job interview after high school or university leads to a lifetime career. Then, young men would become apprentices after primary school, and if the job did not interest them, they would simply leave. It was not unusual to change jobs frequently and go back home several times. In the process many were left unqualified and found themselves over the age limit for learning a profession. Adults worried about the young who only thought about themselves and had no tenacity. Mizoguchi's sister, too, was anxious about him though it must have been a difficult time for Mizoguchi himself.

Film Studios in the 1920s

Mizoguchi was friendly with Tomioka Tadashi, a young actor in the Nikkatsu studio at Mukojima, and with a few other artists as well. Tomioka asked Mizoguchi whether he would consider becoming an actor in action films, like himself, and introduced him to the director Wakayama Osamu. However, it turned out that while there was no requirement for an actor, there was an opening for an assistant. Mizoguchi thus became an assistant director in 1920 when he was twenty-two years old.

When Mizoguchi announced that he wanted to join a film studio, his father and sister were not in favour of it but agreed reluctantly at his insistence. It was a normal reaction because in the common imagination films were associated with *yakuza* and wastrels. About ten years after Mizoguchi joined Nikkatsu Studio in Mukojima, the scriptwriter Yoda Yoshikata, who had joined the Kyoto Nikkatsu Studio in Uzumasa, had this to say about the people working at the studio in the early 1930s.

> The Senbon gang was led by a man who fought for the underdog and was involved with Nikkatsu. The head of the Nikkatsu Studio, Ikenaga Hirohisa, was himself a member of the gang which by and large controlled everyone working in the departments that dealt with large or small equipment or lights. Many of the older people sported tattoos. The owner of the small restaurant 'Ronda' – built soon after the studio came up – the

transport division, and Nagata Masakazu or 'Machan' who would often buttonhole people and harangue them and who also acted as a guide at the studio, were all associated with the Senbon gang and almost all these fellows were from the same primary school as I was. Most people associated with action films at the time, both actors as well as those in other jobs, were young, and as one can imagine there was not one who had not gone through an uncertain and aimless period in his life. Fights were common and those beaten up were carried away and plunged into the developing bath. I have seen young men coming out from the bath dyed an apricot colour. There seemed to be no reason for this. There were even times when someone who became an assistant director would be taken to the back and pummelled by the young actors. I also heard of a cameraman who came to work drunk and carrying a knife. (Yoshikata Yoda, *Mizoguchi Kenji, The Man and the Art* (Mizoguchi Kenji no hito to geijutsu))

Nagata Masakazu, nicknamed Machan, soon became responsible for Number One Film, an independent production company. He had Mizoguchi make the immortal classics *Osaka Elegy* and *Sisters of the Gion.* As the head of Daiei in the 1940s and 1950s, he was also the producer of a series of famous films made by Mizoguchi in his last years.

Yoda Yoshikata's comments on the Nikkatsu studio in Kyoto in the 1930s are fairly representative since most Japanese film studios of the day were much the

FIGURE 2 Left to right: Mizoguchi Kenji at twenty-eight, actress Sakai Yoneko and distributor Kawakita Nagamasa. Photograph taken at the Nikkatsu Kyoto Studio in 1926.

same. Their transformation into modern companies started when Toho began producing films in the style of a properly managed company. This led to a decline in the acceptance of yakuza and other shady characters, and to a reduction in the fear psychosis surrounding the industry. A period of militarism began from the end of the 1930s. People in the film world stopped being wayward and supported the spread of this ideology by making very serious films that went on to receive awards.

But maybe there was something good about it being normal to see yakuza and other layabouts. In any case, because it was that sort of a world, formal qualifications were not expected from those working in the studios. Some were university graduates and some, like Mizoguchi, had only done primary school. Interestingly, those who belonged to left-wing movements, those thrown out of universities or fired from companies, were easily absorbed here. Although the yakuza and the leftists held diametrically opposed positions, they joined ranks when it came to their common enemy – the police. Initially, Yoda Yoshikata was a bank employee but because of his involvement with the movement, he was fired from his job and joined the film studio.

An assistant director named Seikichi Terakado would often pick fights with the master, Mizoguchi. But such was the force of his ideas that Mizoguchi would incorporate many of them into his ambitious projects. Not much is known about Seikichi Terakado's life. According to one version he had secretly entered the Soviet Union, graduated from the Far Eastern Communist University, returned to Japan and joined a left-wing cadre. It appears he used the pen name of Terakado Seiken, a popular Edo period writer, and that he had converted, discarding his ideology to be able to cast an ironic look at the world. It was only in cinema that someone like him could work with the yakuza. Strange was this world where a successful yakuza – who had moved up in the world to become an industrialist – and the left-wing cadre – which had fallen as his ideology crumbled – could live in harmony.

In was quite normal for people to view young people like Mizoguchi, who had neither a fixed job nor a skill, just a great love for literature and art, as simply immature. The film industry was one of the few places willing to employ them. There is no evidence to show that Mizoguchi had any passionate interest in cinema – nor had Japanese cinema reached a stage where it was possible to be passionate about it.

After a little over a year at the studio, Mizoguchi – true to his nature – wanted to quit. It was Suzu who persuaded him to stay on. Nikkatsu was in turmoil over the banning of *onnagata* (men who play women's roles) and all of a sudden there was an opportunity for Mizoguchi to become a director. The idea of quitting vanished.

In an interview with Kawaguchi Matsutaro, Mizoguchi speaks about the conditions prevailing in the film studio:

Mizoguchi: At first I said I wanted to be an actor. That wasn't possible so I became an assistant director. Assistant directors sometimes acted as well.

Kawaguchi: You did everything, didn't you?

Mizoguchi: In today's terms I was a sceneshifter. I did the job of an actor, of a technician. I even did the developing.

Kawaguchi: In the old days assistant directors held the reflector, directed the lights and did whatever had to be done. Today there are unions, and the reflector is the responsibility of the light boys. [Abbreviated – *TS*]

Kawaguchi: There were no lights then, were there?

Mizoguchi: Lights did begin to be used around that time. Stage footlights and the dark stage as opposed to the natural lights of the glass stage.

Kawaguchi: The dark stage was there from the beginning ... (*Laughs*)

Mizoguchi: Well, not everyone knew about reflectors at that time. The year I joined a location team arrived from America. When we went to see them they were using a reflector with silver paper. I began to do the same as it was really convenient. Then I began to use silver paper on the shoji (a room divider or door consisting of translucent paper over a wooden frame) as well. (*Laughs*)

Directors and the Nikkatsu Mukojima Film Studio

The renowned cameraman, Ohbora Gengo, recalls that Mizoguchi was a polite and industrious young man. He first worked as an assistant to Oguchi Tadashi, one of Japanese cinema's earliest directors. In an early interview, Mizoguchi said Ohbora had previously worked in the Shinpa (New School Theatre) group, but little is known about his life there. Mizoguchi joined them in 1908, the year after the Yoshizawa house established a film studio in Meguro Gyojinzaka. The studio had a creative department which collected stories and another which trained actors for in-house productions. He worked under the section chief and melodrama writer, Sato Koroku. In 1913, when the Japan Motion Pictures Limited Company (Nikkatsu) built a glass-roofed film studio where you could film under natural light (the so-called glass stage), the prolific Sato Koroku shifted there as playwright and director. Using mainly New School Theatre material he made twenty films in 1918 – including *The Forsaken Mother* and *Rain of Tears* – nineteen in 1919 and twenty in 1920, when Mizoguchi worked as his assistant.

According to the critic Kishi Matsuo, who based his writing on what he had heard from Kinugasa Teinosuke, a star at the Nikkatsu Mukojima Film Studio, the situation there was as follows:

Oguchi followed a strict routine of two days on the set and three days on location, producing a film in a few days. He was really prolific. People like Kinugasa Teinosuke, who joined the company because of their passion for films, and Tanaka Eizo who worked briefly as an assistant to Oguchi, wondered whether this was the right approach. In those days they just read the script out aloud. No directions were given on how to act and most things were left to the cameraman. (*Collected Works of Japanese Film Directors* (Nihon Eiga kantoku zenshu) Kinemajunpo-sha)

However, not all directors were like Oguchi Tadashi. Suzuki Kensaku, for instance, was a stickler for getting things right. It was said that when he started a film, no one knew when it would be completed. He was perhaps the first Japanese director to experiment with realism. In *Man's Pain* (1923) – his most representative film – one of the actors who had to play the role of a starving man was ordered not to eat for a while. He obeyed faithfully and played the role in a starved and weakened state. It was just a walk-on role but the cameraman made a mistake in the speed of the film. The result was that while the man was supposed to drag himself along slowly, what actually appeared was him flashing comically across the screen. The actor exclaimed, 'I'll kill that damned Suzuki.' He took a gun to the studio and chased the director. This is a story that I heard directly from Inagaki Hiroshi, a young actor at the studio and who later won the Golden Lion at the Venice Film Festival for his film, *The Rickshaw Man*.

Frustrated with the Modern Theatre movement (Shingeki) that had come under the influence of Western theatre, Tanaka Eizo joined the film studio and worked briefly as Oguchi Tadashi's assistant. His artistic and richly pictorial work captured the Japanese spirit and skilfully guided actors in painting delicate psychological portraits. After working for Oguchi Tadashi, Mizoguchi became an assistant to Tanaka Eizo and learnt a great deal from him. However, directors like Suzuki Kensaku or Tanaka Eizo, or actors with artistic ambitions like Kinugasa Teinosuke, were still the exception.

Today an assistant director is an aspiring artist who stands at the top of the industry, and belongs to a select super class. When Mizoguchi entered the film world he may have been called an assistant director but his job was little more than that of a general handyman. Even the director had nothing to do with guiding the performance or devising new cinematic techniques. He had merely to ensure that shooting went according to schedule. The camera was fixed for each scene and actors performed as they saw fit. The director would sit next to the camera, read the scenario out aloud, make sure that the actor was within the frame and just fix the basic movements. It was not a job that required any special training; for an assistant director, primary level education sufficed to be accepted. Within two years of assiduous work as an assistant doing everything that was asked of him, Mizoguchi was promoted to director.

However, unlike Mizoguchi, not everyone who became a director had only had basic education. Wakayama Osamu, the director who took Mizoguchi into the Nikkatsu studio, was twelve years older than Mizoguchi (he was born in 1886) and had finished middle school. Suzuki Kensaku, from whom Mizoguchi learnt how to construct a drama, was thirteen years his senior, and had graduated from a commercial school. Tanaka Eizo, Mizoguchi's master and twelve years older than him, was an intellectual who had struggled to graduate from a technical college. He went on to study at the Tokyo Actors School.

Among Mizoguchi's contemporaries, director Murata Minoru – a friendly rival who worked in the same studio at the end of the silent film era – was the scion of a rich family which supported the choices he made. After graduating from the elite school attached to the Tokyo Higher Teachers' College, he worked in the Modern Theatre movement. He was first a stage actor, and later a film director; he was four years older than Mizoguchi.

Kinugasa Teinosuke, who was two years older than Mizoguchi, also came from an affluent family. He did primary school, studied English, and at fifteen left home to become an actor in the New School Theatre movement. When Mizoguchi joined Nikkatsu Mukojima Studio, he was a popular *onnagata* star, but recognizing the limitations of *onnagata* roles, he switched to working as a director. Kinugasa was bored with the basic style of acting in films and felt that by dividing the shot more finely, a work with greater cinematic appeal could be produced.

As a rule, directors did no more than shoot according to schedule. But not all. Suzuki Kensaku felt dissatisfied with the budding realist style, and Tanaka Eizo began to incorporate the aestheticism of the New School Theatre into his cinema. Well before indigenous artistic and technical developments had matured in Japanese films, most directors had been exposed to foreign films – D.W. Griffith, Eric von Stroheim or Chaplin – and Japanese films had felt the impact of *The Cabinet of Dr Caligari.* In Mizoguchi's generation anybody wishing to become a director (irrespective of his educational background) had been awe-struck by foreign films and began joining the studios. Ushihara Kyohiko, a year older than Mizoguchi, was the first graduate from Tokyo Imperial University to want to be a director. But while he did achieve top educational honours, he was denied permission to join industry by the former ruler of Kumamoto, from whom he had received a scholarship. His contemporary Shimazu Yasujiru had passed middle school. Mizoguchi's contemporary Ito Daisuke finished middle school, went to Tokyo to attend lectures at Meiji University, learnt theatre acting under Osanai Kaoru, wrote scripts and then moved to direction. Another contemporary, Uchida Tomu, did two years of middle school, moved to odd jobs, and finally entered the film world. Futagawa Buntaro, a year younger than Mizoguchi, who showed considerable acting skills in the early samurai dramas of Bando Tsumasaburo, left Chuo University. Tasaka Tomotaka, four years younger, left No. 3 High School midway while Gosho Heinosuke, from the same high school, graduated from Keio Commercial College and Yamamoto Kajiro from Keio University.

Slowly graduates from high school and university started joining up, though there were still examples of people like Inagaki Hiroshi (born in 1905) who began as a child actor and therefore hardly attended even primary school, but still went on to became a master. Mizoguchi's disciple, Shindo Kaneto (born in 1912), graduated in science from high school and is today among the top names in Japanese cinema.

Those with basic education found it difficult to compete with their better-educated counterparts. The industry attracted people with grit and determination. Qualities like intelligence were not deemed necessary. They learned to make films by imbibing the craft through a master-disciple apprenticeship. But with each passing year, film-making seemed to demand a higher intellectual understanding and those who could not keep up, like some of the old workmanlike directors, fell by the wayside. Even the technical expertise acquired through years of work was not enough. What was needed to keep pace and stay ahead of the younger lot was a fiercely combative spirit and continuous study.

Time of Self-Cultivation and Aptitude

Mizoguchi became a director at the Nikkatsu Mukojima studio in 1922. In the summer of 1923, when the studio was destroyed in the great Kanto earthquake, Mizoguchi moved to Kyoto where Nikkatsu had another studio. He was to work subsequently with many other studios, moving from Nikkatsu to Shinko Kinema, Daiichi Eiga, Shochiku, Toho, Shin Toho, Daiei and others. His base, however, was Kyoto.

Always sensitive to the new and fashionable, Mizoguchi feared he would fall behind the times if he did not relocate to Tokyo. He tried frequently to work in the capital but for some reason most of his Tokyo work – with the exception of *The Straits of Love and Hate* (1937) – was a failure, either because he had problems adjusting to a new city, or because he was not blessed with a good support staff, or perhaps for both these reasons. Kyoto more than Tokyo had innumerable old-style artisans. Among the staff and actors, many shared Mizoguchi's demand for thorough craftsmanship and dedication. Not one to bother with details himself, Mizoguchi let his staff handle a variety of problems. What he needed most of all was to gather around him a group of excellent and sincere people who understood his working style. He would give them tasks to do, and then would make changes and take the final decision.

Working in Kyoto – the home of the traditional arts – for most of his life had a decisive influence on Mizoguchi. He studied *kabuki, noh* and traditional Japanese dance and music. To study *kabuki* or *bunraku* (traditional puppet theatre) meant learning playwriting techniques and going back to the origins of the performance techniques. *Kabuki*, particularly in Osaka and Kyoto, centred on the role of a handsome youth. Mizoguchi had a deep knowledge of tradition and his extensive study allowed him to produce some artistic masterpieces in the 1940s and 1950s. Films such as *The Life of Oharu, Ugetsu* and *A Story from Chikamastu* are based on material from classical literature and drama which Mizoguchi used with assured knowledge.

It was refreshing to see the way a Tokyo person looked at human relations and customs in the *Kansai* (near Osaka). Mizoguchi's *Osaka Elegy* was the first film to use the Osaka dialect and show Osaka customs.

Close friends of Mizoguchi have said that he was a voracious reader. He worked tirelessly and expected the same effort from those who worked with him. Tanaka Kinuyo, the lead actress in *A Woman of Osaka*, went from Tokyo to Kyoto to meet him. Mizoguchi would send books wrapped in cloth (*furoshiki*) to her hotel through his assistant Sakane Tazuko. This carried on for some time and there was no sign of shooting the film. All he kept telling her was, 'Just read these books, just read them.' *A Woman of Osaka* is a work based on the world of *bunraku* and Tanaka Kinuyo's role is that of a smart, strong wife who encourages her husband to become a master of the *samisen*. The books sent to her were all specialized works on *bunraku*. On a normal working day, Tanaka Kinuyo would be hurrying from one location to another; but this time she found the change relaxing and enjoyed the time she had to read. Mizoguchi believed that to understand *bunraku* one had first to study it carefully.

Like Mizoguchi, Tanaka Kinuyo, too, did not have much of an education, and she took this demand to study as a challenge. The more she read, the more she was fired by a competitive spirit. Mizoguchi's emphasis on reading extended to other actors as well. When Kagawa Kyoko played Anju, the woman slave in *Sansho the Bailiff*, Mizoguchi asked her to study the history of the medieval slave system to understand and identify with the character. Moreover, he wanted his staff to put in the same effort as he did. Yoshimura Kozaburo writes in his memoirs, *The Life of Film*, about how he saw Mizoguchi in a flaming temper on the sets of *My Love Burns*. 'These fellows are all turncoats,' he shouted. 'They are rebels who will destroy Japanese cinema!' Yoshimura Kozaburo wondered what had caused this outburst. It turned out that Mizoguchi was enraged at the way the set was being built and because the shooting was not going as scheduled.

I believe this is behaviour typical of a self-made man whose exaggerated anger is like a flash of lightning, like a father's anger. Self-made men who reach the top often feel that their accomplishment is based not only on their abilities but on sheer hard work. Nothing makes them angrier than when that effort is perceived to be lacking, when people rise in their professions simply because they are better educated, good-looking or naturally gifted.

There is a story of the scriptwriter, Yoda Yoshikata, who arrived in Tokyo and went to one of the city's best restaurants with Mizoguchi. As they entered they found that the cook had wheeled in a wagon next to the tables and was grilling steaks over the charcoal fire with great flair. Mizoguchi was really taken by this and burst out, 'This is it. This is it. If you retreat to a place like Kyoto you don't expect to see such new things.'

What the chef was doing was indeed innovative but Yoda Yoshitaka was embarrassed by Mizoguchi's naïve enthusiasm and by the amused looks of the other guests This interest and absorption in the 'new' to the point that nothing else mattered was typical of the director whose aim was always be a step ahead of the others. In his early days as a director he would often use translations of foreign novels or copies of foreign films. Perhaps his return in later years to a serious, traditional aesthetic was his way of breaking away from this superficial fascination with the 'new'.

Several instances illustrate Mizoguchi's almost comic love for the new. He was not satisfied just reading the novels he liked, he also read books that were being talked about by his friends. If a friend – Seikichi Terakado for instance – discussed a new literary trend or an intellectual problem, and if Mizoguchi was asked if he had read about it, he would never admit he hadn't. He would say something to the effect that he had a general idea. He would then immediately send out his assistant to buy a book that explained the problem and read it at one go. Thus, not to outdone by smart young men, he would bluff his way through. Often he would just recycle what he had heard but understood only superficially.

During the filming of *Ugetsu*, he asked Yoda Yoshikata for some revision in the first script, stressing that Yoda must study Salvador Dali. It is not clear how far Mizoguchi actually understood Dali, or Dali's relevance to his own work. Yoda understood the words to mean that since Mizoguchi was looking at Dali he wanted a surrealist treatment, and he therefore rewrote the scenario with an abundance of surrealist imagery. But this, it seems, was not what the director had wanted him to do. However, since Mizoguchi had asked for a revision and the script had been revised, he did not admit that it was not what he wanted. Irritated, he took the script to the Daiei head, Nagata Masakazu. When Nagata said that he could not understand it, Mizoguchi felt justified in reverting to the original script. After that Mizoguchi never spoke of Dali again.

This is how Mizoguchi would regurgitate undigested ideas. But his sensitivity about his modest education prevented him from being able to laugh at his lack of a broad knowledge base. This is not to say that all university graduates have a basic understanding of Salvador Dali and surrealism; but the well-educated are at least secure in their learning and rarely feel embarrassed that they do not know what that is outside their field of learning; they are frank, not apologetic, about their ignorance. People like Mizoguchi have a sense of insecurity about their poor education and lack of a well-rounded culture. They tend to store up unrelated bits of information and rarely confess their ignorance, fearing that they will be looked upon as fools.

Bluffing means pretending to know something that you don't. It is generally taken as a sign of shallowness. Mizoguchi bluffed without any constraint, unafraid that he would be exposed. He went further, straining to prove that his bluff was not a lie. Deception is an integral part of the world of cinema. It is not criticized for being superficial; rather, it is praised as an indication of a lovable childishness. Mizoguchi demanded a colossal effort from those around him and for this was feared and respected. That he would not permit cutting corners became part of a respected tradition in the cinema world and was passed on with pride. It boosted the morale of his colleagues and it made it easier to get good budgets.

Mizoguchi once told Tanaka Kinuyo that Japanese actors did not really know the life of the bourgeoisie and they could not play bourgeois characters. Tanaka took this as a challenge and immediately bought a fine residence to see what living there felt like. Although she lived alone and felt that a hotel was far more convenient than a large house, she took this as a game and played it in earnest when she bought the house. Mizoguchi seemed to have been surrounded by people who took up the challenges he threw at them in earnest. Sometimes it was more than a game and some came out as losers.

Earlier, in the era of silent films, Irie Takako, a lead actress and production supervisor, had got Mizoguchi to produce many well-known films. In later years when she had lost her star status, she made a comeback with the help of her many friends. She was given a small role in Mizoguchi's film, *Princess Yang Kwei-fei*. He made her practise this simple role repeatedly and, getting quite ill-tempered, refused to be satisfied. He had agreed to taking her on because the company had demanded it; in no way, he claimed, was he working to help unemployed actresses. Irie Takako understood Mizoguchi's feelings and withdrew from the role. He then had the company ask for the famous actress Sugimura Haruko. Irie Takako felt so insulted that she gave up acting for good. Mizoguchi's close friends, who knew how big a star Irie Takako had been in his earlier films, were incensed. They felt he was being really heartless. But Mizoguchi maintained that if a person was not useful for his work he would have no compunction in getting rid of him or her. Since he himself put in so much work, he added, so too, should his co-workers. Only those who could keep up with his enthusiasm could make a name for themselves in his films.

In the early days of the talkies Yamada Isuzu appeared in *Osaka Elegy* and *Sisters of the Gion*, two masterpieces that made a name for Mizoguchi. The daughter of an actor father and an artist mother, she became an actress herself at the age of fourteen, playing roles of winsome young girls. In her autobiography, *Together with Films* (Eiga to tomo ni, 1953), she recalls these two landmark works which marked her transition from a sweet young thing to a great actress:

Mizoguchi-san was always very nice but when work started he became difficult. Physically too, the work was extremely strenuous. I am certain it was in *The Downfall of Osen* (1934) that for long hours I had my head stuck in a washing bowl half-alive and half-dead. But for Mizoguchi-san it was all quite normal.

However, during a break on a cold day waiting for the set to be cleared, if I said, 'It is cold isn't it', he would cover me with an overcoat. I thought that if he really is like this it would be better if he were a little kinder during work as well.

In those days the critics labelled him a sadist. Certainly he was extremely ambitious about his work, and as an artist he had a passion for thoroughness. However, I was never afraid of that. I never uttered a complaint. While making a film the relationship between a director and an actor can be, on the surface at least, acrimonious. But it sparkles inside. Mizoguchi's technique is a typical example of this.

Among Mizoguchi's early supporters quite a few were self-made men – Kawaguchi Matsutaro and Nagata Masakazu among others. The scriptwriter Yoda Yoshikata was an alumnus of a commercial school. Many of the actors were not what can be called intellectuals but they were certainly able to handle Mizoguchi's provocative pretence.

In the introduction to *The Collected Screenplays of Yoda Yoshikata* (Yoda Yoshikata scenarioshu, 1946) Mizoguchi wrote:

> Yoda-kun worked very hard for many years for me, just like a wife. I basically hate talking. Really, I think words lack freedom. I always think impatiently so that before speaking I am already irritated at not finding the proper words. So I always come across as some raging beast. People think I say things unnecessarily, but it's not I who am at fault. It is language itself that is to blame. Yoda-kun understood that about me so he would let me have my say and carry on with his work.
>
> I think no one understands Yoda-kun's working style better than me. His first draft is never very interesting. When I point this out he changes it dramatically and produces a really outrageous second draft. I don't know how many times I have been embarrassed by such revisions. Even if the first wasn't really interesting, by and large it achieved what it set out to do. The second draft is almost the opposite of the first. If you tell him what you think of it he will bring a third draft. At this point an unrecognisable glow is released. [Abbreviated from original – *TS*]

–2–

Encountering the New School Theatre

History and Background of Japanese Melodrama

Soap operas are extremely popular on television today. Directed mainly at the house-wife, they show elegant, well-groomed women in their thirties and forties who spend an inordinate amount of time trying to form relationships with men. The men regard these beautiful women as something more than mere objects of sexual desire; they also respect their character and spirit. Middle-aged women who constitute the majority of the viewers, have begun to feel that they should receive this kind of respectful attention in their own relations with men. But reality is very different from soap operas, and the attitudes of men vary greatly with age. Men in Japan can be highhanded, but in younger men this arrogance appears to be on the decline.

The possibilities of ordinary friendships between the sexes in the younger generation have given rise to a special type of soap opera where the 'respectful' treatment of women is so ludicrous it appears exaggerated. If it's equality that we're after, then this artificially imposed attitude towards women is the reverse of male imperiousness. On the other hand, if male violence against women has decreased, it is because the idea of gender equality has gained acceptance in society. Perhaps soap operas have played a role in promoting these ideas.

Respect towards women was difficult to find during the Edo or the Meiji period. In *kabuki*, highborn princesses are treated with great respect not because of their innate character but because of their social status.

Newspaper articles on crime inform us that the incidence of adultery in the early Meiji period was very high. We know of cases where a mother petitioned against the father's relations with their adopted daughter (1872, in Tokyo); where a daughter was raped by her real father and, when enticed into other relationships, surrendered to the police (1873, in Tokyo); where a husband who petitioned against his wife's adulterous relationship was in turn accused by his wife of relations with his own stepmother. In all these cases, both parties were punished. We also have an instance of a wife accusing her husband of an illicit relationship, and though the man was given three years' imprisonment, the wife, because she had accused her husband, had to pay a fine of seven yen fifty sen (1873, in Shimane).

Many unsavoury and incestuous relations within the family were treated as crimes. For example, in 1873 (Meiji 6) in Tokyo's Honjho Yanagishima-cho district, a father raped his daughter during his wife's absence. The daughter ran away to live with a family running a restaurant, but she was called back to nurse her ailing father. Subsequently, a complaint was lodged at the local police station (*koban*) that she was being sold off as a concubine. However, the father died while the case was being heard. This young woman was quoted as saying, 'I have lost my moral standing because of this transgression and deserve to be given life imprisonment. When I was young I was put in debt for thirty-five yen' (*Tokyo Nichinichi Shinbun*, 30 October 1873). This was large sum in those days. The court actually threatened this woman who sought punishment against her rapist father, who later sold her as a concubine. She was told that because she was young the court was being generous, and that she actually deserved to be given a life sentence. I do not know what happened to her – she disappeared from the records. Did she pay off the debt, one wonders? It was a time when poor women with financial problems sold themselves to brothels.

But these crime stories about ordinary women in the early Meiji period in Japan also show that not all women who were ill-treated by men sat and wept quietly, and resigned themselves to their fate. A fair number retaliated by taking their cases to court. However, any fightback by women was seen as a crime under the law. In case of an appeal against adultery committed by a man, not only would the man be punished, but the wife, too, would be sentenced. It was not that women had a poor understanding of human rights – they were crushed by the courts. And while it is unclear how people reacted to the logic of the court, there is, in fact, little evidence to show that people thought of it as unfair (apart from those women who fought back, like a mouse cornered by a cat). It is likely that most people accepted the judgements as correct.

True, this was a part of feudal thinking which sought to justify male dominance; but it was also supported by the notion of male-female discrimination inherent in Confucianism and the form that Buddhism took in Japan. The idea that women are born sinners meant that even a compassionate Bodhisattva would find it difficult to save her. Women must subordinate themselves to men – this was the credo of the times, and its practice stands clearly revealed when women were punished, even when they were the victims.

The true story of the murder of Takahashi Oden, known as the Vampire, became notorious in the early Meiji period. Although Takahashi Oden's plight should have aroused public sympathy, she was called a vampire (wicked woman) precisely because of the kind of thinking described above. Since a woman's very existence was regarded as fundamentally a sin, all she could do was try and live modestly and chastely to prevent her true nature from surfacing. She must not try and exercise her own judgement, but must depend on the judgement of men. In fact it was preferable for a raped woman to believe that the devil in her had lured the man into committing the crime, rather than to blame the man's evil nature. If she thought for herself or acted independently, she would be giving free rein to wickedness, and the consequences would be frightening. Such ideas were deeply rooted, and they showed up in exaggerated stories. Takahashi Oden's story is an example of this.

Conversations with the Demon Takahashi Oden, written in 1879 under the pen name Kanagaki Robun, is regarded as the most representative work to define the role of women before modern melodrama came to Japan, although the first work in the period of women's modern melodrama is *Hototogisu*. Written by Tokutomi Roka and serialized in a newspaper in 1898, this is a landmark novel because the woman with a pure heart is extolled as a man's ideal object of devotion. Based on a traditional theme from the feudal period, the novel initially stirred the people who saw it as the tragedy of a young wife harassed by her mother-in-law. This very traditional theme captured the hearts of the conservative-minded; however, since it opposed the prevailing attitude of regarding women as contemptible and, on the contrary, praised them as objects of worship, it explains why it became one of the avant-garde works of popular culture of the new age.

It is well known that the model for Nami, the heroine of the novel, was the daughter of the aristocrat, General Oyama Iwao. Had she been a character in *kabuki*, she would have been a princess. The feudal notion of status underlies the respectful and courteous style in which her noble character is described. When it became a best-seller, this work set the trend for tragic family novels which soon began to be serialized in newspapers. Their popularity continued until the Taisho period. Most of them had either a daughter of an aristocrat or a woman of high status as the heroine or, alternatively, a woman from an old family who was wooed by a young man from a noble house whom she then married. Initially the idea of honouring women developed as an extension of the feudal notion of prostrating oneself before a princess.

Tokutomi Roka attacks the ill treatment of the daughter-in-law by the mother-in-law and defends her fundamental rights. This was the result of the deep influence of Christianity, the new philosophy of the times. Children of the educated upper classes welcomed it as modern and even fashionable. How far Christian philosophy actually respects women is another matter; after all, in Catholicism, God is the father. The basic idea is that by honouring the father, you honour the male. However, Christianity entered Japan not just as a religion but as a new Western fashion, and the worship of women was integral to it.

What does worshipping women mean? Medieval chivalric romances show us that this became a part of Western thought with the introduction of Madonna-worship in Christianity. The worship of Mother Mary cannot be separated from the essential teachings of Christianity. Why should this be so, especially in Catholicism where it is a sturdily held belief? The worship of Mother Mary is particularly strong in Italy, as is the power of the mother within the family; so, too, in the Philippines, with its tradition of matrilineal families. Under Spanish domination Filipinos were converted to Catholicism and there arose a unique form of Christianity in which the worship of Mother Mary became even more entrenched than in the original religion, perhaps because the idea of the absolute power of the father in Christianity did not harmonize with the country's indigenous culture. It is through the worship of Mother Mary that a balance was struck with the worship of the patriarch.

The chivalric romances of knights are full of adulterous stories. The knights are supposed to set out on their adventures because of their Christian faith but, in reality, it is either for the sake of their lord's honour or because of their passionate love for a woman, sometimes the wife of a senior knight. As Christianity forbids adultery, it is contradictory that knights smitten by adulterous love set out in its name. This, too, is an expression of an unorthodox philosophy, arising out of a secret resistance to the authoritarianism of Christianity's male-centredness which demands absolute obedience to a patriarchal God. In these romances of chivalrous knights, it is from the woman more than from God the Father that the man derives his sense of honour, leading to the idea that the knight will battle against his lord who is the husband of the noblewoman whom he seeks to honour through his worship.

All of this is very different from Japanese *bushido* which is often compared to the spirit of chivalry among knights. According to the code of chivalry, should a conflict arise between the knight's love for his lady and his loyalty to his lord, the knight must without hesitation choose his lady love. In the code of *bushido*, on the other hand, the samurai must unhesitatingly choose loyalty to his lord and sacrifice his love for the lady. If a person – perhaps a merchant rather than a samurai – fails to do so, the lovers must commit suicide together; they would thus fulfil at one stroke their love for each other and apologize to their lord for their transgression. I take the argument further by stating that the tradition of fighting the lord for the love of a woman, although feudal in its origin, has become the basic philosophy for modern individualism and democracy.

Tales of chivalric knights were very popular in medieval Europe, but they died out because many of the stories were rather absurd. But the idea of the hero winning the heroine at the end, however, became the archetype of all Western melodrama. When this melodrama entered Japan after the Meiji period through novels, plays and films, the Japanese found to their astonishment that the dignity lay with the women, while the men went down on their knees before them. Intellectually, too, women were represented in a much better light than they were in Japan.

The playwright Akimoto Matsuyo, who was born in 1911, reminisces about the plays he went to see as a child with his mother:

> The plays we saw in those days were mostly *kabuki* and those I liked were all about a world steeped in violent terror. People were killed, or killed themselves for love. It was the hour of death and the place soaked in blood, women were lamenting, and men and women in strange costumes, dancing.

I saw only one truly wonderful actress in those plays: Matsui Sumako in the role of Katushya in *Resurrection* and that scene is engraved in my memory. The arrogant, laughing face of the Western 'lady' pouring scorn on the elegantly dressed Nekhlyudov who pays a call on her – it was a scene out of hell. Even as my eyes were captivated by the wonderful scene, I noted with surprise that there were women like this in the West. Yet it was only on that one occasion that this kind of a 'lady' appeared in a play. All the other plays had sad Japanese women or women who were murdered. (Akimoto Matsuyo, *The Time of My Mother* (Saigetsu no naka no haha) in *Plays and the Artistic Life* (Gikyoku to jisseikatsu), Heibonsha Publishers)

Resurrection was a Modern Theatre play based, quite patently, on Tolstoy's story, and Matsui Sumako was the renowned stage star about whom Mizoguchi Kenji would make a film, *The Love of Sumako the Actress* in 1947, showing her as a pioneer of the women's liberation movement. Akimoto Matsuyo probably saw *Resurrection* in the latter half of the 1910s, but by then women had begun to be depicted with a certain dignity. New and modern scenes that portrayed a more respectful attitude towards women, and expressed men's remorse for their wrongdoing were viewed with surprise. But such plays began to influence young women to think differently. After all, there was no tradition of tales of chivalry in Japanese culture. On the contrary, women were either looked upon as impure, as in Buddhism, or discriminated against, as in Confucianism. No wonder 'women were always crying and sad' or were being killed in both *kabuki* and the New School Theatre.

The concept of double suicide, a much-loved theme, where a weak-willed but handsome man falls in love with a prostitute in the pleasure quarters and the two end up killing themselves, was very different. Love as an ideal – which people began to take some pride in – was a new notion, transmitted to Japan from the West in the Meiji period. Viewed as the product of an advanced civilization, it was adopted by a small section of progressive intellectuals of the upper classes. *The Little Cuckoo* (Hototogisu), written by Tokutomi Roka, an upper-class samurai, was heavily influenced by Western melodrama.

The Western concept of love grew into a model beloved of aristocratic women. The woman protagonist of *The Little Cuckoo* had to belong to the upper classes. But Japanese upper-class women, unlike Western noblewomen, were never trained to fight male oppression. The female protagonist in this play happily accepts the love of her husband but never questions his cruelty towards his mother. As for the mother, she merely laments her fate till her dying day. This Japanese-style melodrama, combining the celebration of a love marriage and the feudal maltreatment of brides, touched middle-class women deeply when it was serialized in a newspaper; and with its adaptation to the stage and the screen its influence extended to the lower classes as well.

This best-seller inspired innumerable romances or so-called family novels – *My Fault* (Ono ga tsumi), *The Mother and Son-in-Law* (Nasanu naka), *Whirpool*

(Uzumaki), etc. – what gained wide popularity from the late Meiji to the Taisho period. Family novels were what women loved to read. Unlike today's 'home drama' they contained a message for women from good families who were unaware of the world outside: there are many predators, the novels said, who will seduce and ruin you, so it is important to be cautious.

New School Theatre – Origins of Modern Film

Most such novels, were dramatized for the stage, and became big hits of the New School Theatre. They established a new theatrical style in the late nineteenth century based on innovations of *kabuki* and old-style drama. Since it was difficult to portray Western manners in the exaggerated *kabuki* style, these innovations helped to express them as realistically as possible. However, *kabuki* continued to exert a strong influence, and this was evident in the way many plays were structured. For one, women's roles were played not by women but by *onnagata*; for another, the influence was embedded in the musical rhythms and intonations of the lines and in the *ukiyoe*-like beauty of the form – something much more important than realism.

The two leading male roles were based on long-accepted concepts: that of a strong and reliable man who does not form any attachments; and that of a frivolous and unreliable but handsome man, a matinee idol, specializing in love scenes. Scripts were written with these star roles in mind.

The end of the *onnagata* and the matinee idol coincided with the rise of realism. With the Modern Theatre movement in the early 1900s, the Western play began to be directly copied and transplanted. Although *shinpa* means 'new', it was already something of a traditional form when compared to the newness of the Modern Theatre, *shingeki*. But the Modern Theatre tended to be highbrow, avant-garde and political, and was alien to the vast majority. Until the 1920s, the most popular theatrical form among the masses remained *shinpa*.

While the early actors and directors of period films were mainly from *kabuki*, most of the actors, scriptwriters and directors of modern drama films, *gendaigeki eiga*, were from *shinpa* theatre. Kinugasa Teinosuke, for instance, became an *onnagata* star at Nikkatsu Mukojima after leaving *shinpa* theatre where he had also been an *onnagata*. Eventually, when realism in film spelt the end of the *onnagata*, he switched to directing. Just as period films were based on *kabuki*, modern drama films have their origins in *shinpa*, which is why modern drama films were initially known as *shinpa* films.

In their content, *shinpa* films were influenced by Western romantic melodrama, while *kabuki* influenced the form of modern drama films. The preferred material for these films was the dramatization of family novels, since the ordinary viewer found the Western-inspired love stories between men and women of the nobility or the upper classes too fanciful. Here, through a variety of devices, melodrama made the lives of the elite a part of the life of the ordinary people. However, for the Japanese, adopting the Western idea of love was not easy. All 'decent', respectable people deemed it a superficial Western modernism, vulgar and 'loose'. A marriage partner would normally be found either by parents or, at the very least, on the advice of parents or some older person. Professions such as geisha, artist or actor were not considered desirable. It was natural, therefore, that male or female leads would be chosen from such dubious backgrounds.

Most of the *shinpa* plays written in the Meiji and Taisho period appear absurdly outdated today, and are largely forgotten except for three that were based on Izumi Kyoka's original stories: *Portrait of a Bride*, *Cascading White Threads* and *The Nihon Bridge*. These hits, these classics of *shinpa*, continue to enthral contemporary audiences when performed by well-known actors. What explains their popularity is that the protagonist is either a geisha or a female artist. These women, unlike ladies of the upper classes, are venerable and priceless objects, but they cannot exercise their independence. Familiar with the hardships of life, they know how to differentiate between an honest man and the man who makes empty promises; they desperately want to leave behind their artificial lives and take the honourable path. Like Katushya in *Resurrection*, they cannot laugh openly in the presence of men; but they do resemble characters from Western melodrama for, while ruing their entanglement in an unhappy love, they believe love to be sublime.

When Mizoguchi Kenji joined the Nikkatsu Mukojima Film Studio which specialized in making such *shinpa* films, the *onnagata* were still around. They continued to train in the *kabuki* style, but no close-up shots could be taken because – for example – their Adam's apple showed up! It was now being argued that women's roles should be played by women. Soon, the *onnagata* star, Kinugasa Teinosuke, became a director and returned to Makino Films.

Oguri Takeo, who replaced Kinusaga, starred in the first few films Mizoguchi made. Mizoguchi had already made *My Fault* (1926), *Nihonbashi* (1929), *Cascading White Threads* (1933) and some others in the style of *shinpa* plays. Working with the Nikkatsu Mukojima Film Studio meant adapting Western romances to fit the Japanese cultural climate. This much said, it was neither easy to change the spirit of glorifying men and underplaying women, nor did the viewers expect to see it.

Shinpa Films in the Nikkatsu Mukojima Film Studio: The Case of *The Quiet Two*

As far as I know, of all the *shinpa* films made at the Mukojima Nikkatsu Film Studio, only one – *The Quiet Two* – based on the original script by Yanagawa Shunyo, is extant. Its rights were then in the hands of the Matsuda Film Company.

Nothing is known of when it was made, who the director was or who else was involved. What we do know is that Nakayama Utako had a role in it, and that she joined Nikkatsu in 1920. The studio was destroyed in the Great Kanto earthquake in 1923 and it was probably around this time – when Mizoguchi was an assistant director – that the film was made. Inagaki Hiroshi, then an actor at the studio, says it may have been directed by Ohbora Gengo.

Although my generation is not really nostalgic about the Nikkatsu Mukojima Film Studio, we are nonetheless deeply interested in the style and content of the films it produced and the stars who acted in them, for this is where Kinugasa Teinosuke and Mizoguchi Kenji began their careers. In these films lay the origin of women's melodrama, and it is to this melodrama that contemporary television drama is directly linked. This is also the very emotional world that Kinugasa Teinosuke lovingly cultivated. Simultaneously, it forms the basis for the tragedy of women in Mizoguchi's films.

Mizoguchi was a pioneer in bringing modern realism into Japanese films. But because of his great stature and success, there are debates about whether he was a natural realist, or whether he worked from a perspective of critical realism or from a humanist vision. Before we discuss Mizoguchi from the modern perspective, we should note that he was first and foremost a *shinpa* director, and his films make this clear. *Cascading White Threads* and *The Story of the Late Chrysanthemums* were archetypal *shinpa* plays. These late works – so praised by the young *nouvelle vague* directors of Europe who understood their artistic base – show a typical *shinpa* sensibility. I recall several scenes where this influence is visible: the last scene in *Sansho the Bailiff*, when mother and child meet again on the coast of Sado; or the place from where Hasegawa Kazuo and Kagawa Kyoko escape in *A Story from Chikamatsu*. Here we see two people dear to each other but kept apart by social pressures. We see the time it takes before they can be united. It is infinitely moving to watch as they fumble and try to understand each other's feelings, the hesitant exchange of words, the slow dawning of realization. The viewer can see how solid the wall is that separates them, and how their differences slowly disappear.

The use of *tatami* mats in Japanese daily life obstructs vigorous movement such as running. However, the repetitive use of scenes of sitting, standing or reclining becomes a powerful means of expressing how the psychological barrier between two people is slowly broken down by their mutual passion. This style of expression is typical of Mizoguchi. His famous technique of 'one-scene one-cut' taken as a long shot is expressly designed to bring out, bit by bit, every nuance of psychological tension between the two, a tension established by this slow change, this step-by-step transformation. The use of shot-reverse-shot or close-ups would have speeded up the movement unnecessarily.

This gradual expression of love, this 'aesthetic of a deep psychological barrier', was part of the puppet *joruri* (*ningyo joruri*) style as well as an intrinsic part of *kabuki*, developed during the feudal age. It was modernized by *shinpa* at the end of the Meiji and Taisho periods, an era when class divisions were dissolving. These trends were reflected in contemporary *shinpa* theatre, where a large number of plays used the theme of love between people of different social classes. 'The aesthetic of a deep psychological barrier', used as a blackmail tactic in *joruri* and *kabuki*, became in *shinpa* a way to heighten its theatricality and aesthetic appeal. It was a reflection of the rapid increase in class mobility during the Meiji and Taisho periods, which saw innumerable cases of love between people of different social stations. But since people's ways of thinking change slowly, this kind of love was suppressed. Even those consumed by it had to fight a strong urge to resist change. *Shinpa* often used romantic themes based on strong passions that set hearts on fire, but the outward displays of these passions were portrayed in extremely slow movements, presenting a unique self-restrained style.

This style left a powerful, lifelong influence on the way Mizoguchi selected his themes and on the artistic and dramatization techniques he used. In his realistic works, Mizoguchi tried hard – at least intellectually – to avoid the cloying sweetness of *shinpa* expression. However, the harder he tried, the more manifest it became in his later works, where it appeared in a refined and pure form. Mizoguchi cultivated the *shinpa* style when he rose from being assistant director to director in the Mukojima Nikkatsu Film Studio. Yanagawa Shunyo wrote the original story (in a somewhat crude and outdated style) for *The Quiet Two*, but the scriptwriter is unknown.

The heroine is a geisha named Namiji (Nakayama Utako), who has a patron, Shibue Teruo (Arai Jun), the profligate son of a bourgeois. They have one son, but Teruo keeps his existence secret. Inevitably, Teruo has a fiancée, Mieko (actress unknown), an upper-class woman. The need to preserve family honour demands that the two should marry, but Teruo is caught in a dilemma, because he does not want to abandon Namiji.

Mieko's younger brother, Ryukichi (Miyajima Katsuo), accidentally finds out about Teruo and Namiji and informs Teruo's grandfather, Muraki (Araki Shinobu). An angry Muraki upbraids Teruo. He summons Namiji to a restaurant (ryotei), where he asks her to give up the relationship. Namiji tearfully pleads that their love is deep and abiding and that they even have a son. However, she resigns herself to her fate and tells her beloved Teruo when he comes to see her, that they must part ways.

Shortly after Teruo and Mieko get married, Namiji falls ill. Her son is taken to Teruo's house, since Namiji's mother feels that this is best for the child. When she is better, Namiji, who cannot bear to be separated from her child, goes to Teruo's house to get him back. There she sees what a wonderful job Mieko is doing bringing up her child just as her own. Namiji thanks her and leaves.

Teruo also suffers from the pain that he has caused these two women. He goes to Karafuto (Sakhalin) to establish a business. His wife, Mieko, and the child follow him. Subsequently Namiji also goes to Karafuto.

Another character in the story is Tozawa, a doctor. He has had a relationship with Mieko before she married Teruo. Tozawa harasses Mieko in several ways, and even attempts to abduct her. He, too, comes to Karafuto, where he instigates the Ainu to agitate, and once again tries to abduct Mieko. Accidentally – if inevitably – Namiji and Teruo rescue Mieko. It leads to a happy ending.

In *kabuki* and *shinpa* a geisha is, all too often, asked to break her relationship with her patron and give up her beloved; or perhaps this film is a remake of *The Lady of the Camelias* (Tsubaki Hime) by Dumas Fils. The influence of American westerns may have led to creating characters who try to set up new businesses in far-flung, snow-bound Karafuto, or evil men who instigate and oppress the *Ainu*. Or again, it could have been a direct outcome of the widely seen action films set in Alaska.

In terms of photography there are very few location shots. Apart from some outdoor shots – outside the house, on a road, in the grounds of a Shinto shrine – most of the shooting is done on the sets, with an extensive use of backdrop scenery for the shots of Mukojima Park, the Karafuto white birches and even for snow-fields.

Another characteristic of these films is the absence of inter-titles. The trend in *shinpa* tragedy films was that different people took charge of different roles and explained the captions, even when no explanation was called for. To have one person explaining captions was unnecessary; to have several doing it was a posi-tive nuisance. In these films, however, there were no captions between sequence changes – only the insertion of a brief but beautifully illustrated inter-title, summing up the main aspects of the sequence. This was used in over twenty films: *Duty and Duty*, *Worrying about Mother*, *Predicament*, *Regarding Desire*, *To the Land of Snow Out of Desire and Duty*, *Drops of Blood on the Snow* and *Instigation,* to name a few. Under the influence of Brechtian theatre, Godard, too, experimented with this technique of an inter-title at the start of a sequence in *It's My Life* in 1962. But the technique was not really new.

The Quiet Two has some 300 shots. In a talkie projection, this amounts to about fifty minutes running time, in silent film, some eighty minutes. Today, a film of about the same length has about 600 shots. In the silent film era – i.e. in the early Showa period – films usually had about 1,000 shots. The larger number of shots would slow down the tempo.

When Mizoguchi and others started making talkies, they used about a hundred shots. The number of shots in *The Quiet Two* cannot be regarded as exceptionally few. However, Kaeriyama Norimasa and others who had called for an improve-ment in Japanese film-making were critical when shots increased. They argued that leaving the camera on and shooting endlessly as if in front of a stage only made films boring. This is true if you watch *The Quiet Two* today. Despite the mere 300 shots, the overall feeling is that the film is too long because the camera was kept running. Also, there are no moving shots to allow for a change in composition within one shot. And when a change in the shot does occur, there is no significant change in the camera angle; at best, it changes from a full to a medium shot. Nor is there any change in the image. For instance, in an indoor shot of a person standing, the camera would be pulled back in order to get the full person in the frame. But if the person sat down, the upper part of the frame would be left empty because the camera would have to be moved forward considerably to make the image fit the full size. This was why in crucial scenes you would sometimes find the titles running across the bust of the character.

Today, when two people are engaged in a conversation, B is filmed from A's perspective and A from B's. This shot-reverse-shot technique was not known at that time. To be sure, the relationship between distance and the person being photographed was understood, but there was no understanding of how to change the camera position to show the person being photographed from different angles. This induced the feel of a slow tempo despite the relatively small number of shots.

Made about three years after *The Quiet Two*, the period drama, *The Blood of a Big Snake* by Futagawa Buntaro, has scenes that demonstrated a very competent use of shot-reverse-shot. The conversation between the two principal characters and the last great fight scene are two fine examples. The tempo is leisurely, with a slow camera moving far back to show the movement of the policeman (*torite*) as he watches the protagonist being killed. Here Futagawa uses something close to a flashback by swiftly building up very different shots. Seeing *The Quiet Two* and *The Blood of a Big Snake* today, one can see why, at the beginning of 1927, Japanese films were, technically speaking, at a major turning point. On the one hand, then, you had *shinpa* theatre films which avoided shot-reverse-shots and on the other, the new samurai action films which had the moving camera as well as the shot-reverse-shot.

Mizoguchi used a crane to set up his camera movements. He liked to build up a change in composition slowly. This is when he developed the moving camera technique and put it to good effect. He resembled the studio in his dislike of the shot-reverse-shot. He was not in favour of change.

His contemporary, Kinugasa Teinosuke, who was also an intrinsic part of Nikkatsu Mukojima, was his polar opposite. In *A Page of Madness* (1926), he used a montage of magnificent images to show rapid progress. Mizoguchi's aversion to montage had progressive critics lashing out at him for his *shinpa*-style plots and his outdated form. He stuck to these, not because he had not gone beyond *shinpa* forms, but because he did not wish to break the actors' performance. However, the overall impression was that he did not wish to progress beyond the Nikkatsu Mukojima group. Mizoguchi was, to put it accurately, a Nikkatsu Mukojima 'type' of director. Throughout his life he was consistent in his belief that the basis of cinematic expression was not montage or camera work, but the performance of the actor.

To return to *The Quiet Two*, I find it most interesting that the story of *To the Land of Snow Out of Desire and Duty*, stresses willpower (*iji*). As a rule *shinpa* plays, as *kabuki sewamono* (realistic drama of manners), deal with the dilemma between duty and 'human feelings'. This film, too, poses oppositions between 'desire and duty', 'bound by compassion' and 'dilemma'. Namiji does not want to break off her relations with her lover Teruo, nor does she want to lose her child. This is the 'human feeling' (*ninjo*) in her. And duty (*giri*), as opposed to 'humanity', is that her child is being affectionately brought up by Teruo's legitimate wife, Mieko. Namiji finally wearies of the dilemma and withdraws. And yet, if this were only her personal stress, it would not provide the right 'drama', for there can be no drama around the sole idea of 'dilemma between duty and feeling'.

Basically, the drama arises from the discord and complications between kindred spirits, each of whom pursues his own interests. Even *giri-ninjo* drama cannot consist of mere lamentations and endurance of suffering; there has to be some subjective self-assertion. This happens in *The Quiet Two*, with the use of the word 'willpower' (*iji*). Namiji is discriminated against because of the prevailing belief that a geisha, simply by giving birth to her patron's son, cannot assume that she will become his wife. As a woman, she cannot oppose this discrimination. However, this discrimination itself becomes the basis of the 'willpower' that builds up in her as she desperately pleads with Teruo's grandfather. It also emerges from her actions as she, a lone woman, follows Teruo to snowbound Karafuto (Sakhalin). *Giri* and *ninjo* can only form the basis for a drama. The dramatic power, which gathers momentum and moves to a climax, comes alive through willpower. In the so-called *giri-ninjo* drama *giri* and *ninjo* should not be regarded as opposing concepts. The opposition, rather, is between the concept of '*giri-ninjo*' and 'willpower'.

In a society that is not conscious of the need to publicly protest against discriminatory practices, the anger is turned inwards. Irrationally perhaps, it emerges as steely resolve or obstinacy (*iji*). Translated into modern terms, the drama of *giri-ninjo* in *kabuki* or *shinpa* becomes, in large measure, a fight against discrimination. Japan's feudal society was thoroughly iniquitous, but one where paternalism often devised ways to attenuate the friction caused by discrimination. When encountered by those who refused to accept its reality, it became for them the source of deep hatred that turned into burning resolve (*iji*). Namiji in *The Quiet Two* thinks her patron loves her, but when she realizes that he is, first and foremost, a patron, and she just a geisha, her bitterness crystallizes into determination. The so-called '*giri-ninjo* drama' should be re-examined for what it is – a 'drama of honour against discrimination'. More importantly, I believe Mizoguchi took these elements of determination and resolve from *shinpa* drama and gave them added weight and depth in the context of realistic drama in *Osaka Elegy* and his later works.

Westernization of Shinpa Films – The Case of *Baptism by Fire*

The story of *Baptism by Fire* (directed by Wakayama Osamu who also worked with Nikkatsu Mukojima Film Studio) is taken from the programme of the Nikkatsu group first-run theatre, the Sanyukan:

> Sekiko (Okada Yoshiko), the much loved daughter of a university professor, Tanizaki Haruo, suffers from consumption. The doctor pronounces it incurable. Her prayers lead to a miraculous recovery, though, and she becomes a devout Christian dedicating her life to her religious beliefs by joining a nunnery in Hakodate.
>
> That their beloved daughter has buried herself in a Christian nunnery is an unbearable torment for her parents, who call her back and marry her off to Soma Eiji (Yamada), a chief engineer in a company. Sekiko, who has little sexual knowledge and has given little thought to it until now, suddenly comes face to face with it. Her heart is that of a pure maiden, and when she wakes up after what seems like a dream of her wedding night, she laments her irrevocably lost youth and maidenly pride, all for the lust of a domineering man. Learning that there was another woman who had once loved her husband, she cries, 'A loveless marriage is a misfortune but when two people who love each other cannot be together, it is an even greater misfortune. I will go back and hope this will help these people ...'
>
> Sokichi (Tagawa Junkichi), the son of an employee, is another devout Christian whose hymns to God bring deep solace to the lonely and grieving Sekiko. As if their souls and bodies had merged into one, the two unthinkingly begin singing hymns under the setting winter sun. Brought together and bound by religious fervour, they soon fall in love and become lovers.
>
> Three years later, on a stormy night a man is driving through the outskirts of a small town near the Hakone pass. His wife, with a baby clasped to her, works at her embroidery at home. For three years Sokichi, a driver, had been toiling hard for the sake of his beloved wife and child. However, he is tragically killed when he loses control of the car and crashes down a cliff. After Sokichi's death, Sekiko feels insecure and, yearning for her parents, returns to Tokyo. She wonders how she can face them and chooses to live alone in a small room with her baby. But, friendless and forlorn, she is forced to abandon her child.
>
> Quite by chance, her brother, a university graduate and now a manager in a hospital, comes across the abandoned child and brings him up tenderly as his own. Sekiko, a loving mother, decides to secretly visit her baby at the hospital. At the same time Soma Eiji has been injured in his factory and admitted to the same hospital. Sekiko sees Kyoko, the woman supervisor of the factory, sitting by Eiji's pillow nursing him, and feels very happy for Eiji. She also sees that the child she had to abandon is being raised by her elder brother. Sekiko returns once again to the arms of the Virgin Mary at the nunnery.
>
> And the bells of the nunnery toll!

Along with Tanaka Eizo and Suzuki Kensaku, Wakayama was an important director at Nikkatsu Studio. Indeed, it was he who introduced the young Mizoguchi to Nikkatsu. It was here that Mizoguchi learned film-making.

Baptism by Fire is not regarded as a masterpiece. Judging by the story, I think it fits the typical pattern of women's melodrama. The heroine, played by Okada Yoshiko, is not the daughter of a nobleman but of a university professor, and was part of the elite. She is also a Christian, something particularly suitable for a heroine in the popular Western-style love stories based on the worship of upper-class women. In tales of chivalry, the greater the spiritual dignity of a woman, the more passionate the knight's attraction to her.

It is difficult to judge today just how far the film captures this idea or to what degree the heroine is aglow with pride and spirituality. The idea of a chaste beauty has little meaning today. Besides, the link between Okada's ignorance of sex and her Christian beliefs is weak, and it is open to question whether the film manages to express the dignity of a noblewoman.

It must be remembered that in those years women had just begun making an appearance in Japanese cinema and that until a couple of years before, *onnagata* had been at the peak of their popularity. Ironically, *onnagata* expressed the eroticism or coquetry of a certain kind of woman better than women actors themselves. And even after women began acting, they found it difficult initially to break away from the style of the *onnagata* which had by then become the model.

In the family novels of the late Meiji-Taisho period it was widely accepted that the young heroine would fall in love with a man from the nobility, or at least with someone from the upper classes. This was plainly based on class-consciousness and on the assumption that love as a spiritual bond would be meaningless for ordinary people who regarded it as a Western notion. However, in *Baptism by Fire*, a young illegitimate son, a driver, not only loves the heroine but worships her and treats her with respect. The proletariat takes on the role of the knight.

This is by no means the first work to express this idea, and in all likelihood it was influenced by American films. But there is no mistaking that it is a cut above the run-of- the-mill family novels, an experiment that planted the idea of romantic melodrama as an expression of Western upper-class thinking. The trouble is that these proletarian knights are unable to fulfil their hopes. They either die in accidents, throwing the heroines once again into hardship and sorrow; or, when they discover that there is another knight who waits on the lady, they enter a monastery.

The story of *Baptism by Fire* brings together two notions of tradition: the Japanese, where the child is looked after by the parents, and the Western, where a man protects a woman. The solution of sending the first lover to a monastery is not part of Japanese ethos, but based on a Western image of the world. Melodramas that belong to the world of women-worshipping chivalrous knights did not match the Japanese reality of the 1920s. The problem faced by Japanese scriptwriters, then, was how best to adapt Western melodramas to their own customs and make them acceptable.

In 1933 Wakayama Osamu, director of *Baptism by Fire* wrote a story on which Mizoguchi based his first film, *Resurrection of Love*. The story, according to the programme of the Asakusa Sanyukan is as follows:

Wnno Youtei (Yamamoto Kaichi) lives on a rice paddy ridge where the water is pure, the mountains beautiful and the rivers abundant. He has two daughters, is a leading modern potter, and the object of everyone's envy. However, what appears beautiful from the outside always hides something dark underneath. Wnno is a deeply sorrowful man, disheartened by the fact that has no male heir.

Hishida Yuichi (Koizumi Kasuke) hatches a plan and sets out for the capital. He comes to Wnno and waits patiently till he is accepted as a disciple. Hishida's perseverance wins over his teacher. Wnno is delighted that there will now be someone to perpetuate his name.

For this to happen, Hishida must marry Wnno's daughter. In the proper order of things the elder daughter Tamie should be married first. But she has a birthmark over half her face and it is clear that Hishida dislikes her. Though the father quite naturally wants her married and is torn by pity, he leaves Tamie (onnagata, Mori Kiyoshi) to her fate and announces the wedding of Hishida and Sayuriko (onnagata, Oguri Takeo) in order to secure an heir.

Hishida is very happy. He had always loved Sayuriko and he can now marry her. But Sayuriko is distressed at the thought that she, a beauty, must give up her life to marry the ugly Hishida when she already has a lover, Murota (Yoshimura Tetsuo), the son of a wealthy man.

Wnno goes up to Kyoto for the marriage ceremony. It is the evening of the happy day but a distraught Sayuriko and Murota clasp each other and decide to end their lives by drowning. Learning of this betrayal, Hishida's frustration turns to anger and then to despair. But at the very moment that he decides to kill himself, he remembers the promise he had made to Wnno of becoming his successor. It dawns on him that he is not the master of his destiny and cannot throw his life away because of a passion.

Awakening as it were, from a dream, he marries the other daughter, Tamie, and vows to his teacher to live single-mindedly for a sublime and pure art, and keep his name alive. There is a new light of happiness on this day when love has been resurrected and a peaceful breeze blows over the shimmering waters of the bountiful river.

This film by Mizoguchi, a simple melodrama, was not received with any great acclaim. Writing in *Contemporary Japanese Filmmakers* (Gendai nihon eiga jinden), Kishi Matsuo says that this work resembles the later 'pro-ide' (proletarian ideology) films. Since large portions were chopped by the censors, Mizoguchi used the *biwa* (Japanese lute) to link the shots. When Koizumi Kasuke dressed up for the role of the idiot, Mizoguchi called it a *biwa* play.

Where exactly is the 'pro-ide' in this film? It is quite unbelievable that Hishida is an imbecile, as Mizoguchi seems to recall. But the film-maker remembered this only at a much later date, and the pro-ide may have been apparent in the original; perhaps the film is the revised version made after it passed the censors and the original story could indeed have been based on proletarian ideology. Which is doubtless why the story is difficult to follow.

The Resurrection of Love is different from *Baptism by Fire*. If the latter falls within the framework of the melodramas of knightly romance, the former draws upon the tradition of *Resurrection*. A man is the cause of a woman's misfortune and unhappiness, and the consciousness of this crime drives him to atonement. This motif is the same as Nekhlyudov's behaviour towards Katushya. *Resurrection* was one of the more popular plays of the early Taisho period, and one of the early superstars of *shingeki*, Matsui Sumako, was widely admired for her role as Katushya. The play was made into a film many times at the Nikkatsu studios.

If melodramas of knightly romance are an expression of an internalized reaction to the worship of a male god in Christianity, then Tolstoy's *Resurrection*, while fundamentally demolishing this tradition, once again draws it back into the Christian fold, where the burden of sexual relations can be released through confession. In *Resurrection of Love*, we have a Christian position. Having brought misfortune and unhappiness upon a woman, a man cannot simply confess and leave. 'Living for a sublime and pure art' becomes the retribution for the crime. In this case it is simultaneously a way to provide succour to the girl's father and to the 'house' (*ie*). The religion of God is turned into a religion of the house.

Mizoguchi would later make a number of films where an important leitmotif was that of a man living to atone for his crimes against a woman, a direction that modern Japanese romantic melodramas were already exploring. It was thus a legacy from his seniors in the industry.

–3–

From New School Theatre to Naturalism-Realism

The Support of a Sister and the World of Shingeki

When the Great Kanto earthquake happened in 1923, the young Mizoguchi was living in his sister Suzu's house. Later, as she and her family moved from place to place, he would provide them refuge in a house in Nikkatsu's Mukojima Studios. Unfortunately, the house burnt down in a fire. Suzu then took the family to the residence of Matsudaira Tadamasa in Ehara, Shinagawa. This large estate was spread over an area of 3,000 *tsubo* (1 tsubo = 36 sq ft). The main house covered 400 *tsubo*, and there were a number of other empty houses as well. Suzu and her family were given one of the unoccupied houses and they turned it into their permanent home.

For all that, Suzu's status was akin to a servant's. Her patron Matsudaira Tadamasa's mother and his legal wife both treated her like one of their employees, although they betrayed no sign of jealousy. That the wife and mistress lived together didn't ever appear to be a problem. The servants took pride in their employment in a *daimyo* house, but the *yashiki* – the people who held the real reins of power – kept away from her. Suzu, from downtown Tokyo and unused to the lifestyle of the nobility, thus lived in virtual isolation.

It was the beginning of a troubled life for her. Friends would come and visit her, and many a time there was talk of leaving. But for the sake of the children, Suzu refused an alimony of 50,000 yen, choosing, instead, to remain near her lord. Unfortunately for her, this man would not reprimand anyone who troubled her and her children – not even the servants. He was afraid of their opposition. In 1926, Matsudaira Tadamasa's wife died, but Suzu's position remained unchanged. However, he did move Suzu and her family, including her brother, to another unoccupied house that was remodelled as a grand Western-style building. Thereafter, whenever Mizoguchi – who had by then become a director and was working in Kyoto – came to Tokyo he would use the house as his own, coming and going as he pleased. He would bring along many of his friends from the studio, ask his sister to entertain them and borrow money from her as well.

After Japan's defeat in the war and the abolition of the nobility system in 1947,

Matsudaira and Suzu were free to marry. They did so immediately. Unfortunately, the fortunes of the Matsudaira family declined soon afterwards.

In *Osaka Elegy*, Mizoguchi used the actor Takekawa Seiichi to portray an old, self-centred, petty man who embezzles company money. He considers himself successful, but is a burden on his daughter. Many years later, Mizoguchi told Yoda Yoshikata that he used memories of his father to create the character of the old man, right down to the smallest gesture. Mizoguchi may have been quite contemptuous of his father, but from what he learned of him from Suzu's children, Matsudaira Tadanori and Kawakatsu Kyoko, it appears that the father was gentle and likeable, if somewhat petty. What did Mizoguchi really think of his father when he was young? What did he think of Matsudaira Tadamasa who provided him with economic security?

In all likelihood, the workaholic Mizoguchi (indeed he was a martinet with colleagues, abusive and scornful of those who he believed shirked work) regarded his father as a defeatist. A good man though the father was, he had no standing in society. At the same time, it is difficult to believe that Mizoguchi respected Matsudaira Tadamasa because of his wealth. If the old egotist in *Osaka Elegy* is modelled on the father, then the spineless lord in *The Life of Oharu* and the emperor Genshu in *Princess Yang Kwei-fei* are definitely cast in the image of Matsudaira Tadamasa.

All his life Mizoguchi worked on stories of women helping weak-willed men. The women may have been outwardly feeble, but they were of an indomitable spirit and had the strength to cope with tragedy. Even stories that do not, at first glance, fit this pattern are actually variations on this theme, and it is exceptional for a man to use his power to help a woman in distress. Mizoguchi may certainly have used traits of character of people close to him – Suzu, Zentaro or Matsudaira Tadamasa for instance – but there is little evidence to show that he was as disapproving of them as he shows in his films, or indeed that he even had any quarrel with them.

In general, Mizoguchi was a likeable person. But at work his personality underwent a dramatic change. The Mizoguchi who hated his father – or more accurately, the father figure in his films – was simply a part of the imaginative structure of his work; his disdain was like his disdain for vacillating matinee idols. I believe that while artists begin with certain characteristics and give them shape, the opposite can also happen. A role has a certain function. It is one way of narrating a particular story. By investing that role with his own feelings, an actor or performer fleshes it out and gives it life. That the character of the small-minded, weak, egotist in *Osaka Elegy* who manages to stabilize his life through his daughter's sacrifice has been modelled on his father, shows the depth of Mizoguchi's animosity to him. What meaning did love and hate within the family structure hold for Mizoguchi?

For most people these are not major problems, even if problems of love and hate within family relationships are complex. When we were young, family relationships were so close and binding that we could not break free of them. With the passage of time they became memories and we could look back on calmly. When Mizoguchi entered the film industry and became a director, it was not with just any studio that he worked, but with Nikkatsu, the specialist in *shinpa* tragedies. Initially he thought of becoming an actor, and it was really by accident that took up direction, a role that suited his personality better. And he – who till then had never worked for any length of time at any one job and was nothing but a source of worry for Suzu – would go on to cut quite a figure as a director.

Shinpa tragedies were traditional plays with themes of love and hate within family relationships. It was impossible for Mizoguchi not to deal with them. In the process, consciously or otherwise, he used his own family relationships upon which to base his work. But it was precisely because he was the kind of director who could not help bringing his personal concerns to his films that he raised them, through naturalism-realism, far above the repetitive, traditional patterns typical of formulaic *shinpa* tragedy films.

Friends and acquaintances of Mizoguchi agreed that he was unyielding on several issues. A large number of incidents have been cited to corroborate this. Since his films made him appear an authority on family relationships, once he made up his mind, he was not averse to bringing the love and conflict from within his own family into his work.

Shinpa tragedies favoured the world of the geisha, the patron and the red light (Blossoms and Willows) district as their subject matter. Suzu, a geisha, was close to a member of the nobility; through her and her patron, Mizoguchi became familiar with the ambience and people of this world. Yodogawa Nagaharu, in *The Three Great Films* (1950), has this to say of the protagonist Umemura Yoko in Mizoguchi's *The Nihon Bridge* (1929):

> taking small steps she walks down a corridor to a rendezvous with her patron waiting in a room (*zashiki*) away from the main building. She opens the sliding paper door (*shoji*), takes out a pouch wrapped in paper from the folds of her *obi* and swiftly hands it to her accompanying maid. That gesture of quickly handing over wrapped money is the geisha personified. His understanding of the small details of women living at that time was superb.

None could have depicted the world of the Nihonbashi geisha better. For most people, such sundry details may hold no particular significance, but for Mizoguchi it was an active internalisation of complex memories of his feelings for his sister.

In a famous essay entitled 'The Power of the Sister' (Imoto no chikara), anthropologist Yanagida Kunio states that for Japanese men a brother's memories of a sister's pure love is a major spiritual support. This love has its roots in an entrenched cultural memory where the elder sister plays the role of a medium (*miko*). In more recent times, cultural anthropologist, Iwata Keiji, has pointed out in *The Anthropology of the Gods* that the custom of women using magic to protect their men when they set out on a journey is still widely prevalent in South-East Asia. This, he adds, may well lie at the origin of Yanagida Kunio's argument.

While I cannot make any judgements about the early Japanese people, I do tend to agree that even in contemporary Japan, bonds between brothers are not as strong as those between an elder brother and a younger sister, or those between a younger brother and the elder sister. Under the influence of Confucian ethics, a strong distinction is made on the basis of age. An elder brother can often be like a father to the younger brother, but the two can never be equal. Over a period of time, this led to a system of primogeniture, which explains why the relationship between the elder and younger brother is like the relationship between a master and a subordinate. In American companies such as Warner Brothers, brothers are equal managers. In Japan, on the contrary, if the elder brother is the chairperson, the younger brother will usually be a department head; he will never occupy a position of equality. This is also why discord among brothers is common. But the relationship between the brother and sister, on the contrary, is supported by a pure love and is, therefore, easy to maintain.

From a different note, distinctions based on sex are very clear in European culture. As children, brothers and sisters sleep in different rooms, unlike in Japan where there is nothing strange about brothers and sisters sleeping in the same room. In fact, from early childhood, the elder brother or sister looks after younger siblings in a way that strengthens kinship ties between the opposite sexes. It is perhaps this aspect of Japanese culture that invests stories of love between brothers and sisters with a special meaning.

A well-known line in a popular song called 'The Avenue of Life' (Jinsei no namikimichi) goes: 'Don't cry little sister, don't cry little sister … have you forgotten the tearful voice of your elder brother who promised to look after you?' Yosano Akiko's famous anti-war poem, 'Brother Do Not Give Your Life', is about an older sister remembering her younger brother who has gone off to war. The old tale of *Sansho the Bailiff* is all about an older sister sacrificing herself to save her younger brother. Koda Aya's *Younger Brother*, a novel centring on an older sister's devotion to her wastrel of a younger brother, was made into a cinematic masterpiece by Ichikawa Kon. Murou Saisei's novel, *Older Brother-Younger Sister*, a story about the love between an older brother and a younger sister, was filmed three times, in 1936, 1953 and 1976. All three films are masterpieces. The violent older brother may beat his younger sister; nevertheless, he loves her deeply.

In European or American cinema, we come across very few films that deal with the love between siblings of the opposite sex. Japan, on the other hand, has many stories of this kind. Mizoguchi rarely wrote a story himself, but was naturally drawn to such material and subjects, and it was in these stories that he found his métier.

Strength of a Woman's Will

Many of Mizoguchi's early *shinpa* tragedies have stories featuring an elderly woman performer or geisha who renounces the world, sacrifices herself and destroys her body. The man is tortured by the consciousness of his crime. Examples of such films are *The Downfall of Osen*, *The Nihon Bridge* and *Cascading White Threads*. *The Nihon Bridge* has an older sister and a younger brother; in *The Downfall of Osen*, the young man calls the woman 'older sister', although the two are not really related. Apart from the early films there are others such as *Osaka Elegy*, *The Story of the Late Chrysanthemums* and *Sansho the Bailiff* where ambitious young men, chasing success, sacrifice an elder or a younger sister, or even a wife who plays the role of an elder sister. In almost all these films, a father or a patriarchal head has a crucial part in driving a woman to self-sacrifice. The younger men are powerless to overthrow him and it is the women who take the pressure put on these younger men and end up sacrificing themselves. In the process, the young men are greatly tormented.

The triangular relationship between the young man, the father (or father figure) and the young woman reflects Mizoguchi's personal feelings. But more than the desire to express a deeply felt need, it was his confidence that he had in his grasp a world he knew and understood, that drove him to depict it. He knew it made him the 'best'; he could use it as a trump card. Mizoguchi was a naturally competitive man who needed at all times to feel superior to his colleagues and was fearful of being overtaken by his juniors. To stay ahead he made a wide variety of films: some of the popular variety, others expressionist or avant-garde, films with a leftist approach, as well as films that were thematically just the reverse, i.e. those in praise of the Japanese invasion of the Asian mainland.

After the Second World War, Mizoguchi made educational films on post-war democracy. However, once Japanese films began to be exported, his own work – aimed mainly at the export market – proved to be fairly poor (*The Princess Yang Kwe-fei*). It has been repeatedly emphasized that in the years between the Japan-China war and the Pacific war, Mizoguchi did not make any films in direct praise of the war. However, a close examination of the history of Japanese cinema shows that many did follow the popular trend. They expressed his intense desire to be part of the world of cinema, to be right on top. (In this he was the polar opposite of Ozu Yasujiro who, throughout his life, pursued one style and two or three motifs.) But while he tried his hand at a variety of new trends, his best depictions remained those of the 'elder sister', and the 'geisha or performer', the adoring 'younger brother' and the 'father or head' who makes her bend – sometimes against her will – in the interest of the family. This sourcing of material from the world he knew made him a master at depicting women.

A film may be largely based on an individual's sentiments, but it cannot be merely an autobiographical novel. Even if some of Mizoguchi's films were close to being autobiographical novels, they were not like the usual films of the time. Films need to be put in a popular story form (or appear to be within a popular story form) even when grounded in personal feelings. Suzu can be called a mistress as she lived in a large mansion and seemed to be loved by her patron. However, in a popular story, the mistress is a concubine – she must bear the burden of being a woman. The story of an older sister working as a geisha and paying her younger brother's school fees was common in *shinpa* theatre, beginning with *The Nihon Bridge* written by Izumi Kyoka. Naturally, the greater the suffering a geisha endured, the more pathetic would the story appear.

The basis of *shinpa* tragedy theatre was to show the will of a woman who is lashed by cruel fate. It took on an even more concrete form in the case of a fallen woman. As a director in a *shinpa* tragedy studio, Mizoguchi's heroines ranged from geishas and prostitutes to fallen women. The heroine of *The Nihon Bridge* is the first-ranking geisha from the red-light district; the heroine of *The Downfall of Osen* is a prostitute; the heroine of *And Yet They Go* is also a prostitute who works in a place called Chabuya, a brothel for foreigners.

It does not follow, however, that every *shinpa* tragedy spoke of women's cruel fate. These plays were basically popular entertainment. Showing the pitiful fate of women would not have entertained people if the story been one of unmitigated misery. It had to be presented with a degree of lightness. For instance, if the story was about a nobleman's mistress having to abandon her child, it had a certain amount of pathos. If it was about a woman who had to sell her body and become a prostitute, it would fall in the category of wretchedness. Given the ethical values prevalent in society, the life of a geisha or the mistress of a nobleman could be shown only in a beautiful and melodramatic way. If the life of a prostitute were to be realistically depicted, it would have been unsavoury and obscene.

That Mizoguchi often made a geisha the heroine of his films is not exceptional; this was a common theme in a *shinpa* films. But it was his desire to pursue realism that led him to show prostitutes or the women working in Chabuya. From the end of the Taisho to the early Showa period, naturalism-realism was well entrenched in the world of literature. In fact, it was the prevailing social orthodoxy that needed to be overturned. Given his competitive spirit, Mizoguchi worked to raise *shinpa* tragedy films to the level of naturalism-realism. The search for realism in literature coincided with the rise of the autobiographical, or 'I-novel'. The larger abstract question 'what is truth?' transformed into a more concrete and specific question 'what is reality?' and the actual life of the writer became the unquestioned reality. But the life of the writer has often been regarded as isolated from society. In the 'I-novel' the social aspect of reality is weakly expressed. Mizoguchi went completely counter to this trend. He took the truth of individual feelings expressed in *shinpa* tragedy films, and raised it to a social level to show that it embodied a universal truth. It is through this process that he drew close to naturalism-realism.

Naturalism Realism – *Mistress of a Foreigner* and *And Yet They Go*

In *Mizoguchi Kenji: The Man and His Art* (Mizoguchi Kenji hito to geijutsu), Yoda Yoshikata writes:

> I think the two films, *Mistress of a Foreigner* and *And Yet They Go*, made in 1931, the year of the Manchurian Incident, are the foundations of Mizoguchi's art … This is because Mizoguchi gave naturalism-realism his own unique strength and perspective. Another important reason is that with Mistress of a Foreigner he began to use the then special technique of one scene-one cut …
>
> I can never forget my initial response to *And Yet They Go* in the preview theatre – the overwhelming feeling that this was the kind of film I wanted to see. I was young and wanted to write about films – films that had both good and evil, films covered with grime as it were, but being inexperienced, I did not know what to expect in such films. I read Molière and Maupassant and felt something of their attraction, but above all I loved the work of Tanizaki Junichiro. The censors hacked *And Yet They Go*, and it was painful watching it when it was released.

Sadly, neither the films nor the scripts of *Mistress of a Foreigner* or *And Yet They Go* survive today. *And Yet They Go*, in particular, was so heavily censored that it must have been very difficult to evaluate it critically. Both the original works on which the two films are based are available. The popular novelist, Juichiya Gisaburo, author of *Mistress of a Foreigner,* wrote it as a mixture of novel and reportage. *And Yet They Go* was based on the novel by Shimomura Chiaki. A few films seem completely unconnected to the original stories on which they are based. This was not the case here, since the story, the theme and the nature of the central characters can be perfectly understood on their own. One can quite understand why these 'became the foundations of Mizoguchi's art'. A closer look might make this clearer.

Mistress of a Foreigner is the sad tale of Izu Shimoda. Black ships come to Shimoda, where Townsend Harris opens a consular office. He stays on for a year to press the *bakufu* to open up the country. Okichi, a geisha, is given to him as a mistress. The people of Shimoda think of foreigners as beasts and are afraid of them. They see Okichi as a woman monster – a woman whose chastity had been sold to a beast – and they abhor her as unclean. She leaves her home, and from the commissioner's office is carried in procession in a palanquin to the counsellor's office. The people of the town watch this procession with disgust.

Juichiya Gisaburo then introduces two men into the story: Tsuru, a carpenter on a ship and Okichi's young fiancé; and Isa Shinjiro, an employee at the commissioner's office. When Okichi is ordered to go from the commissioner's office to Harris, the American counsellor, she can only appeal to Tsuru to help her refuse. However, Tsuru decides to go to Edo where he is told he can be a samurai. One night he comes to tell

Okichi that he is leaving because he wants to become successful. Okichi begs him to help her to escape with him:

'How can I run away with you? There is such a strict guard over you.'

'What! Are you afraid ? Really Tsuru-san!'

'Shouldn't I be? What if the office guard or the barrier guards catch us?'

'If we are caught … bite your tongue … you always used to say that you would die with me.'

'What are you saying Okichi … such frightful things.'

'No, just kill me! Kill me! If you want to become a samurai, then do it.'

'What are you saying? Don't talk of dying!'

'It's all right if you don't want to be with me.'

'Don't be absurd.'

'Then … Tsuru-san …Tsuru-san … I can't take this any more. Oh how bitter this is.'

The exchange with Okichi continues in this colloquial style, but Tsuru has no fighting spirit and desperately wants to make off.

'Tsuru-san, you also … you remember that great commotion. At that time Koaruki-san used to look up to Nirayama-san, they used to meet, isn't it? But where will a woman run? She hid in the house and couldn't leave … The foreigner was a beast of debauchery…Tsuru-san.

'No matter how much that beast … that beast loved his wife, his wife, his own wife, he used her freely … Tsuru-san, give up trying to become like a true samurai.

'For me, even with this, I am a woman, a Japanese woman. If I could be with you, if the village headman would allow it … because I want to be with you … even if I have to suffer imprisonment … I really want to become Tsuru-san's wife.'

Tsuru also breaks down and weeps.

'Tsuru-san … Tsuru-san.'

'This is truly regrettable …'

When the crow's cry is heard, Tsuru's face is visible as he drags his sandals from the rear entrance of Okichi's house.

Suzu, too, was given away as a geisha. When Mizoguchi was about seven or eight, Viscount Matsudaira bought her contract and gave her her freedom. It is not clear whether Mizoguchi was aware of this but in any case he was too young to help his only elder sister. What is certain is that he repeatedly portrayed characters like Tsuru who had neither pride nor self-respect. Such men were always shown to have high-spirited and strong-willed elder sisters, or a woman he refers to as 'elder sister', or a lover who he lets down when she appeals to him for help.

Okada Tokihiko in *The Nihon Bridge* and *Cascading White Threads*, Natsukawa Daijiro in *The Downfall of Osen* and Hanayagi Shotaro in *The Story of the Late Chrysanthemums* are such characters. Particularly interesting is the humble company employee played by Hara Kensaku in *Osaka Elegy*. When asked by his lover (played by Yamada Isuzu) to raise money and replace what her father has blown up, he can do nothing. When she makes a plan and sends him to her dangerous elder brother, a pimp, he is speechless with fright. When the police catch him, all he can say is that he has nothing to do with anything, and indeed does nothing to help her. *Osaka Elegy* was Yoda Yoshikata's original script based on Juichiya Gisaburo's work. Hatamoto Akiichi's dramatization of *Mistress of a Foreigner* is similar to Mizoguchi Kenji's and though there is no direct link, the character of Tsuru resembles the Hatamoto dramatization so closely that Tsuru might well have been his reincarnation. Perhaps Mizoguchi secretly depicted these characters as his self-portraits.

In *Mistress of a Foreigner*, Isa Shinjiro, the employee in the Commissioner's office, chases Tsuru off to Edo and comes to Okichi's house where, he explains with great gentleness and in nationalistic terms, the reason why she must become the American's mistress: Osho (Wang Zhao Ying), a woman close to the Chinese Emperor is, for reasons of state, being sent across the Amur River to a foreign country in the north, and as she goes she says, 'The year? ... Kichi? ... Wasn't it the same age as Kichi? I was seventeen.'

That's the kind of story it is. More than being beguiled by the crafty employee, Okichi loses heart at Tusru's betrayal and decides to become the counsellor's mistress. She takes good care of Harris, but when he returns to America, people see her as strange and reject her. Okichi ends up as a pathetic alcoholic. Tsuru may be a self-portrayal of Mizoguchi, but there is no trace of Mizoguchi's father in the role of the canny Isa Shinjiro. Mizoguchi's father was a petty man and a loser in life, while Isa Shinjiro is smart and capable. The only similarity is that he lives off the sacrifices of women, or of those weaker than himself.

In *The Straits of Love and Hate*, Shimizu Masao plays the son of a *Shinshu ryokan* owner. He falls in love and elopes with the maid (played by Yamaji Fumiko), but abandons her when he finds that he cannot make ends meet, and returns to his father. An unreliable man, a strong-willed woman and a stubborn, crafty and cruel patriarch who will not let the two live: with some variations, these human relations formed the core of Mizoguchi's art.

One can offer an ironic counter explanation here. Mizoguchi was well acquainted with the life of a concubine who is loved by a great lord in the mansion but mistreated by the heiress's maid. Such a story had all the elements of a typical *shinpa* tragedy. Re-reading this today, one may be surprised to learn that the family novel became the basis of No-Farce (*kyogen*), a form close to *shinpa* tragedy. There were many stories of family conflicts between the wife of a viscount or baron and his mistress, or stories about illegitimate children. Yanagawa Shunyo's *Bygone Friends*, Kikuchi Youho's *My Fault*, Watanabe Untei's *Whirlpool* were all part of this genre. These serialized newspaper novels were made into *shinpa*-type plays in the Taisho period. The masses loved the world of the nobles because they were rich, close to the imperial house and vested with power and authority.

If Mizoguchi's only intention been to show a world he knew well, he could have simply used the well-established patterns of *shinpa* tragedy. However, he did not do so until the decline of the nobility in the post-war period. I would like to examine the reasons behind this.

Search for Realism: *A Woman of Pleasure*

Mizoguchi lived off a viscount because of his elder sister's connections. It enabled him to escape poverty and pursue his own interests. As and when he chose, he would give up work he found unsuitable and return to his sister's house; through her, and because of his good relations with the Viscount, he got many things done for himself. He may have been wary of his father who also lived with them, a dislike that would inevitably reflect on him and his work. Perhaps – being brought up poor – he cultivated an antipathy to the rich, and out of this arose his compassion for the prostitutes of the lower class. Whatever the reason, for a sensitive young man, this life could not have been a very happy one. Or perhaps he simply disliked showing the life of the nobility. If he had done so he could have ended up with an autobiographical novel. But a film is not just the visualization of private feelings. These feelings have to be given a popular story form. Familiar though he was with the life of a nobleman's concubine, Mizoguchi chose not to write about this. He preferred a similar situation in order to tell an even more pathetic story in *A Woman of Pleasure*. This gave it universality and a greater appeal.

Mizoguchi was familiar with the sort of women portrayed in *A Woman of Pleasure*; it seems that he also bought himself many prostitutes, and was acquainted with geisha, prostitutes (*shogi*), independent prostitutes (*shisho*), part-time maid/part-time prostitutes (*yatona*), and prostitutes who worked with foreigners, as in Kobe. In his later years, when his wife suffered mental problems, this only strengthened his self-condemnation.

From his young days, when he lived off his sister in Asakusa, it appears that Mizoguchi frequented the nearby Yoshiwara red-light district, often returning early in the morning. In what was to be his last work, *Street of Shame*, he speaks of the final days of the Yoshiwara district before the anti-prostitution law was passed and it was closed down. He knew the world of prostitutes early in life, partly because of Suzu, and partly because he matured sexually when he was very young.

He never made any advances to 'decent' women and nor was there any scandal with the many actresses he worked with. The story of his unrequited love for the actress Tanaka Kinuyo in his later years is known, but those who knew them unanimously agree that Mizoguchi behaved like a naive adolescent; the slightest mention of Tanaka Kinuyo's name would embarrass him, and it is quite possibly he never told Tanaka Kinuyo that he loved her.

While he was bold with prostitutes, he was bashful with 'decent' women, a trait he shared with older Japanese men. As far as women were concerned, Mizoguchi was neither a naturally debauched person nor a particularly domineering one. His only obsession was to chase success and make a name for himself.

—4—

Social Realism

The Time of Leftist Films – *Metropolitan Symphony*

Among the *shinpa* tragedies that Mizoguchi made were *The Song of Failure* (1923), *A Paper Doll's Whisper of Spring* (1926), *Cascading White Threads* (1933), *The Downfall of Osen* (1935), and its most shining example, *The Story of the Late Chrysanthemums* (1939). Kabuki forms greatly influenced *shinpa* tragedy films, but rendered it almost impossible to make realistic plays. By the 1930s these styles were chiefly used to depict the customs and manners of the Meiji period.

Films such as *A Picture of Madame Yuki* (1950), *Lady Yu*, *Lady Musashino* (1951) and others, while made in the contemporary mode, have a clearly recognizable *shinpa* tragedy style. *Kabuki* and *shinpa* are characterized by the 'conflict between a pleasure-loving man and money and power'. The emotional landscape of this conflict is developed in a very picturesque way. Many critics argue that Mizoguchi developed realism in Japanese films with works such as *Osaka Elegy* and *Sisters of the Gion*. In these two *shinpa*-influenced films, however, he went into a decline.

For Mizoguchi the elements of *shinpa* were fundamental and, as a diligent and ambitious man he continued to experiment with new forms that took him in different directions. The film *813* (1923) was a mystery based on the translation of one of Morris Lupin's 'Arsene Lupin' series; *Foggy Harbour* (1923) was part of a series of 'a very dark human drama'; *Blood and Spirit* (1923) was influenced by *The Cabinet of Dr Caligari*, and other works of German expressionism. The Ministry of Education commissioned *The Song of My Village* (1925) as an educational film for rural youth. On the one hand he made *No Money No Fight* (1925), an ironical film on war, and on the other, patriotic films, such as *Imperial Favour* (1927). The three films of *The Life of a Man* (1928) were comedies based on a comic book (*manga*).

Mizoguchi was ever sensitive to prevailing fashions, constantly experimenting, yet aware of his shortcomings and doing his best to overcome them. Riding rashly on the wave of the popularity of militarism just after the Manchurian Incident, he made *The Dawn of Manchuria*; *The Song of the Camp* came the year after the start of the Japan-China war. However, when the war entered a more serious phase and broadened into the Pacific war – a time when the government forced film-makers to make propaganda films in its support – he turned his back on war films and sought escape in art films.

Keiko films, or films with a leftist bent, became popular in the 1920s and 1930s. After the First World War, a long-drawn-out economic depression that began with a fall in agricultural prices turned into a full-blown financial crisis (1927), led to the failure of many banks and to social instability. The right-wing movement spread rapidly, and from 1926 onwards, the labour movement, too, gathered considerable strength. The world of letters saw the growth of a proletarian literature movement. New right-wing figures dominated literary magazines. Writers of other persuasions, including established names since the Meiji period, found it difficult to publish their writings, and the only ones who flourished were those who supported the rightist ideology. In the world of cinema, propaganda films from the Soviet Union by directors such as Eisenstein or Pudovkin injected a far greater modernism than had hitherto been perceptible. The films were new not just in terms of ideas but also in terms of their form and perspective.

In this contradictory situation, young and ambitious film-makers began taking an interest in the rightist trend. Both the press and the audience at large welcomed films that fitted into this framework and that were likely to become hits. Even managers of film companies that had originally been against rightist thinking, were convinced that if films made money, they were fine.

Simultaneously, leftist (*keiko*) films were also acceptable. Directors who had specialized in melodramas and had evinced no particular interest in right-wing ideas, as well as the big names from period drama, had so far been making films based on the ideology of 'humanity and loyalty' (*jingi chuko*). They now began to insert left-wing ideas into their films and *keiko* films grew in popularity.

The severe repression of left-wing thought and the merciless censoring of *keiko* films can hardly be over-emphasized. The more a work demonstrated a clear ideology, the more it was hacked, making it impossible at times to follow the story. The popularity of most of these films did not last more than a couple of years. By 1931 the left-wing movement had begun to show signs of receding. In the face of severe repression and complete control exercised by the government, anything remotely resembling a *keiko* film was banned. Among the better-known examples of *keiko* films are: Uchida Tomu's, *Living Dolls* – the story of the failure of an insincere but talented man who cannot survive within the structure of a capitalist society; Suzuki Shigeyoshi's *What Made Her Do It?* – a traditional melodrama of a gentle young girl who is treated cruelly by society; Ito Daisuke's *The Killing Sword* – a period piece, based on a peasant rebellion; and Tasaka Tomotaka's *Look at this Mother* – the story of a widow with a child, who loses her job.

Mizoguchi's *Metropolitan Symphony* is the greatest of the *keiko* films.

Fujii, the son of the chairperson of a large company, announces his marriage to Reiko (Irie Takako), a banker's daughter. A woman working in a café [*translator's note*: by

FIGURE 3 Natsukawa Shizue (left) and Kosugi Isamu in *Metropolitan Symphony* (1929).

implication a loose woman], Osome (Natsukawa Shizue), whom he plans to abandon, arranges a meeting with Fujii at a hotel. Here he persuades her to agree to a break-up. On her way back from the hotel, Osome runs into an old friend, Genzo (Kosugi Isamu), a worker. Genzo's life in his fishing village has been ruined by Fujii's company and he has been forced to come to Tokyo.

Genzo actually works at a construction site in Fujii's company where he quarrels with Fujii's father and is thrown out. Reiko, who has heard Genzo's story, is struck by his courage and feels very sympathetic towards him. One day, Genzo's company friends wish to take a break and head for the slums of Fukagawa to distribute charity. This is when Genzo insults Reiko, telling her she is listless and apathetic, with no desire to work or to live. He calls her a wooden doll.

Fujii's father wants him to marry Reiko quickly as he is trying to get a loan from her father. Reiko, however, thinks Fujii is a fool and will not accept him. Fujii wants to get rid of Osome, who is pregnant, by buying her off, but Osome flies into a rage and suffers a miscarriage in Genzo's house.

Meanwhile, a panicky call about the collapse of a building that Fujii's company is constructing throws the celebratory party into confusion. Osome and Genzo sneak into

Fujii's house seeking revenge. By this time, however, both Fujii's company and Reiko's father's Yamada Bank have gone bankrupt.

What comes across as a shallow melodrama condemning the bourgeois and praising the proletariat seems to have actually been a powerful work. Iida Shinbi, in a review written for *Kinema Junpo*, 21 September 1929, commends the film in the following words:

> Scene changes bring out the sharp contrast between the rich and the poor. The occasional use of montage has an effect of reticence and grace. The editing has been well thought-out in the way in which the characters are introduced, particularly the industrialist Fujii and his profligate son, the rich Yamada and his flapper daughter, and the big magnates of the financial world. The montage has a direct impact on the viewer, allowing the director to convey succinctly that which is difficult to say.

He adds that the strong depiction of the workers, the fishing village that Genzo has been forced to leave, the scenes of conflict between the fishing company and the fishermen, and the working men's district in the rain, all leave a lasting impression. Not only was this the best Japanese film of 1929, it won accolades abroad as well.

What was exhibited in Japan, however, was a heavily censored version. Tomoda Junichiro wrote an indignant review in *Kinema Junpo* on 1 January 1930.

> The Japanese censor system rejected a work praised by the rest of the world. The company asked Mizoguchi Kenji to make changes ... The changed *Metropolitan Symphony* passed through the censors without any cuts and was released. What this teaches us is that the censor system is a system [set up] to ruin films. So let us talk about how *Metropolitan Symphony* was ruined.
>
> In the uncensored version of the film the life of the bourgeois is shown as one of deception, corruption and idle leisure in contrast to the simple life of the oppressed proletariat. It seeks to strengthen the proletariat's feelings of enmity against the capitalist. In the revised version, the sense of a class enemy is barely apparent in the last scene when Genzo and Osome look at the fallen Fujii house and laugh loudly. Reiko is a thorough capitalist when she comes to Tomigawa town in Fukagawa to help the poor, and doesn't believe what Genzo tells her – in fact, she tells him to 'stop lying!' However, the scene which shows her terrible confusion has been cut completely. The contrast between bourgeois life and proletarian life has been destroyed.
>
> In the title shot, the caption, 'You do not need to spend any money to kill the labourer, if it doesn't rain for even ten days, that is enough' has also been cut. In fact, almost all the scenes showing the proletariat have been sliced.

Although *Metropolitan Symphony* is rarely seen as a complete work, it has won critical acclaim. Unfortunately, in the version normally screened many important scenes have been deleted. This makes it unbalanced and no more than 'a marriage of convenience, play and leisure and love, the invasion of capitalism into the countryside, charity groups, capitalist economic activities, the collapse of capitalism, ending with the exposure of the bourgeoisie' (from the earlier quoted Tomoda Junichiro). In this form it could not even have made it to the list of the best ten.

In *And Yet They Go* (1931), Mizoguchi faced the same drastic cuts by the censors and for a while he stopped making such films. The censors used the power of the police to make matters difficult, effectively throttling them. For all that, there was undeniably an internal weakness: far from believing in leftist ideas, film-makers had done no more than jump onto a popular bandwagon.

Suzuki Shigeyoshi, director of *What Made Her Do It?* – the biggest hit among all the *keiko* films – began to make short propaganda films for the Department of the Army as soon as the popularity of *keiko* films began to wane. His assistant director, Kimura Sotoji, was said to have been deeply impressed by leftist ideas. He was also reputed to be a major driving force in *keiko* films after he showed *Youth Across the River*, perhaps the last *keiko* film, in 1933. Yet, when the Sino-Japanese War broke out, he also made a name with *Kaigun Bakugekitai*, a propaganda film for the Navy. Tasaka Tomotaka, director of *Look at This Mother*, received an award for *Five Scouts*, one of his earliest militaristic-artistic films made at the beginning of the Sino-Japanese War. Thereafter, he became one of the more prominent supporters of the war.

Even Mizoguchi made films in support of militarism – *Imperial Favour* (1927), *Dawn in Manchuria* (1932) and *The Song of the Camp* (1938) – without any of them ever achieving success. He simply could not become a militarist even when he tried.

How does one assess the value of *keiko* films today when not one has survived?

Motif of Westernization – *Oyuki, the Madonna* and *Poppy*

After the heavy censorship of *Metropolitan Symphony* and *And Yet They Go*, Mizoguchi stopped making *keiko* films. Yoda Yoshikata recalls that when Mizoguchi was making these films and stressing proletarian ideology, he was actually under investigation by the police and was quite frightened by the experience. It was enough to terrify anyone, and Mizoguchi could hardly be accused of cowardice. But what is certain is that he was no left-wing fighter either.

Mizoguchi moved for a while to Shinko Films, and buried himself in the Meiji period and in emotional works, among them *The Festival of Gion* (1933) and *The Jinpu Gang* (1934). Alongside, he made *Oyuki, the Madonna* (1935) and *Poppy* (1935) with the independent company, Daiichi Eiga.

The Festival of Gion has been lost, but it is said to have been a very good film, the story of unrequited love set against the backdrop of the collapse of an important merchant family. *The Jinpu Gang* was a man-centred film, as against

Mizoguchi's normal practice of focusing on the woman. Another film, *Chushingura*, is also lost. From this point on, Mizoguchi began to concentrate on studying a particular period and on focusing increasingly on a bygone world, giving the impression that had fallen behind the ranks of the leading directors.

In any case, new and younger directors such as Ozu Yasujiro, Shimizu Hiroshi, Yamanaka Sadao, Itami Mansaku, Gosho Heinosuke and Inagaki Hiroshi had begun making a name for themselves. Compared to their fresh vision, Mizoguchi – with his stressing on tiny details to create a Meiji environment – seemed like an old, established director, who bore no resemblance to his youthfulness of the 1930s.

Oyuki, the Madonna is based on Kawaguchi Matsutaro's adaptation of Maupassant's *The Lump of Fat*. To this story Mizoguchi added some of his own elements. Maupassant's original work, set during the Franco-Prussian War, is the story of a group of people who try to flee the battleground in a horse carriage. The bourgeois use the expression 'lump of fat' to refer sarcastically to the prostitute who is riding along with them. When they are caught by the enemy, they offer to send her to the commander as a human sacrifice. This done, when they leave the battlefield the next day, all they do is censure her and call her vulgar.

The scene shifts to the Seinan war in Kyushu. At one stage, government forces are seen trying to control the horse carriage. As a new element to the original story,

FIGURE 4 Yamada Isuzu (left) and Hara Komako in *Oyuki, the Madonna* (1935).

the film shows these forces being defeated in battle. The commander flees and hides in the home of the female protagonist, a *saké* server.

The original work is a critique of bourgeois selfishness. Maria is shown as a humble woman, protected by a young man out to make a success of himself in the world, a Mizoguchi theme so visible in other films – *The Nihon Bridge, Cascading White Threads, The Downfall of Osen, Osaka Elegy* and *The Story of the Late Chrysanthemums*.

Poppy, a novel by Natsume Soseki, was made into a film based on a script by Ito Daisuke. Mizoguchi was not comfortable with cerebral themes and his teaming up with Natsume Soseki, one of the most intellectual of modern Japanese authors, would suggest an ill-matched pair. However, there is a deep realism in the depiction of the life of the Westernized elite, and his portrayal of the sensibilities of ordinary people (*shomin*) would be difficult to match today. It is a quintessential Mizoguchi:

> The poor young man has been looked after by an old-fashioned scholar of Chinese (*kangakusha*). He comes to Tokyo to study and become a modern intellectual. He falls in love with a cold and arrogant woman from an upper-class, Westernized family. To use this love to gain an entry into the upper classes he must break his vow to the teacher who has looked after him and whose daughter he has promised to marry.

FIGURE 5 Ohkura Chiyoko (left) and Miyake Kuniko in *Poppy* (1935).

The teacher's daughter, played by Okura Chiyoko, has believed implicitly in the love of this young man since she was a child. She is shy and sweet, an 'unworldly daughter' (*oboko musume*). The film has scenes that are typically associated with such a character; for instance when she realizes that the young man no longer loves her, she wails like it is the end of the world. All the old nuances of *shinpa* tragedies are deeply etched in her acting, something that a contemporary actress would find hard to evoke.

Social Criticism: *Sisters of the Gion*

In 1936, the Daiichi Film Company under Nagata Masakazu was facing management problems. Mizoguchi decided that even if the company were to collapse, he would somehow leave behind an ambitious work. It led to the making of *Osaka Elegy* and *Sisters of the Gion*, and proved that the Japanese film industry could, on occasion, produce a great work despite adverse circumstances.

At the time these two films were made, the police were ruthlessly suppressing *keiko* films. It was hardly opportune to make a left-wing critique of the social system. But by using the perspective of discrimination against women, Mizoguchi chose to approach the problem from a different, yet permissible angle. In any case this theme was much closer to Mizoguchi's concerns than leftist ideology.

Osaka Elegy uses sharp realism to look at the familiar story of a fallen woman (*furyu shojo*) and the road to her downfall. *Sisters of the Gion,* which examines discrimination against women through the story of a geisha, is a harsh criticism of the feudal nature of the profession. The two films argue that it is only natural for women to resent the prejudice they face in a male-dominated society and turn to crime to fight it. Aside from the clarity of the argument, and the dark and tragic content of the films, these films exude a lively, exhilarating strength. One obvious reason is that Yamada Isuzu, whose father was a *shinpa* actor and mother a *samisen* performer, played the protagonist's role in both films. Brought up as a child of these traditional artists, Yamada Isuzu fell in love with the actress Tsukita Ichiro. She was at loggerheads with her father when Mizoguchi, who was aware of her problem, directed her. She transposed to the screen some of this spirit of resistance and, keenly aware of what was being demanded of her, brought an intense passion to her roles.

In one unforgettable scene in *Sisters of the Gion*, the young geisha is sitting in front of the mirror and applying make-up as she prepares to leave the house (*yashiki*). It is a 'one scene-one cut' shot where the camera is placed in front, at a slight angle, giving the suggestion of a bird's-eye view. The camera is not always fixed and neither is the editing frozen. This much said, this scene, even within an altogether great film, is a particularly moving one.

When a geisha applies make-up, it is a moment of great solemnity, not unlike a samurai preparing his body for a duel, a sportsman warming up before a match, or a writer sitting at his desk gathering his thoughts. This is what the scene conveys with great intensity.

Our usual, preconceived notions would have us believe that the heavy make-up of a geisha is a sham, no more than a tool to beguile men with. But if we were to ask instead how far the face of a geisha changes with makeup, we would begin to wonder, question the act and look for its meaning.

Normally, the style of photography is meant to satisfy our curiosity about the application of make-up. The close-ups of parts of her body – as when the liquid face-paint is applied on the skin, when the tongue moistens the lipstick, or the eyelashes are being fixed – are carefully planned to create this montage of the moment. With these techniques, a director can freeze the moment, critique it or, even as he shows the form, introduce an element of surprise.

But Mizoguchi did none of this. He used neither close-ups nor montage, and not just in these scenes; in fact, he *never* used these techniques in any of his films. And by rejecting them, he actually conveyed the solemnity of the moment for the geisha. This was a truly fresh discovery.

All this was shown largely through Yamada Isuzu's acting skills. Mizoguchi merely left the camera running in front of her. In a sense, this was not something new. However, I believe that the very act of a geisha applying make-up – regardless of whether it is shown in an interesting way or as an exotic ritual – is a very solemn one. Being the actress she was, Yamada Isuzu understood implicitly the power of Mizoguchi's vision. Not many would have grasped the gravity of the act.

As a rule, we pay little attention to everyday human actions; but if we were to observe them carefully, we would see their inherent beauty. He who can perceive and convey this beauty has the makings of a director. But not all are so gifted. It requires effort and exceptional skill to capture and express a beautiful thing in a readily understandable way. For, no matter how much thought goes into capturing the moment, it may just come out flat.

What is important is to experience the joy of discovering that there is so much beauty even in the commonplace that it makes you forget yourself. In his search for that beauty, Mizoguchi went beyond the affectation and ostentatious style of a geisha's daily life. He saw its gravity. He observed without prejudice. The scales fell from his eyes and he developed a unique way of looking, a way that was grounded in society. *Sisters of the Gion* presents the customs of Gion in Kyoto in the mid-1930s:

Two sisters work independently as geishas. The older one is Umekichi (Umemura Yoko), the younger one is Omochya (Yamada Isuzu). Umekichi is a more traditional geisha, very much part of the giri-ninjo world. Her earlier patron was a man named Yoshizawa (Shiga), a wholesale silk dealer whose business has collapsed. Yoshizawa leaves his house after a fight with his wife and though he is penniless, Umekichi gives him shelter.

The younger sister is an exception among the geishas of Gion. She has graduated from a women's high school and is a modern woman. She cannot bear to see her elder sister's traditional behaviour and is angered by the absurd idea of duty (*giri*) that a geisha has to perform for a man who is just enjoying himself. She, therefore, hatches a plan.

First she woos the head clerk (*banto*) of a cloth store who is in love with her and gets him to make some clothes for her elder sister. She thinks that if her sister ventures out in a beautiful kimono and sits in a good seat in the theatre, she will perhaps attract a better patron. She also talks to an antique dealer, asks him to become her elder sister's patron and repay the contract fee that Yoshizawa has given. She returns Yoshizawa's money and asks him to leave. Completely in the dark about these machinations, the elder sister is surprised when Yoshizawa suddenly departs. The younger sister tells her that all men are alike, and urges her to accept the antique dealer as a patron.

Aware that the head clerk steals goods from the kimono store, Kudo (Shindo Eitaro), the owner, barges into Omochya's house to reclaim his goods. Omochya manages to persuade Kudo into becoming her patron.

Everything seems to be proceeding according to plan when suddenly disaster strikes. The elder sister accidentally finds out where Yoshizawa has gone. She is furious when she learns that her younger sister has manipulated her. The head clerk of the kimono store, who has suddenly been rejected by the younger sister and has lost his job as well, gets together with his taxi-driver friend to plan revenge against Omochya. They take her for a ride and throw her out of the moving car.

Omochya suffers serious injuries and is taken to hospital. While she is nursed by her elder sister, she asks, 'Why do the men of this world bully us, why must they bully us?' The elder sister, who is always preaching to the younger one about observing *giri-ninjo* faithfully, replies that despite her sincerity she feels Yoshizawa, who has found a new job at his wife's village, has forgotten her.

This film was evaluated as a realist film, a bitter exposure of the tough life of the geisha, far removed from its external glamour. People were moved by its stinging indictment of the system – socially, ethically and in class terms – and by its strong depiction of the new breed of woman who would fight male selfishness. Many films in post-war Japan exposed or condemned social injustice, and from that perspective *Sisters of the Gion*, although it may lack a fresh approach, still had an indestructible brightness that set it apart from others.

At one level, this is a story of a geisha who conceives of a crude plan to ensnare a man into supporting her. The film uses this plot to approach the question of women's position with great seriousness and to argue that within the means available to them, this is the only way they can resist men.

So far, Mizoguchi had been respected as an experienced director. With these two films however he was given the ultimate accolade – 'master'. *Osaka Elegy*, *Sisters of the Gion* and films by Ozu Yasujiro and Uchida Tomu used realism, as a means to analyse society. This was truly one of the golden ages of Japanese cinema.

Complications of Class-Consciousness: *The Straits of Love and Hate*

With *The Straits of Love and Hate* (1937), a film with a strong melodramatic content, Mizoguchi proved that he could craft a polished work. Made at the Shinko Kinema studios it was based on a work by Kawaguchi Matsutaro. The original, however, was not a fully formed story. Yoda Yoshikata thought up a plot about a mother and daughter as a pair of comic (*manzai*) performers. When he discussed this with Kawaguchi Matsutaro and Mizoguchi Kenji, Kawaguchi suggested, 'Let's do another *Resurrection*.' Yoda then incorporated the suggestion into his own story and wrote a script.

Kawaguchi Matsutaro, an important *shinpa* tragedy writer and performer, kept Mizoguchi in touch with *shinpa*. *The Straits of Love and Hate* has the air of a *shinpa* melodrama. It is difficult to see Tolstoy's *Resurrection* in the film. Yet the two do share some common traits – self-sacrificing women who fall in love with rich young men and are abandoned by them. They lead difficult lives and end up as whores.

However, Nekhlyudov, the protagonist of Resurrection is different. True, he causes an accident with Katushya because of his youthful impetuosity, but basically he is a wonderful young man. He repents, has noble intentions of helping Katushya and is determined to lead a respectable life.

In *The Straits of Love and Hate*, Kenkichi, the young owner of a hotel (*ryokan*) in rural Shinshu, is a weak young man who cannot look his father in the eye. Kenkichi elopes with Ofumi (Yamaji Fumiko), a maid, to Tokyo, where he idles away his time living off her earnings. His father arrives from the village just when they run out of money. He forces his son to leave Ofumi who has been looking after him. Living in the same pension as Ofumi is an accordion player, Yoshitaro (Kawazu Seizaburo), with the air of a yakuza. While Ofumi encourages his friendship, she still has to take care of the son she had with Kenkichi. The son is looked after by a wet-nurse, while she works as a waitress. Her life deteriorates. She ends up an alcoholic.

As time passes, she and Yoshitaro become comic (*manzai*) performers and join a travelling troupe that tours the countryside. She takes her child along with her. When they arrive at the town where Kenkichi lives, he comes to see their performance. A part of Ofumi believes that Kenkichi will see in her *manzai* performance the story of her abandonment, and of how she has brought up his child. Full of remorse, he will take her and their child back to his house. But Kenkichi's father browbeats his son, telling him to reflect on whether Ofumi is really the kind of woman he can take home. Kenkichi, as expected, can only make meek excuses and try and persuade his father. But he is unable to take a firm stand. Disgusted, Ofumi decides that this is not the home that she wants to live in. Picking up her child, she leaves Kenkichi and continues her travels with Yoshitaro.

The portrayal of Kenkichi's character in *The Straits of Love and Hate* is distinctly different from *Resurrection,* and the film comes across wonderfully as a

Japanese story. Kenkichi is not, like Nekhlyudov, a man with a strong sense of individuality; rather, he is someone who tamely follows his father, always fluttering about nervously, a typical example of a profligate son of a wealthy rural patriarch.

Yoda Yoshikata took Kawaguchi Matsutaro's suggestion about *Resurrection*, but blended it with the story of a woman *manzai* performer that he had in mind. In transforming the scene where Nekhlyudov sees the exiled Katushya to suit *manzai*, he transformed it into something far more interesting. In *Resurrection*, Nekhlyudov appears in court as a juror where he once again, unexpectedly, meets Maskurov (Kachushya), a woman of ill-repute, who is being questioned about a murder. In *The Straits of Love and Hate*, Kenkichi sees Ofumi doing a duet with Yoshitaro in a small village theatre, performing her role with lightness and humour despite being abandoned by a man, bearing his child and earning an unsavoury reputation.

In old Japan, pitiful bodies of unfortunate people (*ingamono*) were displayed to the public for money. Some of them were actually malformed, but most were fakes; others had gained notoriety for all kinds of criminal offences. These pathetic groups were exhibited along with the play.

If you allow me a slight digression, I would like to add that the tradition of *ingamono* has been intellectually continued in the I-novel, one of the more developed forms in modern Japanese literature. Other modern forms of this practice are the currently popular TV programmes where viewers reveal embarrassing personal facts just to make people laugh. The psychology that connects these current practices to the earlier one is that regardless of whether exposing one's shame evokes contempt or support, it does serve to unburden oneself.

In the years that *shinpa* tragedies were popular in the Taisho period, *Resurrection* had often been translated and performed as a play, or had been made into a film. In Japan's modernizing society, the story of unrequited love in a feudal setting with strict clan divisions was the sort of drama that evoked an easy response. Love between people of different social status was unimaginable. Even when Japan became more democratic and when status-consciousness began to decline, the problems of staging such a play persisted. Only in a society where class distinctions are rapidly collapsing can the melodrama of love between people of different social status be easily accepted.

Love is used to give shape to, and make visible, a notion of class. The conflict in the story between those who wish to maintain the status quo and those in love who wish to change it, creates the basis for the drama. In Japan *shinpa* plays such themes were popular from the late 1890s to the late 1930s, a time when the film *Tree of Love* became a great hit.

Tolstoy's *Resurrection* – as a model of a drama of unrequited love in a class-conscious society – was avidly studied by the Japanese artists of the time. Tolstoy was concerned about destroying the system of class distinctions. Believing that the nobility itself could renounce these distinctions, he made Nekhlyudov, a nobleman like him, behave as a humanist. In some ways it was a naïve if self-satisfying idea. But of course he knew there was no simple solution to the problem. Katushya refuses Nekhlyudov's help and decides to live with a 'political criminal', and in her choice lies the kernel of class conflict. In the translations of *Resurrection* available then, class conflict was vague. The accent seemed to be on how a man and woman lose themselves when they take to serious crime, but once they recognize their error, they embark on the path of repentance.

Ofumi briefly accepts Kenkichi's offer of help in *The Straits of Love and Hate*, but then refuses it and returns to Yoshitaro. She is convinced that only the poor can understand the poor – not because she is conscious of class, but because she has moved away from Kenkichi's timid and haphazard life.

The ruling classes in Japan never managed to establish a ruling ideology. Unlike Russia or Europe, which threw up thinkers like Tolstoy from within a class-ridden society, the Japanese did not go beyond their superficiality. Here lies the sharp difference between the two worlds.

That is why – until the translator himself clarified that *The Straits of Love and Hate* was a translation of *Resurrection* – it was difficult to figure out how it could be so brilliantly transformed into a Japanese drama!

The Death of Mizoguchi's Younger Brother – Yoshio

In 1938, Mizoguchi's younger brother, Yoshio, died at the age of thirty-three. He had graduated from the English Literature Department of Hosei University and had worked for Toshiba Corporation. Suddenly and without warning, he began to act effeminate and nervous. In some ways he was naïve and exceptionally pure-hearted.

He had read a good deal of Marx and leaned towards Marxism. He would lecture for hours, sometimes writing characters in the air with his fingers to explain his point to his sister's elder son, Matsudaira Tadanori. Unable to muster the courage to buy books himself, he would send his nephew to the bookseller while he watched hidden behind an electric pole. In 1933, when Kobayashi Takiji (an outstanding writer of the proletarian literary movement) was tortured to death by the police, Yoshio began fearing that he, too, would be killed. He refused to answer the phone, and would simply stand around and shiver. He even tried to commit suicide by jumping from the office window. He finally became anorexic and was admitted to hospital.

Mizoguchi genuinely loved his brother. One day he went with Matsudaira Tadanori to visit him. Yoshio stood gazing at a point in the sky through a large hole in the wall. He was getting thinner by the day, and began resembling a dry stick. Looking at him, Mizoguchi told his nephew repeatedly, 'This is the face of the best human being.'

Yoshio is said to have uttered a sound and, without any apparent pain, collapsed and died. It was as if he had prepared himself to die, like a living Bodhisattva. His nephew, Tadanori, while conceding that Yoshio was not mentally normal, believed that he died because his aimless search for perfection was no match compared to Mizoguchi's zest for life.

–5–

The Fate of Matinee Idols

Genealogy of the Lead Actor and the Matinee Idol

One of the striking characteristics of Mizoguchi's cinema was that it had very few strong male characters. The central figure was usually a woman. The men who played opposite her were either the ineffectual kind whom she protected, as in *The Downfall of Osen, The Story of the Late Chrysanthemums* etc., or the unreliable kind as in *Osaka Elegy, The Straits of Love and Hate, A Picture of Madame Yuki*. They could be weak and contemptible, first abandoning her, then taking revenge, as in *Sisters of the Gion* and *Street of Shame*. There could also be insensitive, proclaiming their progressive ideology, then showing their disdain as in *My Love Burns*, or oppressing women and pushing them into prostitution. Viewing Mizoguchi's oeuvre is like observing the whole gamut of worthless Japanese men, and the women who put up with them and help them.

However, strong, reliable and wonderful men *do* occasionally appear in his films: Oishi Kuranosuke in *Chushingura* and Tairano Kiyomori in *Taira Clan Saga* are ideal men. But they are the exceptions, and not particularly admired for their roles.

In *A Story from Chikamatsu,* Mohei – who valiantly protects the heroine Osan and ultimately dies a heroic death – is one such exception. In popular Western romances the hero is, at least initially, modest with women. In a certain number of Japanese films, on the other hand, when the lovers are caught and the man is taken to prison for adultery, he assumes a macho image, slapping his chest, smiling confidently and displaying all of a sudden heroic qualities that he had not possessed before.

Zushio, in *Sansho the Bailiff,* escapes to save himself from slavery, but returns to the manor (*shoen*) to liberate other slaves, and finally helps his mother, who is herself a slave. However, what detracts somewhat from his hero-like image is that he runs away on learning of his younger sister's sacrifice. In the original story it is the determined, strong-willed elder sister who helps her weak, unreliable younger brother escape. This is understandable; it is the strong helping the weak. In the film, however, Mizoguchi changed the character of the brother who is able to escape thanks to the sacrifice of a weak, *younger* sister. In changing the ages of the two lead characters for convenience, Mizoguchi considerably reduced the sense of manliness of the male lead.

On this one point, Kurosawa Akira is just the opposite of Mizoguchi. Kurosawa's main objective is to demonstrate the strength, vigour and magnificence of the man, to bring out his full strength and glory, with the woman providing full support.

The basis of Mizoguchi and Kurosawa's almost diametrically antithetical styles lies in their temperament and character. But a more fundamental reason can be found in Japanese culture itself, in its two-layered male and female structure. Mizoguchi and Kurosawa represent its two facets.

Kabuki has two kinds of male protagonists. The lead actor is strong, impressive, deeply considerate and very 'male'. He resembles the hero of Western theatre but is different from the heroes of chivalric ballads since in *kabuki* love is never a major consideration. The other is the matinee idol – a handsome man, kind to women, pure of heart, a man who cannot live without the love of the other sex, and who is almost always in love. Most characters of the latter kind are weak, somewhat rash and insincere, and lack 'manly' solidity. In *Chushingura*, for instance, Ohboshi Yuranosuke (Oishi Kuranosuke) is the lead character and Hayano Kanpei is the matinee idol. In the play *Kanjincho*, Benkei is the lead character while Yoshitsune is the matinee idol.

Basically, *kabuki* has a ruffian and a gentleman. We also have period pieces (*jidaigeki*) and the in-between tales (*sewamono*). The period pieces – rich and vibrant spectacles with dramatic entrances by the hero or the ruffian – require a lead actor. Romantic tragedies need a gentleman, while the matinee idol is usually seen in *sewamono* where you have a realistic depiction of the prevailing social customs among merchants.

I am not sure that men and women view *kabuki* along these divided lines. By and large, men seem to like the roles of ruffians and period pieces, perhaps because they can see in the lead actor a representation of the 'real man'. Women like the gentlemen and *sewamono* pieces where the matinee idol, even when somewhat unreliable, is considerate and caring, and treats them as equals. They have no particular fondness for the lead actor, no matter how reliable or noble he is.

In his book, *A History of Film People: Mizoguchi Kenji* (Jinbutsu nihon eiga shi 1 (Mizoguchi Kenji), Kishi Matsuo quotes from an article written by Manpontei for a film magazine, *The Age of Films* (Eiga jidai) in the late 1920s:

> Mizoguchi's character and appearance were appropriate for the role of a romantic character. Temperamentally, he maintained his composure whether he was being praised or criticised. He had the style of a nobleman and this was evident in his clothes and accessories. He transformed the usual image of the artist into something more refined. Women who met him even once, were attracted by his defenceless, shy demeanour. He

was pure of heart and highly emotional. A certain type of woman finds these traits very attractive.

A real matinee idol!

There is a story about Mizoguchi, the young and upcoming director in 1925. He met a homeless woman, Ichijo Yuriko in Kiyamachi, Kyoto. Yuriko was a half-maid/half-prostitute (*yatona*), and lived with a friend who was said to have once been a geisha in Tokyo. Mizoguchi and Yuriko formed a relationship but fought and argued incessantly. One day Yuriko slashed Mizoguchi's back with a razor. The incident, reported in the newspapers, caused a scandal and Mizoguchi, who was shooting *Shining in the Red Sunset,* was thrown out and replaced by Saegusa Genjiro. Yuriko was arrested, but because Mizoguchi gave her a really sympathetic defence, she was released without being prosecuted. However, the head of the studio, Ikenaga Hirohisa, separated the two and Yuriko returned to Tokyo.

Had it ended here, it would have been no more than a simple scandal. But being a sympathetic young man, Mizoguchi began worrying that Yuriko would commit suicide. He went to Tokyo to look for her. A Tokyo *ryokan* (hotel) owner, the friend of a friend, helped him in his search. They found her working as a live-in maid in a hotel in Tawarachyo. Mizoguchi stayed there with her. Much was tolerated of the young Mizoguchi because he would give the impression of a defenceless, unassuming, pure and beautiful man who women could easily fall in love with. But for all his resemblance to a young matinee idol, he did not, like the young man in *A Story from Chikamatsu*, try a double suicide for a woman's love. He was, in fact, a bit of a coward. Kishi Matsuo describes how the love affair between Mizoguchi and Yuriko ended:

> Mizoguchi was taken back to the *ryokan* where he hung around, watched a film, read a book. He would get up late in the mornings and go to a temple bathhouse next door. (The priest was related to the Imperial house.) Many people connected with the arts came to this neighbourhood. Among them was a minstrel (*naniwabushi katari*) with whom Mizoguchi would occasionally chat. One day the minstrel said, 'I am sorry, but I would like to give you my opinion. You are young and cannot become a woman's pimp. Leave her, get back to Kyoto as quickly as possible and work hard at your job. Don't worry, you will soon forget this woman.'
>
> Mizoguchi refrained from answering; but he turned over the minstrel's words in his mind and decided to follow his advice. He returned to Kyoto and to his job at Nikkatsu. This was towards the end of autumn 1925. Yuriko, who couldn't afford the *ryokan*, left to become a prostitute in Suzaki, and then disappeared. Later, Mizoguchi was to repeatedly use this story of a man who elopes with a woman, leaves her and goes away, in fact simply abandons her.

Kishi Matsuo says that this kind of story was first used in *And Yet they Go* (1931):

> At the beginning of the film, the man and woman have eloped, but the man is made to go back. The woman is left all alone and treated as someone of ill-repute. This may have been a simple scene, but Mizoguchi showed he was a master by the way he held the long shot of the stares of cold contempt that people cast on the woman.

This film is no longer available, but similar scenes can be found in *The Straits of Love and Hate* (1937), *The Story of the Late Chrysanthemums* (1939) and *The Life of Oharu* (1952).

Mizoguchi, who played the role of a matinee idol in his own life, was a genius at portraying matinee idols in his work. His research into this character may have led him to discover more about himself, but it is also true that he worked for a studio that made films based on contemporary dramas. In Japan, studios making period films and those making contemporary dramas were different. Period dramas were made largely in Kyoto, while contemporary dramas were made in Tokyo. When the Tokyo studio was destroyed in the Kanto earthquake, Mizoguchi began making contemporary dramas in the Kyoto studio after autumn 1923. However, while the studio, which was a part of Nikkatsu, did shift to Kyoto, Nikkatsu period dramas and contemporary dramas were produced independently.

As a rule, contemporary drama films had matinee idols as their main protagonists, while period drama films had lead actors. In fact, the image of the ideal lead actor in *kabuki* was incorporated in its entirety into period films. Onoe Matsunosuke, Okochi Denjiro, Bando Tsumasaburo, Mifune Toshiro and Katsu Shintaro were lead actors in typical period films, while Takakura Ken acted in films of chivalry. Which is why it is impossible to imagine Mifune Toshiro in a love scene. The lead actors and the kind of films in which they performed had a large male following, although some women also admired these films.

Matinee idols featured in period drama as well. The most representative of these was Hasegawa Kazuo. As a matinee idol on the *kabuki* stage, he specialized in romantic and emotional roles (*wagoto*) even after he became a star in period films. His large fan following was almost exclusively female and each woman felt that his glances were meant for her alone. Hasaegawa Kazuo was an exceptional talent among period actors.

The fans who saw the male ideal of period drama in the bold and rough (*aragoto*) style of actors such as Okochi Denjiro or Bando Tsumasaburo, described Hasegawa as effeminate (*niyake*) and were indifferent to his style. Effeminate meant someone who spent his time pursuing women, someone neither sober nor reliable. In his last years, Hasegawa acted in Mizoguchi's *The Story of the Late Chrysanthemums*, a cinematic version of a *kabuki* and a 'romantic and emotional' (*wagoto*) masterpiece. Hasegawa, with his vast *wagoto* repertoire – although he was getting on in years and did not look like a young romantic hero any more –

gave a most convincing performance. The Western audience, though, seemed to dislike his style, finding it strange that a weak and unreliable man should do love scenes. Ever since chivalric ballads developed in the West, the traditional hero had always been strong and trustworthy. Mifune Toshiro is not always considered one of the top-ranking Japanese actors, but he does represent the ideal of the strong Japanese male, at least for the West.

In the feudal period, the standing pose (*tachiyaku*) [*Translator's note:* this presents the whole body, as opposed to poses where the actor is sitting, etc.] was appreciated because form was an important element in the social structure. However, as Western influence increased in the Meiji period, the question of how to preserve this pose became problematic. The ideal for a *tachiyaku* is the samurai, but the samurai, as a class, were abolished and samurai-like behaviour was considered passé. Intellectuals replaced the samurai as the leaders of society and, as they learned from the West, they began stressing the idea of love as against the wild behaviour of the ruffian (*aragoto*) in *kabuki*. In a sense, they were left midway, neither able to appreciate the beauty of the traditional *tachiyaku* poses nor attracted to the Western hero. And period drama films continued to have their fans for those who still wanted to see men behaving like men. About 40 per cent of all Japanese films made between 1900 and 1950 (excluding the US Occupation) were period drama films, which is most unusual and calls for an explanation.

If we were to link this to the world of publishing, we would see that from the end of the Meiji period to the end of the Taisho, quick, easy-to-read novels had the largest sales. Their protagonists were, by and large, like the *tachiyaku* of *kabuki*. The stories had similar characters – masterful heroes, fencers, champions of the underdog and rebels – and were written in the traditional narrative style, but used the methods of a modern novel. Most of the period drama films based their scripts on material from these stories and popular novels.

Melodrama and the Matinee Idol Stars

While male readers welcomed the role of the *tachiyaku* type of protagonist in stories and popular literature, female readers were entertained by family novels which began appearing at the end of the nineteenth century and by the films and plays based on them.

There appeared a flood of films with social messages. The popular novel, *Konjiki yasha*, shows how people with social ambitions face serious problems in pursuing a successful life; *The Little Cuckoo* describes a daughter-in-law being ill-treated by her mother-in-law; in *My Fault*, a young girl is misled and seduced by a villain but overcomes her misfortune; while in *Bygone Friends,* the pure love of a mother-in-law actually resolves problems. These films showed women enduring adversity or being used by men, as also men trying to help unhappy women.

The films depended on stirring women emotionally – they showed traits of the female character and women's stoic acceptance of their fate. Even when the ending was happy, numerous scenes of the unhappy woman brought out her lover's weakness and unreliability, his rashness and frivolity. The male role had to be that of a matinee idol. The origin of the female character's trials and tribulations lay in her love for a weak and frivolous man. In Japan, good, reliable men, i.e. the *tachiyaku* variety, do not display their love. The roots of this reserve can be traced to Confucianism where it was not considered refined for a man to make a public display of his love for a woman. Rather, it was regarded as a somewhat charming weakness. Only a matinee idol character – confident of his appeal to women and sensitive to them – could bare his emotions.

A popular Edo period, humorous, poetic form called *senryu* said that 'an amorous man has neither money nor power.' This was an apt description of a matinee idol. Several examples can be found in stories of heroines falling in love with just such a man *sans* money or power, suffering on his behalf and finding happiness at the end. The main section of *A Story from Chikamatsu* is well known in *kabuki* for the *wagoto* character. The matinee idol who is in an unhappy situation falls in love. Despite his beloved's brave efforts to help him (he has no money, power or intelligence) and no matter how hard he tries, he cannot to extricate himself from his misfortune. Finally both are driven to suicide.

Modern women's melodrama, whose star was usually a matinee idol, established itself as an important part of modern cinema. It played up the heroine's courage, the man's shallowness, was popular with women and had a happy end. Among the well-known matinee idols were were Okada Tokihiko in the 1920s, Uehara Ken in the 1930s, Ikebe Ryo in the 1940s and Sata Keiji in the 1950s.

The *tachiyaku* character appeared in modern plays too. The influence of American films led to the creation of characters that occasionally combined the fine aspects of both the *tachiyaku* and the matinee idol, resulting in a strong, reliable and sensitive male protagonist (Hayakawa Sessyu is an admirable example). The superstars of Western, particularly American films, possessed these qualities which so attracted Japanese fans and film-makers. In Japan, actors such Suzuki Denmei in the 1920s, Ohinata Den or Saburi Sin in the 1930s, Tsuruta Koji in the 1950s and Ishihara Yujiro in the 1960s, are all representative of this model. Hayakawa Sessyu also combined within him the qualities of a *tachiyaku* and a matinee idol.

Unlike Nakadai Tatsuya, these actors were never labelled effeminate by the general public. Moreover, unlike the heroes of American cinema – Clark Gable or Gary Cooper, for example – who would enact love scenes even as they grew old, Japanese male leads did not play such roles forever. Once they reached middle age they either stopped acting altogether, or performed roles without too many female characters around them. They also had the option of acting the strict teacher to frivolous young men, or taking on pure *tachiyaku* roles. The choice was theirs. Japanese actors popular with Western audiences (Hayakawa Sessyu, Mifune Toshiro and Nakadai Tatsuya, for example) have generally been *tachiyaku*-type actors.

Most of the female protagonists in Mizoguchi's films had to die in the end because of their love for a weak man. In *Cascading White Threads* (1933), the woman protagonist is sentenced to death for killing (in self-defence) the money-lender from whom she has taken a large loan to pay for her lover's studies. The prosecutor tells her that the lover can come to her defence and testify if he wishes. But the irresolute man fails to do so. In *The Downfall of Osen* (1935) too, the female protagonist is in love with an irresponsible fellow, no older in age than her younger brother. She sends him money for his studies, suffers a mental breakdown and is convinced she has paralysis. The lover who, thanks to her help, has become a doctor, does nothing to help her.

The hero in *A Story from Chikamatsu* (1954), based on Chikamatsu Monzaemon's work, is thoroughly ineffectual. All he can do is suffer the death penalty with his lover for their adulterous relationship. Mizoguchi was dissatisfied with the matinee idol character and never made films based on family novels which showed stoic women loving unstable men, suffering, and then finding happiness quite by accident. What he did make, though, were films where the woman who falls in love with a weak man emerges the stronger for it.

The matinee idol character was also idolized by women who were both attracted to the magnificence of the *tachiyaku*, and repelled by his tyrannical ways. What they found most appealing in the matinee idol was his sensitivity, gentleness and expression of love, as against the *tachiyaku* who kept them at an arm's length. Even if such a character was essentially weak, women wanted him to be pure and sincere. And this is exactly how Mizoguchi used them, as can be seen in the performances of Okada Tokihiko in *Cascading White Threads* and Natsukawa Daijiro in *The Downfall of Osen*. He was to change only later.

Dual Structure of Culture and the Fate of Matinee Idols – *Osaka Elegy*

The film that marks Mizoguchi's handling of realism in Japanese cinema is the invaluable *Osaka Elegy*, a work that will long be remembered for Yamada Isuzu's lively portrayal of Ayako, the young, rebellious, main character.

Ayako is a telephone operator in a medicine store in Osaka. Her father embezzles company money, goes off fishing and complains all day long. Ayako, who has no wish to see her father in jail, feels she must somehow raise the stolen money. She is in love with Nishimura, a colleague, and decides to discuss the problem with him. Inevitably, Nishimura gives her no support.

Asai, the owner of the company where Ayako works, asks her to become his mistress. Ayako agrees on the condition that he quietly returns to the company the money

FIGURE 6 Yamada Isuzu (left) in *Sisters of the Gion* (1936).

her father has embezzled. She quits her company job and starts living a luxurious life with Asai. One day she accidentally meets Nishimura, who proposes to her. She does not tell him about her situation, but thinks that she would indeed like to marry him.

Asai's wife discovers that Ayako is his mistress. Asai cannot face her and is forced to leave Ayako. Delighted by her freedom, Ayako plans to go to Nishimura's house. On the way, however, she meets her younger sister, who informs her that their younger brother has left his university because there is no money to pay his fees.

Ayako decides that she must raise this money. She calls Nishimura and Fujino – a stockbroker who has frequently given her suggestive looks – to her apartment. Fujino arrives, and just as he gets into an amorous mood, Nishimura appears. Ayako tells Fujino that Nishimura is her husband, and demands money from Fujino for trying to commit adultery with a married woman. Fujino goes straight to the police and files a complaint. Nishimura and Ayako are arrested. The shy Nishimura calls Ayako intimidating, and accuses her of fooling and using him. Ayako, in the next room, listens in astonishment to Nishimura's statement.

Ayako returns home after her father frees her from police custody. But her furious younger brother feels they should have nothing to do with a promiscuous woman, indeed they should forbid her from entering the house. Her father has never told anyone that Ayako had returned the money he had embezzled. Nor has Ayako mentioned that the blackmail about adultery was to raise money for her brother's education. Ayako does not justify what she did, but she does expect to be warmly received in the family fold. What happens is the reverse: she is abused and labelled a loose woman by her brother and berated by her sister; as for her loathsome father, he refuses to explain that the crime she committed was in the interest of the family.

When Ayako understands that those nearest and dearest to her are cold and unforgiving she runs out of the house without offering any explanation. In the last scene we see her standing on a bridge, leaning against the railing, looking down at the waters on a gloomy night.

In this story Nishimura has the exaggerated weakness of a matinee idol. A good young man he may be, but he cannot stop Ayako from taking this thoughtless step. When the police arrest him as an accomplice, his only instinct is to protect himself, without a thought in his head for her. Looking as if he would at any moment break into uncontrollable tears, he ends up making damaging statements.

Hara Kensaku, who played Nishimura, was not a pure matinee idol type. He played many different roles, including *tachiyaku*, or the dashing hero in period drama for children, but never one of someonee so utterly cowardly, and it surprised us all. His incredible acting skill, though, gave the character credibility. For instance, when Ayako threatens Fujino, Nishimura retreats silently to a corner of the room, trying to make himself as small as possible. His seated figure looking the other way, is both pitiful and funny. He truly comes across as a person who, suddenly and without warning, is turned into an accomplice of blackmail by the woman he loves. All he can think of is that this frightening time will somehow pass quickly. I don't see any real man wanting to cut so disgraceful a figure.

For all these weaknesses, the matinee idol was normally depicted with sympathy. But in this film Mizoguchi was merciless. The woman protagonist gradually awakens to the spinelessness of her lover, and is shaken by the coldness of her father and brother. She then grows taller than any man; her demeanour exudes a steely resolve as she sets off to meet the challenge. All the major moments in *Osaka Elegy* are long shots, with only one close-up being used at the end to show Ayako's expression. And the face of young Yamada Isuzu (as Ayako) wears a fiercely determined expression as if to suggest that she will henceforth rely only on herself.

We have a similar situation in *The Straits of Love and Hate* (1937):

The character of the protagonist (played by Yamaji Fumiko) changes completely in the course of this film. In the first half, she is a maid in a hotel (*ryokan*) in a rural town. She is loved by the son of the owner, and becomes pregnant, but his father will not let them get married. The son runs off to town with her.

Unfortunately, he is the typical 'amorous man with no money or power'. He neither works nor fulfils his obligations. When they have a hard time trying to make ends meet, he simply dumps her and returns to his father's *ryokan* in the countryside.

Up to this point Fumiko – like all heroines of romantic melodrama – is submissive and pliant, and flutters at the mere confession of love, even by an unreliable man. Then her character does a volte-face. She puts her child in foster care, begins working in a bar to provide for him, becomes a comic (*manzai*) performer in a travelling troupe, and is transformed into a woman more hardened than any man.

Her troupe arrives at the rural town where her former lover is now the owner of the *ryokan*. He meets her and once again declares that he would like to marry her formally and bring her and the child to live with him. This time, she flatly refuses – not only because of past bitterness, but because she is now brimming with a new-found confidence and no longer needs any help from the faint-hearted.

This was the first time that Yamaji Fumiko – who had so far starred only in traditional women's melodrama – acted in a Mizoguchi film. She amazed her fans by her performance of a lower-class woman with a core of great strength. Shindo Kaneto, the art assistant for this film, was equally surprised by Yamaji's transformation, and decided to become Mizoguchi's disciple.

These two male roles – the *tachiyaku* and the matinee idol – arose out of the dual structure of the feudal culture in Japan and were consolidated through popular plays. The experiment to transform the roles into one of the chivalric hero (strong, reliable, loving), born of the popular Western tradition, happened during the time of the modernization and Westernization of Japanese cinema. The tradition was difficult to adapt and often left one with an unnatural impression. Mizoguchi began from the popular and conventional melodrama for women that brought together a

FIGURE 7 Yamada Isuzu in *Osaka Elegy* (1936).

pitiable woman and a weak and handsome man (*nimaeme*), but went on to imbue the woman with a supreme strength of character. He was moving towards a stringent criticism of his vacillation. There may be several reasons why he swerved away so completely from the original *shinpa*-type melodrama.

First, it was Yoda Yoshikata who wrote the script for *Osaka Elegy*. Yoda had been an unknown figure until then. But once trained by Mizoguchi, he worked extensively for him and was to write most of his future scripts. What now begins to appear as a characteristic in Mizoguchi's films – distaste for the weak and handsome man – may have been Yoda's personal approach.

But occasionally, Yoda Yoshikata wrote scripts for other directors as well. In his script for Inoue Kintaro's *Crow in the Moonlight*, he gives a sympathetic portrayal of a characteristic *shinpa* protagonist. Other films (Itami Mansaku's *Just Take it Out*, Yamanaka Sadao's, *The Village Tattooed Man*, Gosho Heinosuke's *The Baggage of Life* and Ozu Yasujiro's *Tokyo Hotel*) made in 1935, a year before *Osaka Elegy*, explored a kind of realism different from the realism of *keiko* films that had been popular five years earlier. The new films were calmer works, out to create a sense of wonder in people through their sharp observations of reality.

When Mizoguchi saw these young film-makers making a name for themselves through their realistic works, he must have wanted to outstrip them with an even more 'realistic' film. In all likelihood, he incorporated a self-critique into his investigation of realism.

In his later years when he made *Women of the Night* (1948), he went to Yoshiwara Hospital to study the behaviour of *panpan* (prostitutes during the US occupation – street walkers) who were under treatment for various venereal diseases. The director of the hospital gave him details about their afflictions and said, 'Far from being the result of a crime committed by these girls, it is above all a crime committed by men.' At that moment Mizoguchi cried out, 'You are right. It's my crime.' This story was related by Itoya Hisao, the producer who went along with him.

Mizoguchi owed many debts to women. His first wife had once slashed him with a razor following a lover's spat. During the shooting of *Osaka Elegy* his second wife was not mentally stable. Mizoguchi took the blame for her problem on himself and on his relationship with women. His bias against the conventional *shinpa* melodrama grew out of his personal experience.

In his later films he increasingly attacked male meanness, cowardice, wiliness, violence and discrimination towards women. And yet he was not overly disparaging of the matinee idol character – or else he may have lost his female following altogether!

This is especially true of *The Story of the Late Chrysanthemums*, a cinematic version of a highly evaluated *shinpa* play, with the most famous *onnagata*, Hanayagi Shotaro, in the role of the matinee idol role. The conditions for this role suited him perfectly. He is a beautiful and untrustworthy young man who finally grows up only when he is helped by a woman's love and sacrifice; also, he was tall while the woman protagonist was short. Mizoguchi was criticized for being conservative, for it was believed that he was affirming loyalty through the sacrifice of a short person for a tall person! However, apart from Hanayagi's skilful performance, the childish and selfish matinee idol is not an attractive personality. The woman protagonist (played by Mori Kakuko), though, has great appeal; she conveys a kind of refined human dignity that cannot be contained in a feudal type of loyalty. The character of the matinee idol was used in this film only to bring out the luminescence in the woman.

A Picture of Madame Yuki

A Picture of Madame Yuki (1950), *Lady Yu* (1951) and *Lady Musashino* (1951) are generally regarded as films made at a time of slump in Mizoguchi's creativity, when he revived the *shinpa* type of matinee idol character in a somewhat simplistic way. That character had been outmoded since the 1930s.

The cinematography in these three films is quite extraordinary. In *A Picture of Madame Yuki*, the scene of the mist-covered, reed-filled lake into which the female protagonist is about to throw herself, is an exquisite piece of work. Every single

FIGURE 8 Simizu Masao (left) and Yamaji Fumiko in *The Straits of Love and Hate* (1937).

scene in *Lady Yu* is like viewing a masterpiece of Japanese painting. Particularly lovely is the first scene of a pure Japanese *miai* (introductory meeting between prospective bride and groom) in a Japanese-style garden. *Lady Musashino*, too, has an utterly captivating scene of two lovers strolling in the countryside. Each of these well-composed and highly polished scenes is linked by a pure Japanese sensibility, a picturesque quality and an aesthetic vision that can be seen on the *shinpa* stage.

This is the story of *A Picture of Madame Yuki*:

Madame Yuki is the daughter of a nobleman, a former Viscount, and the wife of a playboy, Naoyuki (Yanagi Eijiro) who has been taken in as a son-in-law (*muko*). The family's fortunes decline rapidly after the Second World War. When the story opens, the Viscount has died. Madame Yuki converts the property, a chalet in Atamii, into a *ryokan*, and employs her loyal retainers. They lead a good life built on the business principles of a samurai house. The husband, Naoyuki, is a foolish lord, nibbling away at what is left of the family fortune. He consorts with friends – his mistress, Ayako (Hamada Yuriko), a former dancer, and a craven black-market broker, Tachioka (Yamamura So). Naoyuki and his friends come to this *ryokan*, throw their weight around and even urge Madame Yuki to leave the running of the *ryokan* to them.

In spite of their offensive behaviour, Madame Yuki does not take a firm stand against her husband – not because she has been brought up like a princess or is ignorant of the ways of the world. During the day she is a worldly upper-class woman, but at night, when her husband clasps her, she is a mass of carnal desire. All she lives for is sexual fulfilment and entreats her husband not to discard her.

She also has a lover – Kikunaka – a novelist who had helped the Viscount's family in the past. He is there at her request, works at the *ryokan* as her advisor and consultant, is honest and sincere, but will not help with her sexual problems. Then Tachioka hatches a plot. Kikunaka is drunk and asleep in his room. Tachioka sends a message asking Madame Yuki to come to Kikunaka's room. Shortly afterwards, he also requests Naoyuki to come to the same room. Naoyuki sees the two together and believes they are in an adulterous relationship. It ends with Madame Yuki's suicide. As for Naoyuki, before he fully understands what is going on, he loses his *ryokan* to Tachioka, who is actually having an affair with Ayako.

I believe Kogure Michiyo (as Madame Yuki) was miscast in this film. In Imai Tadashi's *Blue Mountain Range*, she had played an ageing geisha. Renowned for her sexually attractive persona, she was unsuited for a role of a sexually aroused woman yet with no power to live, a woman so weak as to be mouse-like and dumb before a violent, oppressive, stupid, husband. Strange it is that a woman who is energetic and prosperous to begin with is locked in an unending cycle of worry about her body-mind split even as she presents a contented face to the world. With a little exaggeration I would call it slightly weird!

Uehara Ken's portrayal of Kikunaka, too, was unconvincing. Madame Yuki gives clear signals that she wants to be rescued from her husband; yet Kikunaka remains unmoved and makes no effort to help her. This is completely out of character for a matinee idol.

In *Mizoguchi Kenji, The Man and the Art* (Mizoguchi Kenji no hito to geijutsu), Yoda Yoshikata writes that he was toying with a more believable story at the dramatization stage:

> Regarding the structure of the script, I argued heatedly [with Mizoguchi]. I wanted to use a maid, Hamako, to allow the male protagonist, Kikunaka, to break his relations with Madame Yuki. But Mizoguchi said, 'What's all this? I just don't understand it.'
>
> I said, 'That is not true, I don't see how you can't understand his feelings, the pain he must be going through.'
>
> 'That's literature, not film.' Even then I did not give up.
>
> I said, 'It is not literature at all. It can be a good play.'
>
> 'Your thinking that way is going to be a problem. You just don't understand what people like in films,' he said. This I could understand from people's views on morals and ethics and I asked him if he felt I wasn't looking at Kikunaka's character sympathetically enough. Mizoguchi replied that he felt that people empathised with Kikunaka's character as played by Uehara Ken and he felt that he could not destroy their dreams.

The structure was so planned that Kikunaka's worship of Madame Yuki was platonic and indecisive. In order to overcome this problem, Kikunaka could have gone away with Hamako (Kuga Yoshiko), the beautiful maid, and a way to separate him from Madame Yuki would have been provided. Yoda stressed that it would not have disillusioned Uehara Ken's fans. But Mizoguchi was not convinced. He got a brilliant performance of a dissolute young woman from Michiyo Kogure, famous for her roles as a pure and sincere daughter. Two years earlier even Tanaka Kinuyo, with her pure-as-the-driven-snow image, had played the role of a *panpan* (prostitute).

Mizoguchi's reluctance to dispense with Uehara Ken's pure, matinee idol image was difficult to understand. Consequently, Uehara did not quite measure up to the character of a hero in a romance. The film was left vague and ambiguous, with its indecisive hero and its heroine cutting a poor image. Neither of them evoked any response from the audience. The other negative characters, though – Naoyuki, Ayako, and Tachioka – were successfully portrayed in the recognizable Mizoguchi style.

Perhaps Mizoguchi showed Kikunaka as gentle with Madame Yuki because he saw himself mirrored in him and because he modelled Madame Yuki on his elder sister, Suzu. He was handling the tragedy of a powerless, younger brother unable to help his sister. But, this, naturally, is pure conjecture.

–6–

Art Imitates Life

Mizoguchi's Marriage

In 1927, the actor Nakano Eiji introduced Mizoguchi to Saga Chieko, a dancer in Osaka, whose real name was Tajima Kane. She hailed from Tochigi and was seven years younger than Mizoguchi. Saga Chieko was a spirited woman with a great determination to make her career a success. Mizoguchi fell in love with her and began going to her house to learn dancing. She had started out as a dancer in Tokyo and had married an opera singer. After the Kanto earthquake when there was no work, she moved to Osaka with the help of a gangland boss (*oyabun*) from Kobe, leaving her husband behind. He visited her occasionally in Osaka, but relations between them had turned cold and soon Mizoguchi and she became intimate.

In the summer of the following year, the 'boss' called Mizoguchi, saying he wanted to talk to him about Chieko. Mizoguchi was apprehensive. In the eyes of the law he had committed adultery and to complicate matters the husband was also a *yakuza*. Mizoguchi consulted a scriptwriter friend, Hatamoto Akiichi, and then requested Nagata Masakazu, a young man who worked in the general affairs division of the studio, to act as an intermediary. Nagata Masakazu, a skilful speaker, was often asked to take visitors around the studio premises, something he did very well. It also seems that he had links with the Kyoto Senbon *yakuza* group. Nagata went to Kobe as Mizoguchi's representative to meet the 'boss'. He convinced him that Mizoguchi and Chieko were not intimate but were in love. The 'boss' believed Nagata and agreed to their marriage, which took place on 8 August 1927.

Later, as a producer, Nagata Masakazu set up an independent company, Dai Ichi Eiga. He also set up Daiei, despite the confused situation created by the forced amalgamation of film companies during the Second World War. Because of Nagata's involvement in the events leading to his marriage, Mizoguchi grew to trust him, and many of his masterpieces were made for the Dai Ichi Eiga and Daiei.

Mizoguchi's wife became an actress with the theatre group, 'Elan Vitale', under her earlier stage name as a dancer. She was also actively involved in Mizoguchi's work, always prepared to offer her comments. Though Mizoguchi was occasionally unfaithful, his love for his wife was very strong. Chieko was an aggressive and strong-willed woman and there were frequent arguments with the self-centred Mizoguchi. It appears that she, too, was not always faithful.

Sometime around 1929, Mizoguchi received some money from Matsudaira Tadamasa. Chieko used it to open a bar, the 'Salon Chie', in Tokyo's Ginza district. Suzu helped out whenever she could. One evening, when Mizoguchi visited the bar he saw a number of customers who looked like workers. He left, but returned later and in a fit of temper threw a frying pan at Chieko, and tore the bar apart. In most of their fights, Chieko was usually the winner, but on that day it was Mizoguchi who prevailed, and it resulted in the bar's closure. It appeared to be something more than just the usual friction between husband and wife, and quite clearly, it was some deep sorrow in Mizoguchi's heart that had led to this sudden emotional outburst. The battles between the spouses continued, and perhaps under their strain, Chieko began to suffer from pleurisy. She was an attractive person with a soft heart and everyone who knew her remembers her with affection.

The Last Scene of *The Downfall of Osen*

The Downfall of Osen, made in 1935, is among the handful of Mizoguchi's unsuccessful films that has not been discussed at length. The script, based on Izumi Kyoka's novel, *Baishoku kamo nanban*, was written by Takashima Tatsunosuke. The film was set mainly at the turn of the century.

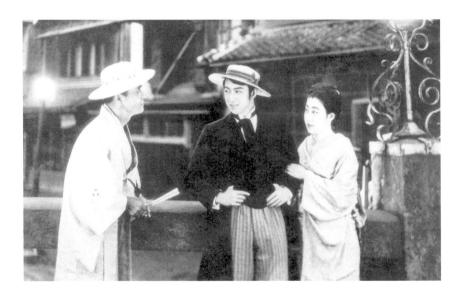

FIGURE 9 Kogule Michiyo (left) and Kuga Yoshiko (right) in *A Picture of Madame Yuki* (1950), © Toho Film Co. Ltd.

The scene is the railway station of Manseibashi. Trains have stopped because of the rain and power failure, the platform is crowded and people are milling around. Hata Sokichi (Natsukawa Daijiro) and Osen (Yamada Isuzu), a young man and woman, are sitting on a bench in the waiting room, lost in thought. Osen's appearance and the light in her eyes make for a strange and particularly disturbing image.

The camera shows Hata in a contemplative mood. It pans across the area, showing Kanda Myojin as it looked about ten years ago.

Actually Manseibashi is easily visible from Kanda Myojin. Among the still extant films of those years, none has shots that give a sense of the geography of the place; neither is this scene shot in a comprehensible way. Today we are familiar with all kinds of flashback techniques and know how to read them. But in those days viewers were not accustomed to this and to use a pan to indicate a flashback was very advanced grammar indeed. Today this comes across as a fault for, given the rhythm of the entire film, it seems like an abrupt leap.

It is a night scene within the precincts of the Kanda Myojin. Sokichi (Natsukawa Daijiro), a seventeen-year-old in a kimono with very short sleeves, stands in a daze under a *gingko* (maidenhair) tree, having just failed in a suicide attempt. Osen, a distraught geisha, trying to escape her pursuers, comes running by. Another group of villains charge in from the opposite side to help her. In the mêlée, Osen sees Sokichi's failed suicide as a warning to her.

The relationships in this scene are initially unclear and confusing. We do not know whether it is a flashback and understandably, contemporary critics were critical of it. But interpreted positively, it can be argued that the writers planned the scene in a way that would show the strange meeting between the two protagonists. They focused their energies on conveying as strongly as possible that the meeting was fated.

Later it becomes clear that Osen is a friend of the ruffians. She had fled the geisha house to join them in the flesh trade but had instead become a moneylender. She has accidentally come upon Sokichi trying to commit suicide.

Osen takes Sokichi to the ruffians' den and persuades them to let Sokichi stay and to tutor him.

The robbers try to get the priest to look the other way as they steal a statue of the Buddha, and it seems that Osen is using her sexual charms on him. The robbers are rough with Sokichi, needling him till he cries before letting him eat. Sokichi puts up with their insults because he feels he has found an elder sister in the beautiful Osen. The basically hard-hearted Osen softens in the face of Sokichi's totally reverential attitude and asks him why he tried to commit suicide.

At this point there is a flashback within a flashback as Sokichi narrates his life. He had left a blind grandmother, his only relative, in the village and gone to Tokyo to study, with every intention of achieving success in life (*shusse*). But with no money to buy a train ticket, he walks along the railway tracks. It's a memorable, desolate scene. With no money for fees either, he cannot find a school to join and in despair he decides to commit suicide.

Osen is deeply sympathetic and says that she will make sure that he gets to school.

The titles for Osen are: 'I think it was the pure heart of your grandmother in the village that made me stop and protect you like an elder sister and bring you back.' They used to have such wonderful, unpretentious titles in films those days. The feeling with which Yamada Isuzu speaks these words, pierces the viewer's heart.

Osen defends Sokichi from the robbers' needling, but unable to bear their persistent humiliation, he tries to kill himself yet again. Sokichi then takes on the ruffians, but just when he and Osen declare that it is immaterial whether they live or die, policemen break into the hideout and rescue them. The robbers are arrested and the two can now start a new life.

They begin living together like elder sister and younger brother. Sokichi starts going to school and Osen pretends she is making money as a seamstress. In reality when Sokichi is not around, she makes a living as a prostitute.

After some time, Osen is arrested on charges of having stolen money and valuables from one of her customers. The scene where Sokichi returns from school just as she is being arrested by the police and about to leave the house is one of the most beautiful in the film.

Without offering an explanation Osen says, 'I have bought some food (*nimono*). It is under the paper in the covered dish and there is *ochazuke* for tomorrow's breakfast.'

In a rage, Sokichi tears a paper (origami) crane, shouting 'You are my demon.' Walking out in a daze, he is hit by a rickshaw, in which a teacher from his school happens to be sitting.

The flashback ends and the scene returns to the Manseibashi station. Sokichi is now a successful man. He has lived with his schoolteacher, he worked his way through university, even went abroad to study, and is now a professor in the Department of Medicine at the Imperial University.

Finally the train arrives. Again, a crowd of people mill around on the platform. Osen, the woman who is sitting in the waiting room, suddenly collapses in a faint. Sokichi comes forward as a doctor to help, pushing through the crowd that has gathered around her. He is surprised to see that she is his former benefactress. Immediately, he has her carried to the university hospital. Before she falls in a faint, Osen's face presents a dreadful sight; it shakes the warm-hearted Sokichi to the core, especially since he knows that he owes his success to her sacrifice.

The last scene is superb. To quote the script: 'Osen's room in the hospital. The doctor (Sokichi), is standing, an unkempt figure, in a room for a single patient. Before him is the mad Osen, who appears like a goddess in a trance. She is making an origami crane. Suddenly, with a frightening expression, she throws the knife she has been using, but continues to fold the crane.

Smiling slightly, crying, looking at Osen who has lost her mind, the doctor laments, forgetting himself, his body and the world; he thinks with sadness of the tragic transience of this world.

'It's me, Sokichi.' Uncontrollable tears stream through his beard as he clings to Osen. Osen looks blankly at Sokichi. Sokichi reflects sadly on his inability to be of any help despite all the power of a human being, all the power of a doctor. He breaks down as he thinks of the inevitable cycle of birth and death, of the purgatory that this world full of sorrow is. All he can do is weep.

'What ...'

'... who?'

'... they have done this to you ...'

As the seasons pass, a woman's entire life can only end in sorrow. Sokichi laments, sometimes aloud, sometimes softly.

The film differed somewhat from this script. The 'knife of fate' in the script is the knife that Sokichi had earlier used in his suicide attempt. In the film he tries to shave but there is no razor. Apart from these little details, the major change is that Osen stares in a deranged way at Sokichi's attempts to show sincerity, making no attempt to come close to him. She shouts, 'Everyone teases my Mune-chan' but shows no sign of recognition. There is no 'clinging' or 'lamenting' in the film; Sokichi just stands there paralysed, in a daze, staring at the strange behaviour of this mad woman.

The film is complex, but an important section – the crime story of the robbers and the way in which the characters have been portrayed – is unfortunately trite.

FIGURE 10 Yamada Isuzu and Natsukawa Daijiro in *The Downfall of Osen* (1935).

From our point of view today, this emotional story amounts to very little and never transcends the antiquated *shinpa* tragedy formula. Apart from the startling impact of the earlier flashback, even the critics must have slept through the film.

This was in 1935. Yet the previous year masterpieces full of a fresh, modern and realistic sensibility had been made: Shimazu Yasujiru's *My Little Neighbour, Yae-chan*, Itami Mansaku's *The Forty-Seven Ronin*, Ozu Yasujiro's *Tokyo Hotel* and Gosho Heinosuke's *The Baggage of Life*. The question is why, until 1936, when he finally caught up with them through *Osaka Elegy* and *The Sisters of the Gion*, was Mizoguchi so immersed in these outdated, emotional stories from the world of the Meiji?

Many of Mizoguchi's films bear his stamp, works that show his firm grasp of his basic objective. Many of his films were masterpieces; but there are also works that are incoherent and inconsistent. I personally feel this is a wonderful film, if just for the scenes of Sokichi and Osen's first meeting, their parting, their reunion and for the last scene with the mad Osen.

Discovering the Pose of Redemption

The greatest tragedy in Mizoguchi's life was his wife's insanity, which caused him deep suffering. This can be vividly seen in the crystallization of an art based on the Buddhist idea of atonement and prayer in his later films, *The Life of Oharu* and *Sansho the Bailiff*.

His wife's illness dated from 1941, but six years earlier Mizoguchi had already made *The Downfall of Osen*; two years earlier, he had made *Cascading White Threads* with a similar motif, and *The Nihon Bridge* six years prior to that. But more than an abiding motif with Mizoguchi himself, it would be more accurate to say that this was the leitmotif in the work of the writer Izumi Kyoka, on whose scripts these three *shinpa* tragedies were based, and a part of Mizoguchi's heart responded to Izumi Kyoka's scripts. Mizoguchi may have moved beyond the old-fashioned *shinpa* to grand realism, but the *shinpa* elements retained their vividness and continued to tempt him. They appeared subliminally in the films of his last years.

While Sokichi laments and cries in the script for Osen who has suffered for him and lost her mind, all he actually does in the film is to stand by her bedside, petrified. In *Sansho the Bailiff*, made in 1954, the protagonist, Zushio (Hanayagi Kisho), after a long life of slavery, goes to Sado to meet his old mother (Tanaka Kinuyo) from whom he has been separated since childhood. He discovers she is blind and unable to stand. At first she is suspicious, but once she realizes that it is her son, she clasps him tightly. This last scene in *Sansho the Bailiff*, is a clear improvement on the last scene of *The Downfall of Osen* where Michoguchi was unable to muster up the sensitivity needed for the scene. He was to do that nineteen years later, in *Sansho the Bailiff*.

The difference is that unlike Osen, who sacrifices herself for Sokichi, the mother in *Sansho the Bailiff* does not do so voluntarily. She is tricked by a slave trader and sold as a prostitute in Sado. Zushio's younger sister Anju's suicide to protect him after he is thrown out of the manor (*shoen*) by Sansho, is the self-sacrifice of an utterly innocent woman. Zushio's reward for Anju's sacrifice is to look for and help his mother, whose once high status had been reduced to that of a prostitute.

That the basis for a man's worldly success was the sacrifice of a woman was particularly true of the Meiji ideology of 'success in life' (*risshin shusse*). It was considered natural for an older or younger sister to work herself to the bone to be able to educate the eldest son or brother. Izumi Kyoka's *shinpa* tragedies were based on such existing practices. Mizoguchi began by giving form to this tragedy and ended by immersing himself in its very essence. He crafted the image of a woman who offers herself as a sacrifice either by disappearing (*The Nihon Bridge*), committing suicide (*Cascading White Threads*) or going mad (*The Downfall of Osen*). The callousness with which men use these acts to their own ends is likened to the heady taste of wine. As examples you have the love scene in *Cascading White Threads* and the scene of separation in *The Downfall of Osen*. Drunk on this wine, the man is suddenly placed in a quandary about whether to acknowledge or apologize to the woman, and is frozen into inaction.

The scene where Zushio first comes close to his mother recalls the moment where Osen comes close to Sokichi. Osen sends the ruffians packing, recalling her own childhood, trying to drive away the fear she has of the men who had turned her into a prostitute, used her, and had now returned to mock her. In *Sansho the Bailiff*, Zushio, who sees in his father's shrine the precious statue of the Buddha as proof of his high status, begins to accept this only when he actually touches it, and then he clasps it tightly. It's a superb build-up of the mood by Tanaka Kinuyo and Hanayagi Kisho as they move tentatively towards each other on the beach and embrace – a rare and finely polished performance.

Mizoguchi found a way to depict love scenes through Buddhism. In art, the discovery of a particular pose or form is the same as discovering its meaning. Precisely because art is a ceaseless discovery of form, discovering the spirit of the form is an act of creation. If the last scene in *Sansho the Bailiff* is imbued with such meaning for us, for Mizoguchi it must have been a moment of beatitude. And for me, it was a moment of spiritual awakening, a reflection of Mizoguchi's understanding.

What effect did Mizoguchi's wife's insanity have on his films? As I have stated before, the motif that links most of his later films is the invocation of woman; an invocation that includes the suggestion of an apology because she is sacred and because of what she endures for the man. We are led to feel that this must surely have had some connection with his wife's illness. In fact, this motif first appeared in Mizoguchi's films well before his wife fell ill and he had examined it repeatedly.

Indeed, Izumi Kyoka, whose novels Mizoguchi used, ad done likewise even earlier.

I recall Oscar Wilde' famous words, 'It's not art that imitates life, it is nature that imitates art.' In Mizoguchi's case, I feel it was not his life that provided the model for his art but rather his art that was the model for his life, an art that transcended his personal vision of life. He based his tragedies on the idea that the fundamental contradiction in society was the inequality of the man-woman relationship. This was expressed most acutely in the evils of the Meiji ideology which sought 'success in life' for men. If this premise were to be accepted, we could perhaps agree that Mizoguchi's life was a kind of martyrdom. Japanese modernization inevitably gave rise to a certain form of tragedy, and Mizoguchi used Izumi Kyoka's works as a sort of filter to concentrate on this tragedy and make it part of his own life. This he achieved in his later years with a series of graceful prayers of devotion to a sacred sacrifice.

−7−

Three Traditional Art Films (*Geidomono*)

War and the Traditional Arts

As Japan's war against China entered its climactic phase in 1937, the film world faced some severe pressures. Government policy demanded that the industry produce films in active support of the war. Not only were socially critical 'realistic' films suppressed, even romances were regarded as irrelevant. Mizoguchi, whose works revealed the essence of a male-dominated society from the perspective of the woman, could no longer make the kind of films he wanted to. In compliance with the government's demands, he did churn out one poor and uncontroversial propaganda film, *The Song of the Camp* (1938). But placed in a difficult situation for the duration of the war, he shifted to making *geidomono*, a film genre that used Japanese traditional arts.

Geidomono are films where the protagonist, male or female, is a practitioner of one of the traditional Japanese arts such as *kabuki*, puppet theatre (*bunraku*), or traditional dance. They stress the rigour of the practice, but add that practice alone is not enough to understand the essence of the art; it is equally vital to face the difficulties of life, build character and sacrifice individual happiness for art. The world of traditional Japanese arts was mostly feudal, monopolizd for generations by a few leading families. Because of the 'follies of youth', the protagonists of *geidomono* films would, at times, make attempts to oppose this feudal structure; this would only result in their exclusion and in the denial of opportunities given to those who obeyed. The hardships they faced would strengthen their character in a way that enabled them to help maintain the feudal order. Only then would they be allowed to return as favoured carriers of the tradition.

The fixed form of the *geidomono* did not conflict with government strictures of self-sacrifice, loyalty to the state and need to practise techniques to win a war. The government did not so much encourage these films as merely tolerate them. Even film-makers who were not active supporters of the war, did not see them as directly pro-war, although the films did represent a compromise with and a subordination to a feudal ethic. Directors could continue to function as artists without damaging their sensibilities. To film-makers, who had till then used romance as a subject, the *geidomono* genre offered one of the few possibilities where romantic themes were permitted, albeit in the context of a feudal ethic, where the woman would sacrifice herself for the man, and the man, on the basis of the woman's sacrifice, would go on to develop his art. Free love was considered an expression of American or English ideology and in most cases not permitted by the censors. *Geidomono* film-makers concentrated on depicting love, not war. Mizoguchi's three *geidomono* films, as they are referred to, are *The Story of the Late Chrysanthemums* (1939), *A Woman of Osaka* (1940) and *The Life of an Actor* (1941).

The Story of the Late Chrysanthemums

The Story of the Late Chrysanthemums is a tragedy, a tragedy that lies not in the unfulfilled love between a handsome man and a beautiful woman, but in the lack of any opposition by the woman to blatant social discrimination. In fact, she actually seems to be supporting it. The story's tragic irony lies in its emotional structure that fully supports a discriminatory and class-conscious society. That in such a society the most discriminated against are often the staunchest supporters of such practices is an ironic but universal truth. But there will come a time when such relationships will be reversed, and it will be possible to distinguish, on the basis of will or intention, between those who oppose and those who just follow.

Set in a feudal society dominated by a few reputed families at the end of the nineteenth century, this is the story of *kabuki* performers and their world of traditional Japanese arts. Over generations, performers from these influential families have monopolized important roles. Onoe Kikugoro, a popular and talented member of a fifth-generation *kabuki* family, is one of the stars who dominates this world. His adopted son, Kikunosuke, is expected to carry forward the name, in the sixth generation. Although Kikunosuke has not yet matured as a performer, he is quickly confirmed as the successor. Thereafter, he seems to lose touch with reality. He spends his time dallying with a geisha and neglecting his art but, aware of the importance of his position, no one remonstrates with him. Only Otoku, a maid employed to look after an infant in the Onoe household, criticizes him openly, telling him that he has yet not matured as a performer and should work harder. Kikunosuke is struck by her candour and falls in love with her. Rumours fly around about their love. Kikunosuke's wife sacks Otoku from her job, and his father, Kikugoro, forbids him from seeing her. Otoku rues her lower social position; by loving Kikunosuke she has caused him a great deal of trouble.

Kikunosuke refuses to listen to his adopted parents and is thrown out of the Onoe house. No one gives him work in *kabuki* in Tokyo. He seeks help from Onoe Tamizo, a powerful figure in the *kabuki* world in Osaka. Tamizo gives him a role. The Osaka audience, seeing his immature performance, laughs at him, and hangs on to retain his role only because of his patron. Otoku arrives from Tokyo and the two begin leading an impoverished life as husband and wife. One day Onoe Tamizo dies and Kikunosuke can no longer get a role on the Osaka stage. Left with no alternative he joins a group that tours villages. Kikunosuke is now a defeated man, but with Otoku's encouragement and because of his personal trials and tribulations, his art improves.

During the tour, the troupe goes bankrupt and is disbanded. Kikunosuke and Otoku hear that another troupe has come to neighbouring Nagoya from Tokyo. Otoku requests them for a role for Kikunosuke. Meanwhile, audiences have begun applauding Kikunosuke's acting skills. The actors ask Onoe Kikugoro to allow Kikunosuke to come back so that he can perform in Tokyo. There is a condition though – Kikunosuke must part from Otoku. She is the only one to be informed of this. As the delighted Kikunosuke boards the train to Tokyo, Otoku quietly leaves for Osaka and returns to the poor dwelling they had shared in their poverty-stricken days.

Kikunosuke is enraged when he realizes that he has been tricked into separation from Otoku. But he soon settles down and becomes a popular actor in Tokyo.

Some years later when the Tokyo Ichiza group goes to Osaka for a performance, Kikunosuke, as the popular star, is feted on the night before the opening. Cheering crowds greet him as he is taken along a canal in a boat decorated with lanterns. While these celebrations are taking place, the landlord of the house that they had lived in comes to tell him that Otoku is dying. Kikunosuke rushes to her bedside to inform her that Kikugoro has agreed to their formal wedding. With these encouraging words he returns to the boat. Otoku dies with the voices of the cheering crowed ringing in her ears.

The film has a number of scenes that do not figure either in the original work or in the script. They appear to have been put together without much thought. There

FIGURE 11 Mori Kakuko (left) and Hanayagi Syotaro in *The Story of the Late Chrysanthemums* (1938).

is one very powerful scene, however, that makes us pause. After Otoku decides to leave for Osaka, she returns to the house where the two had once lived. She enters the dark premises quietly, surprising the daughter of the house who asks, 'Where is Kikunosuke?' and Otoku replies that there is no point in living with a man like him.

The response can be interpreted as one way of dealing with defeat – a way to tell oneself that the decision to leave was one's own. However, there is somewhere nestling within her a deeper anger that goes beyond mere sentimental gloss.

Otoku had criticized Kikunosuke's art in all honesty and it had proved to be a source of inspiration for him. For this, she had been reviled as evil, and as a troublemaker out to grab the famous fifth generation *kabuki* house. For the honest if poor Otoku, this was an insult to her integrity. At a time when the idea of fundamental human rights had not been formulated, the only way to expunge the insult lay in demonstrating that her only desire was to encourage Kikunosuke to improve his performance. And so she leaves without shedding a single tear, carrying herself in a way that seems to ask 'Is this all right? Does this prove my sincerity?' She makes no attempt to reason. Yet, a part of her clearly wonders what sort of man Kikunosuke is and tries to dismiss him from her life.

On the surface, the film is a tale of self-sacrifice and unrequited love. On a deeper level, it uses the plot to extol the victory of a woman defending her human dignity. No position is taken on the protagonist Kikunosuke or his family. The story's structure inevitably results in Otoku's suppression; she is treated disdainfully because of her status. The story reaffirms an essentially male-dominated, class-divided society, and its logic is to strengthen this. Herein lies its tragic irony. Mizoguchi's film is not about love, it is about will, though to what degree this was consciously articulated is not clear. According to the cast and crew, and as far as I personally know, neither the stage version of *The Story of the Late Chrysanthemums*, nor the later film version, went beyond the story of a failed love affair. It is only in Mizoguchi's version that we see the female protagonist fired with intensity, her generous spirit ill matched with the ambitious man trying to succeed in the world.

Mizoguchi's films show a woman's devotion as the basis of a man's success as he complacently waits for happiness to come his way. Compared to the female protagonist who, by the end, has destroyed herself, the male protagonist's happiness comes across as skewed and out of place. Highlighting the male ego could sometimes be mistaken for Mizoguchi's personal support of a patriarchal society. In films such as *The Nihon Bridge*, the protagonist does show an appreciation of, and respect for, the woman for her sacrifice, and even surrenders his elite status; in *Cascading White Threads*, he honours the woman who commits a crime for him by committing suicide himself; and in *The Downfall of Osen*, the protagonist is deeply anguished, because the woman has lost her sanity because of him. On the other hand, films such as *Oyuki, the Madonna, Lady Musashino, The Life of*

Oharu, *Tales of Ugetsu*, *The Woman in the Rumour*, *Princess Yang Kwei-fei* and others have many a male character whose happiness is predicated on the woman's sacrifice. One of the best expressions of this is Kikunosuke in *The Story of the Late Chrysanthemums*.

Was Mizoguchi better disposed towards men? He certainly seemed more forgiving of them. But for all their apparent happiness they are actually being punished and come across as almost moronic in their contentment; the women, on the other hand, seem to shine with innate goodness. Mizoguchi is often critical of male egoism in his films, and *Osaka Elegy*, *Sisters of the Gion*, *Women of the Night*, *My Love Burns* and *The Life of Oharu* demonstrate this clearly.

As Japan modernized from the Meiji period onwards, it was caught up in a 'success in life' boom unique in world history. Even a small farmer, it was felt, could succeed and become a major force in the development of the country if he worked hard and studied well. Many examples can be cited of young men from poor families who were determined to make it. Izumi Kyoka uses this facet of Japan's modernization in his melodramatic novels. Mizoguchi did so too, but viewed it as modern Japan's fundamental crime, and therefore reshaped it and gave it a new perspective. He developed the idea in three stages: first, he compared a woman's devotion and a man's crime; second, he showed a woman becoming aware of the man's egoism and resisting it; and third, he showed a supposedly happy man absorbed in a woman's devotion.

What Mizoguchi ultimately wanted was to reach a stage when the woman can forget the past and excuse the man. Such examples can be found in his work: the religious image at the end of *The Life of Oharu*; the wife who becomes a spirit and waits for her husband and child in *Tales of Ugetsu*; the blind mother who clasps her son in *Sansho the Bailiff*; and the last scene in *A Story from Chikamatsu*, where the female protagonist smiles as she goes with her lover to the execution ground. This, as I see it, was Mizoguchi's orientation in his last years. He was beginning to see a state of enlightenment where the woman would accept the man.

A Woman of Osaka

The Story of the Late Chrysanthemums glamorizes a woman's ability to face trouble, but in reality shows the position of women in a feudal society. In the absence of the very notion of equality between the sexes, women could not 'reasonably' oppose male domination. We cannot, therefore, use this argument to claim that they glamorized the nobility of their suffering. Women of a bygone era had a will of their own. The theme of endurance and suffering in *The Story of the Late Chrysanthemums* continues and surfaces more emphatically in *A Woman of Osaka*. Here, too, Mizoguchi depicts women in the traditional world of the arts. The men want to protect them, but what links these female protagonists is their self-assertion.

A Woman of Osaka is the story of the Bunrakuza, a puppet theatre (*bunraku*) group in Osaka, and is based on the famous puppet play, *Tsubosaka Reikenki* (Miracle Stories).

Ochika, the female protagonist, played by Tanaka Kinuyo, is the well-educated, lovingly brought up daughter of a man who runs a house for meeting with a geisha (*machiai*) near the Matsushima red-light district in Osaka. She looks after Toyosawa Danpei (Bando Kotaro), a famous *samisen* (three-stringed Japanese instrument) player in *bunraku*. One day, as she listens to him perform, he collapses. He is a widower, and unable to take care of himself. She nurses him, and soon becomes his wife. Though determined to help him excel in his art, she ends up housebound, caring for the home.

When Koshiji, the main narrator who performs with Danpei, learns that he has married the cultivated Ochika, he is very happy. His wife, Otaka (Umemura Yoko), however, is strongly against the marriage. She feels that since Danpei's *samisen* has to follow her husband's lead, and since Koshiji is more popular and better paid, he should assume the leadership of the theatre group. This creates an awkward situation because Danpei's wife, Ochika, is both rich and educated. Otaka has a young helper, Okuni (Nakamura Yoshiko), a poor and gentle woman, who has always looked up to her, and who has come with the aim of helping Danpei in his performance. Ochika is aware that Otaka has brought Okuni to help Danpei, but she pretends not to know anything about it. Instead, she looks after Danpei herself and ultimately marries him.

Koshiji and Danpei, a famous duo, have a cordial personal relationship. But relations between their wives steadily worsen. Koshiji's voice is mellifluous, his narration skilful. When reminded of this, the ever-sensitive Danpei feels disheartened. He tries to take the lead with his *samisen*. Otaka sees this as an attempt to ruin Koshiji's sonorous voice, and complains hysterically to Ochika. Not to be outdone, Ochika retorts that Danpei is right in what he is doing. Otaka is silent but Koshiji complains to the head of their group (*tayu*).

However, complaints about fellow members are not well regarded. Koshiji's co-performers ask him to explain why he had spoken privately to the head of their group. Such developments can break up the group, they argue. But fissures have already been created; Danpei and Ochika join a breakaway group and leave with it to tour the provinces.

As fans come to know that it was arguments between the wives that led to the break-up of the popular duo, Ochika finds herself much maligned. People learn that she has ousted Okuni to become Danpei's wife, and they see her as a stubborn woman. She does try to stick to her convictions, but the plain fact is that Koshiji *is* popular.

Okuni is a gentle uncomplaining sort. Bunkichi (Takada Kokichi), a young, aspiring *yakuza* working in the puppet theatre, is sympathetic to her. He tries to extort money from Ochika to help Okuni, saying she is facing difficult days. Bunkichi is beaten up by some neighbourhood toughs and gradually loses his eyesight. Okuni feels responsible and decides to sacrifice her life for him.

Ochika tours with Danpei, helping him to rebuild himself. But the travelling theatre does not do well. Ochika then meets Koshiji and suggests that he collaborate with

Danpei once again. She also tries to get Okuni to look after Haruko, the main actor with whom Danpei had teamed up. Meanwhile, Koshiji sees the original story of *Tsubosaka Reikenki*. It is agreed that Ochika will write the script and Danpei will create the music for the play. However Danpei, who has so far supported Ochika in everything she has done, and had rarely bothered about anything but his art, suddenly explodes with rage and tells her to return to her parents' home.

Danpei commends Okuni's kindness (*ninjo*) in helping Bunkichi who is slowly going blind, adding that Haruko, too, is working hard performing with him. He says that if he were to return to Koshiji, then Haruko would be left all alone. Similarly, if Okuni were persuaded to look after Haruko, Bunkichi would be left on his own. 'You are not the woman,' he says to Ochika, 'who can write the script for *Tsubosaka Reikenki*, the story of a faithful woman who looks after a blind man.'

Ochika leaves Danpei and returns to Osaka. Convinced that she has given up everything for her husband's art, she cannot understand his reaction. Nor can she reconcile herself to the way she is treated. But when she goes to Okuni's poor house, she sees Okuni, her eyes streaming with tears, encouraging the blind Bunkichi to work as a puppeteer; she finally understands the meaning of *ninjo* and rewrites the script of *Tsubosaka Reikenki*.

Danpei reads the script. The first performance of this great masterpiece is held with Haruko (once again played by Osumi, the main actor) and Bunkichi handling the puppets.

Through the stories of Ochika, Otaka and Okuni, and the different paths that they take, *A Woman of Osaka* depicts the lives of women who are closely linked to their husbands' work.

Otaka is the kind of woman we are familiar with. Because of her partial understanding of her husband's art, she forces him towards success and uses his position to raise herself above those around her.

Okuni is willing to sacrifice herself for her husband, but since she lacks a strong sense of self, she is fated to follow others. Yet she is a wise woman, making the best of what fate offers. If her husband works well, she carries on without complaining. Whenever necessary, she works herself to the bone to help him – an ideal woman for a weak, self-serving man, in fact, just the kind of woman who is often friends with handsome men in real life.

Ochika, on the other hand has the ability, the charm and the self-assurance to do a job well when needed. But she is the wife of a *samisen* player, one of the main players in the puppet theatre. People expect her to be modest, to show a greater understanding of her position, but she rejects this societal expectation and acts as she feels she must. From being a wife, she becomes her husband's manager, governing his relations with people on the basis of what is good for him. Unfortunately, if a man does this in his own interest, it is seen as rational, but in a woman it is seen as contradicting the principles of love (*ninjo*). Under the circumstances, do we judge men and women on a par, or do we expect an emotional 'high-mindedness' from women? Perhaps this is something women have to determine for themselves without any interference from men.

Mizoguchi's high-strung, neurotic wife believed she was actively helping her husband in his work. She would criticize his films and deal with his acolytes. Notwithstanding their fights, Mizoguchi relied on her. She lost her mental balance a year after *A Woman of Osaka* was made. It is said that she wrote the words 'I have written Mizoguchi's script' in large letters, one letter on each page. Ochika's character appears to be inseparable from Mizoguchi's own memories, or the memories of someone like him, someone who relies deeply on a woman despite the embarrassment she causes him. Perhaps Mizoguchi saw himself as a 'wonderful' man – not like Koshiji, who followed his wife, but like Danpei, who by and large allowed his wife to exercise her individuality, but controlled it when it mattered.

Sadly, the print of *A Woman of Osaka* has been lost, but from Tanaka Kinuyo's many fans who have written about her tremendous performance as Ochika, we know that she brought to her role the competitive spirit and the love of a woman with a frightening and passionate intensity.

–8–

A Difficult Woman

Defeat and Democracy: *The Victory of Women*

Mizoguchi was neither an active supporter of the war, nor an opponent of government policies. It is said that he immersed himself in *geidomono* (whose themes were self- suppression and self-sacrifice for the glory of Japanese tradition) in order to distance himself from the war. In some ways, then, *geidomono* did support

FIGURE 12 Mizoguchi Kenji in his capacity as the President of the Association of Japanese Film Directors, and as Film Commissioner of the Cabinet, at a ceremony held by the Japanese Government in 1940.

nationalism (*kokusuishugi*). This may have been why the Army, which actually controlled film production, overlooked Mizoguchi's *geidomono*, although Mizoguchi, I believe, tried to ignore the fact that his *geidomono* films did help in nationalist propaganda.

Finally, towards the end of the war, Mizoguchi made a *geidomono* film, *The Sword* (based on the script by Kawaguchi Matsutaro), that was openly in support of the war effort. Is this what one expected of the master? Interestingly, among all his extant films, this is the worst in terms of quality of workmanship. Clearly, Mizoguchi had given up on its production, and one is left with the feeling that *The Sword* would inevitably be a bad film.

Mizoguchi could not have made an artistically interesting theme if he was forced to compromise in any way. During the war the Japanese sword, said to

FIGURE 13 Yamada Isuzu in *The Sword* (1945).

contain the spirit of a samurai, was made into a symbol of militarism, while in popular novels the swordsmith was portrayed as the craftsman of the spirit of nationalism. The film took this popular symbolism and transformed it into one in which the swordsmith forges into the sword the higher spirit of loyalty to the Emperor, and also turns it into a valuable contribution to nationalism. However, Mizoguchi's insincerity was evident even while the film was being made.

And yet *The Sword* holds a special place in the history of film. It is valuable for the number of *shinpa* stars who acted in it. All the same, it is a minor work, shown in the last days of the war when no one went to see films anyway. 'Nationalistic' or not, it had little impact, as that kind of nationalism had died out. After Japan's defeat, Mizoguchi emerged as one of the few directors who had extended little support to the war effort. This should have stood him in good stead in the post-war period, but as it happened, it did not. He was now the President of the Association of Japanese Film Directors and Film Commissioner of the Cabinet, and was happy to be in these positions of honour. I believe most Japanese at that time had a similar approach, and none of the directors thought about the kind of films they would make once the war was over.

After its defeat in the Second World War, Japan was occupied by the American Army. Film production was brought under its control because cinema was seen as one of the best means of reforming Japanese thinking. The US occupation forces

FIGURE 14 Kuwano Michiko (left), Tanaka Kinuyo (centre) and Miura Mitsuko (in front of Tanaka) in *The Victory of Women* (1946).

asked for films that would educate the people in democracy – films calling for the liberation of women, for instance, or films critical of militarism and the feudal system.

Mizoguchi's first post-war film, *The Victory of Women,* had the democratization of the judiciary as its theme. It was released in April 1946, a year after Japan's defeat.

> A lawyer, Hosokawa Hiroko (played by Tanaka Kinuyo), used to plead in court for the liberation of women. In the difficult, impoverished post-war years she can barely eke out a living. Asakura Moto (played by Miura Mitsuko) comes to her house to sell meat. It turns out that Moto, who looks down and out, was Hiroko's school friend. Moto is in great trouble. She had been the sole bread-winner, moving around with her baby while her unemployed husband lay ill at home. When her husband had died, she had killed her child in a fit of madness. Moto now persuades Hiroko to become her lawyer. Hiroko's elder brother-in-law, Kono (Matsumoto Kappei), is a public prosecutor and a shrewd man. During the war, he had sent many democrats to jail for thought crimes (*shiso kenji*). Among them was Hiroko's lover, Yamaoka (Tokudaiji Shin), a university professor who had finally been released but is now ill. He dies while Hiroko is acting as Moto's lawyer.
>
> The lawyers' association demands that Kono, a typical reactionary public prosecutor, be removed from office. Hiroko's confrontation with him during Moto's trial becomes the focus of interest. Kono urges Hiroko through his wife, Michiko (Kuwano Michiko), Hiroko's elder sister, to agree to a compromise, pointing out that she is obliged to him as he had helped her become a lawyer. Hiroko rejects the proposal outright. Kono argues against Moto, saying that a woman who rejects her traditional duties is guilty of a grave misdemeanour. He recommends that she be given a five-year disciplinary punishment. Hiroko disputes this, arguing that Japanese women have all along led a life of subservience to men and been deprived of self-respect in a feudal society. Little wonder, then, that Moto had lost her mental balance when her husband died. She pleads that Moto be declared innocent.

The drama unfolds in this old-fashioned way. The structure of the plot itself – the public prosecutor and lawyer as brother and sister-in-law, and the lawyer's grudge against her brother-in-law – is very much in the nature of a *shinpa* tragedy, not unlike the old *Cascading White Threads.* The stereotyped tawdriness of every character is enough to take your breath away. Most disturbing of all is Moto's helpless state. In sharp contrast Hiroko comes across as a natural leader who articulates the reasons why women must be liberated. Moto merely accepts Hiroko's assertions that she is not responsible for the crime, she slumps dejectedly and thanks Hiroko by prostrating herself before her in the courtroom.

It is strange to see the way the film's intellectual elite – Hiroko and the university professor – is shown teaching the ignorant and the powerless the concept of democracy, without any kind of debate. *The Victory of Women* was considered an anachronistic failure even during its time, and critics like Uryu Tadao wrote about it derisively. It certainly does not show the contemporary level of understanding of democracy in Japan. The same format can be seen in Kurosawa Akira's *No Regrets for Our Youth* and Kinoshita Keisuke's *Morning for the Osone Family*. All these films end with the 'intellectual' supporters of democracy (who had been persecuted during the war), emerging as shining leaders of the people. They project huge, unreasonable expectations from learning, intelligence and ideology. Today, when respect for university professors and progressive intellectuals has declined, it is difficult to re-evaluate them. They appear to ask for a responsible surrender to others. And yet they contain many things – such as the painful sensitivity of youth in *No Regrets for Our Youth* – that are true. I, for one, remember feeling that I too wanted to become the sort of intellectual they described.

A Difficult Woman and an Unrepentant Man – *My Love Burns*

In 1949 Mizoguchi made another typical post-war film to enlighten people about democracy. *My Love Burns* was based on the biography of Fukuda Eiko, a woman activist in the people's rights movement during the Meiji period. I have a feeling this film left a deep impression on my countrymen when it was first released, although it is criticized today. I would be interested to know what kind of reaction it would evoke if it were to be re-evaluated even twenty years on. However, unlike *The Victory of Women*, and because it was made four years after the war, Mizoguchi had time to reflect. The result was brilliant. The fact that it was set in the Meiji period, a world that Mizoguchi could handle with the self-assurance of a puppeteer manipulating a puppet, made it that much easier. However, his ideas of freedom and people's rights were still based on the notion that a few intelligent members of society could teach the ignorant masses.

> Hirayama Eiko, played by Tanaka Kinuyo, leaves Okayama in 1879 for Tokyo. There she throws herself into the people's rights movement, placing her trust initially in Hayase, a fellow activist from her home town. But when she learns that he is a government spy she leaves him. Later she befriends Oi Kentaro, a leader of the movement. During one of the protest movements at the Chichibu Spinning Mills, both are sent to jail. Here, Eiko comes across a woman worker, Chiyo (Mito Mitsuko), who was a tenant farmer for her own family.
>
> When they leave jail, Eiko and Oi set up home together and employ Chiyo as a maid. Some years later, Oi stands for elections and becomes a member of the Imperial Diet. However, Eiko realizes that Oi has a relationship with Chiyo. Oi refuses to acknowledge any error on his part. All he says is that Chiyo is his mistress and that is all there is to it. Eiko is furious and leaves Oi to return to Okayama. The film ends with a scene in the train with Chiyo lovingly following Eiko back.

The film uses a political movement as part of the action, but rarely grapples with politics, and herein lies its weakness. The opposition movement is not dealt with, and the people's rights movement is simplistically shown as good. Apart from Hayase's activities as a spy, the movement's ideology, structure, or even the weakness of human nature are hardly tackled, and we are left with the impression that the leaders are in a bind because their orders are ignored by the ignorant.

As a young boy, I simply worshipped the heroine, but the adults around me who watched the film were not moved. Today I can see why. The film must have struck them as little more than sloganeering. Research on the people's rights movement was, at that time, limited. It was only in the 1960s that theatre, which used political movements as part of its subject matter, moved to a more conscious level, and films such as Oshima Nagisa's *Night and Fog in Japan*, or plays such as Fukuda Yoshiyuki's *Oppekepe* (a popular Meiji period song) and Hanada Kiyoteru's *Memories of the Explosion*, made earlier works seem naive in comparison.

No matter how innocent *My Love Burns* appears today, it is typically Mizoguchi, an indictment of masculinity and showing a distrust of men. The men who surround the passionate heroine are all shameful specimens, not worth helping; the heroine's task is to shatter the illusions about male authority. This is an enduring motif through all of Mizoguchi's work, and is obvious in *Osaka Elegy* as well. Immature as a political film, *Osaka Elegy* is, on this one point, full of spirit.

FIGURE 15 Tanaka Kinuyo (left) and Miyake Kuniko in *My Love Burns* (1949).

Mizoguchi could not deal seriously with democracy as a political ideology, and was determined never to make such political films again. But the theme of women who, despite repeated mental and physical abuse, disillusionment and frustration, do not collapse but achieve a kind of sainthood, becomes clearer in Mizoguchi's later films.

The same year that *My Love Burns* was made, Imai Tadashi, then still a new-wave director, released the critically acclaimed *The Blue Mountain Range*. The two films are extremely sensitive and similar as they both deal with the problem of democracy and man-woman relationships.

The Blue Mountain Range is a story about a huge controversy in a girls' school over an ordinary love letter. A progressive teacher gently chides a group of young girls for the uproar they have created and for behaving like 'little sisters-in-law'. She is ostracized by the local city bosses for her permissive attitude. The school doctor and some spirited former students of the high school get together to help the teacher against the bosses.

Here again, the people who are trying to democratize the girls' school are not the students, teachers or the families, but an intellectual lady teacher (Hara Setsuko) from Tokyo, local intellectuals (the school doctor) and budding young intellectuals (the former students of the high school). The pattern remains the same: the local bosses are defeated by an alliance of progressive, cultured people who enlighten the ignorant schoolgirls. But within this pattern, a number of progressive ideas are advanced. For one, the very correct lady teacher is made the leader in the fight for democracy by the school doctor, who thinks he is too worldly to do it himself; he is backed by the students who are willing to expose the plans of the local bosses. To be able to make a real difference, the snobbish students will have to get their hands dirty, and the lady teacher will represent the call for justice and honour. This division of labour is skilfully executed in the form of a comedy, and the image of true democracy makes an appearance for the first time in popular post-war sensibility.

Democracy as an idea that gives the weak strength is acceptable within these traditional sensibilities. Since ancient times, it has been expressed in a popular saying which says that when respect is given to parents and to children there is no embarrassment in a petticoat government.

The theme that women were the vectors of democracy became the leitmotif of films made during the Occupation, particularly between the years 1944 and 1950. Kinoshita Keisuke's *Morning for the Osone Family* (1946) reaches its climax when a widow, whose family is ruined during the war, opposes her younger brother-in-law, a senior officer, with all her strength once the war is over. In Kurosawa Akira's *No Regrets for Our Youth*, also made in 1946, the wife of an anti-war activist, who is sentenced to death as a spy, manages to survive the war in a village although she has to face terrible persecution. After the war he becomes a leading figure in spreading democracy in the rural areas. In both these films the man represents authority and power. The heroine's confrontation and exposure of the evils inherent in power are used to praise the political awareness of women.

I now detect something in these films that I had overlooked when they were first released. Their heroines come from upper-class families. The widow in *Morning for the Osone Family* has a bourgeois (probably business) background; she is modern in her outlook and fond of a Western lifestyle. Her younger brother-in-law, an army officer, accuses her of goading her husband and children to become liberals, of wanting to split the family unit. In *No Regrets for Our Youth*, the heroine is the daughter of a liberal, top-ranking, university professor. The ideological underpinning that gives her the strength to resist is shown to have been cultivated in the highly-prized bourgeois atmosphere of the family. What this means is that after the war, when people working in film thought of a 'democratic atmosphere', the first thing that came to their mind was either the bourgeois business class or a university professor's family. The audience, too, accepted this categorization since it was widely believed that this intellectual struggle was being fought elsewhere and had no connection with common people.

At a deeper level, democracy was commonly understood to mean that men had to ask women for forgiveness, and this made them angry. In Kurosawa Akira's *Wonderful Sunday*, an impecunious young man lands himself in trouble on his very first date and is frustrated in his attempts to make love to his fiancé. He is turned down and begs forgiveness. Ozu Yasujiro's *The Hen in the Wind* is about a demobilized husband who, when the war is over, agonizes over the fact that he knows his wife has become a prostitute because of the problems she faced while he was away. But he finally accepts the situation.

In terms of form, it is ultimately the husband who forgives his 'erring' wife. But the image projected is that of a man who begins by accusing her unfairly and is then filled with remorse. In Yoshimura Kosaburo's *The Day Our Lives Brightened*, a young ex-army officer joins a gang after the war and gets involved in a spate of crimes. He meets a young woman, the daughter of a senior statesman he had assassinated. She is now a cabaret singer. It is by begging her forgiveness that he finally turns a new leaf.

'All the People Repent' (Ichioku so zange), the servile-sounding slogan used by bureaucrats to subdue citizens before Japan's defeat, aroused sharp resentment. Some people even called it strange. But from what I remember, at least in cinema, the idea that people are born again from a sense of true repentance for some earlier wrongdoing was widely shared. Many films had men making genuine and heartfelt atonements to women. The question is: were there no films before or after this period on this theme? In the very successful traditional melodrama *What's Your Name?* we have an unusual scene of Sada Keiji, hanging his head in front of Kishi Keiko, one of the few films to show man-woman relationships this way.

For all that, no film had a truly deserving protagonist. The only exception that comes to my mind is a film about a mother: *The Mother Caught in a Storm* (1952) by Saeki Kiyoshi, based on the script by Yasumi Toshio. A young army officer, involved in the Nanjing massacre, returns to Japan. He acknowledges his guilt for his crime and returns to China to seek punishment, leaving his mother to face the anguish. This is perhaps the only film to recognize that true atonement demands something more than a mere acknowledgement of guilt. Most other films in which the man asks for forgiveness were based on a popular idea of sexuality and of vulnerable women who generously accepted the man's tears. This, in a sense, is what we can call the 'family version of democracy from above'.

Seen from this perspective, *The Victory of Women* and *My Love Burns* were immature and idealistic failures, but they are also unique, particularly the latter. We have two films here in which the man never repents and the woman never forgives. In *The Victory of Women*, just as the man is about to apologize, the prosecutor (that symbol of male authority), changes his mind and becomes coercive. In *My Love Burns* the men never accept their wrongdoing even when their crime is discovered, and the woman is left with no choice but to fight. This was a recurrent theme with Mizoguchi, even before the war. Later he would paint the miserable condition of women in his realistic films and idolize them in his aesthetic ones. His path was based on two principles: a realistic perspective and the demands of desire.

FIGURE 16 Tanaka Kinuyo (left) and Yamamura So in *The Love of Sumako the Actress* (1947).

Five Women Around Utamaro (1946) shows the Edo period *ukiyoe* painter, Utamaro (Bando Minosuke) as a people's artist who paints erotic pictures of beautiful women and fights suppression by the authorities. This was an eminently suitable subject for Mizoguchi and he depicted the world of Edo with great richness. Yet it proved to be a poor film.

The post-war film *The Love of Sumako the Actress* (1947) with its theme of women's liberation was also intended to educate people on democracy. During the late Meiji and early Taisho period, Matsui Sumako (Tanaka Kinuyo) was the first major star of the *shingeki* theatre movement. Under the tutelage of Shimamura Hogetsu, she metamorphosed from someone plain into someone who could play the role of Nora in Ibsen's *A Doll's House*. Write-ups about her said that, like Nora, Matsui Sumako, too, had escaped from an old family in order to live independently.

Women of the Night

Mizoguchi's finest film, *Women of the Night* (1948), was released a few years after the war.

The story is set in Osaka, three years after Japan's defeat in the Second World War, when the residue of the bombings is still visible.

FIGURE 17 Bando Minosuke (right) in *Five Women around Utamaro* (1946).

Fusako, waiting for her husband who still hasn't returned from the war, is informed of his death; soon afterwards, her sick child also dies. Ill-treated by her husband's younger brother and his wife, she decides to leave her home and becomes a secretary to Kuriyama, the president of a company and her husband's friend during the war.

Kuriyama is an opium smuggler, but he looks after Fusako well, and she ends up as his mistress. She then meets Natsuko, her younger sister, a dancer, who has come back from Korea, and they start living together. One day Fusako returns to the apartment and finds Natsuko sleeping with Kuriyama. She is shattered and runs out of the apartment. Natsuko walks the city looking for Fusako. She is mistaken for a prostitute, picked up by the police and taken to a hospital where she is forcibly examined. She has a venereal disease and is pregnant. She runs into Fusako, who by now hates men and has become like an older sister to the city prostitutes.

Meanwhile, Fusako's husband's elder sister, Kumiko (Tsunoda Tomie), attracted by the glitter of a fast life, has run away with money stolen from the family. Robbed and raped by men hanging around the red-light district, she decides to become a prostitute. This is not easy as she finds that the prostitutes who control the area will not allow her to solicit without their permission. Around this time Fusako, having just run out of the hospital, comes to Kumiko's rescue. She hugs Kumiko under the shadow of the cross on the church, and laments loudly.

FIGURE 18 Tanaka Kinuyo (left) and Takasugi Sanae in *Women of the Night* (1948).

One of the major social problems in post-war Japan was that of *panpan* girls standing around boldly and soliciting customers at every street corner in big metropolises. Many of these girls evoked sympathy. Reduced to poverty after the war, they had found themselves forced into prostitution. But there were also large numbers of promiscuous, immoral women. Mizoguchi saw this as splendid material and he approached it with ferocious realism.

Understandably, the *panpan* girl was completely different from the geisha that Mizoguchi knew so well. She was a new type of prostitute, and it was difficult to understand her lifestyle and her way of thinking. Getting to know the little details of her life was particularly hard; their stories and their character could only be dealt with conceptually. More than painting a true-to-life picture, therefore, the films were obsessed with a crude message of sympathy for the plight of the *panpan* girl.

Nevertheless, in a number of scenes Mizoguchi's direction is truly superb: when Fusako returns to the apartment to find her younger sister sleeping with Kuriyama, and the sight of his harried face; when Kumiko is harassed by a wastrel student (Aoyama Hiroshi) and relieved of her money; when the strumpets attack, and take away the clothes she is wearing. These scenes are masterpieces that contain two of Mizoguchi's specialities: the long shot and the 'one scene-one cut'.

–9–

Recreating the Classics

Is Mizoguchi Old-fashioned?

Since the end of the silent era, Mizoguchi has commanded respect as one of the few, select, great masters in Japanese cinema. But not all critics have been favourably inclined, and some, indeed, have been very critical. Those who praise him as a master, also – on occasion – point out his shortcomings. They claim that he gets caught up in details for their own sake, which slows down the tempo of his films, and that his theme of human relations is based on an archaic psychology devoid of a contemporary feel. In other words, Mizoguchi's films are not modern. Such criticism suddenly abated when Mizoguchi's technique of the 'one scene-one shot' became popular in the West around the 1950s and was highly acclaimed in France. Till then, it was believed that the shorter the shots, the faster the tempo; and a fast tempo was considered 'modern'.

These views flourished particularly after the Second World War, a time when an understanding of democracy was spreading in Japan. Not being modern now meant being pre-modern, and it was around this time that Mizoguchi came in for severe criticism. The most representative piece of writing was by Uryu Tadao, a brilliant mind who launched into film criticism after the war with a piece called 'Investigation into What is Called a Human' (Ningyen no tankyu to iu koto). It was written in 1946 and published in January 1947 as part of an essay, 'Reflections on Japanese Film' (Nihon no eiga e no hansei) in *Film and the Modern Spirit* (Eiga to kindai seishin), and included as well in another collection, *The Genealogy of the Cinematic Spirit* (Eigateki seishin no keifu), brought out by Uryu Tadao in February that same year.

The titles of these two collections indicate that a 'cinematic spirit' had to be a 'modern spirit'. Mizoguchi's films were criticized because they lacked the modern spirit.

Uryu Tadao never once thought that films such as *Sisters of the Gion*, *Osaka Elegy*, and *The Story of the Late Chrysanthemums* were masterpieces; nor did he think that 'this director had brought a fully modernist vision to film. "Rather," he wrote, "I am deeply troubled every time I think that some people have been lauded for their work as leading figures of Japanese cinema.'

Uryu Tadao's rejection of Mizoguchi was total. He argued that it was not possible for the director to use the world of the geisha quarters, *kabuki* and the puppet theatre as Material for cinema, even if it was a world he loved. This was, he felt, a feudal or semi-slave society. If Mizoguchi entered the world of the *geidomono* (traditional crafts) because during the war years he could not make films from a humanist perspective, the very act of delving into this world meant, says Uryu, that 'it is difficult for us to believe that the thing that we want to end is something fundamentally different; we cannot even make an inquiry into how to break out of a feudal society.' If you speak of peasants or workers, it is possible to show the aspirations of the people who want to break free of the conditions prevailing in Japan from the Meiji period, for these conditions have the hallmarks of a feudal or semi-feudal capitalist society.

The world of the geisha and the theatre actor preceded the feudal period. It belonged to a semi-slave society. As long as Mizoguchi chose to portray it, Uryu Tadao believed it was impossible 'for the contemporary Japanese who desire to enter the modern world' to appear in it. He concluded his essay in these words:

> The ethical basis of Mizoguchi's works is a type of duty (*jingi*, also translated as humanity and justice). He posits duty (*giri*) and humanity (*ninjo*) as the very foundation of all human relationships. He has never tried to understand them from an enlightened, critical perspective. Had he done so, had he highlighted the problem through analysis, his work would surely have commanded great respect. But that is not the case. This is also why he has not been able to pursue a completely cinematic expression either.
>
> What he has done is clearly to follow one human relationship but never the human being. His persistent eye is always celebrating [this relationship], but never letting go of the thread that ties a man and a woman, the constraints between people, the form of an artist's concentration, a prostitute's way of thinking. One cannot exorcise the demon within a woman without showing how a suffering man develops as a human being.
>
> He has never analysed. He has never criticised. He has never tried to be scientific. Therefore, he has never tried to think.

Uryu makes several extreme statements, many of them incorrect, and some with just a grain of truth. Firstly, it would not be right to say that Mizoguchi's ethics are founded on a type of justice (*jingi*), that the basis of human relationships is duty (*giri*) and humanity (*ninjo*). But it would be going too far to say that Mizoguchi did not try to 'to understand them from an enlightened, critical perspective'. Established opinion in the history of cinema has it that no film-maker has portrayed the falsity of geisha society as critically as Mizoguchi did. It is clearly wrong to say that 'he has never analysed' or that 'he has never tried to be scientific.' In films such as *Sisters of the Gion* and *Osaka Elegy,* he observes and portrays with a realism rare in cinema, the economic problems which are the basis for the heroines' unhappiness, and how this transforms human relationships and leads to tragedy. Without a scientific analysis at the very core of his work, how could he have achieved this realism? And finally, it is excessive to say that 'he has never tried to think.'

There is something to be said for Uryu's views on how the 'suffering man develops as a human being' or 'exorcise the demon within a woman'; but to suggest there is no value in depicting the 'the thread that ties a man and a woman, the constraints between people, the form of an artist's concentration, a prostitute's way of thinking' is patently wrong. It is idealistic to argue (as Uryu does) that it is better to investigate the 'man himself' rather than (as Mizoguchi does) merely 'human relations'. What separates 'human relations' from the 'man himself'? For instance, by keeping at the heart of the film, 'the thread that ties a man and a woman, the constraints between people' in *The Story of the Late Chrysanthemums*, Mizoguchi successfully 'exorcises the demon within a woman'. If, by 'how the suffering man develops as a human being', Uryu Tadao means that a petit-bourgeois man is successful through intellectual self-discipline in becoming a progressive political activist, then the 'one woman's demon' depicted in *The Story of the Late Chrysanthemums* does not have that sort of progressiveness. Rather, she is ready to give her heart and body for a husband or a lover. This is certainly a feudalistic 'demon'. But then, in a society based on patriarchy and lineage, the heroine has no other means available to her to express her pride as a human being.

It is not as if Mizoguchi had decided that a woman should sacrifice herself for a man. For Mizoguchi the most important thing – more than any ideology or anything else – was to discover the truth of 'one woman's demon'. What comes out clearly in all his films is that even through 'the form of an artist's concentration (devotion), a prostitute's way of thinking', a despised person can discover himself by concentrating completely on the reason for his existence. In his films the geisha, the dissolute young girl and the artist, always steel themselves in the face of agonizing humiliation. The form that this determination takes organically, develops as 'the form of an artist's concentration, a prostitute's way of thinking'. Hence, even in a pattern that Uryu Tadao believes has no value, one can catch a glimpse of the 'devil' in a person. Mizoguchi is one of the few directors who can do this.

For these reasons I cannot agree with Uryu Tadao's rejection of Mizoguchi. Nevertheless, the general view that Mizoguchi, the master film-maker, is now old-fashioned remains. Many argue that his 'one scene-one shot' technique, and the extreme long shot have acted as a conservative and reactionary influence on the progress of cinematic language because they come out of a theatrical and not a cinematic style.

Why does the 'one scene-one shot' appear outdated, why is it considered reactionary? Because, says Uryu Tadao, it was not analytical. And what do we mean by analytical? Is it something that can be split into various parts and be studied? Theoretically, at least, the true essence of something can be discovered by differentiating between its outward expression and the other parts that constitute it.

However, when applying this to cinema it was mistakenly thought that analysis meant breaking up scenes into a number of detailed shots and then putting them together. Because of this misguided notion, the 'one scene-one shot' is not considered analytical as it did not divide the scene. When Uryu Tadao writes that Mizoguchi 'never analysed', he has actually fallen into this trap. A scene in a film, no matter how finely divided, cannot be treated like a concept because the fragments are concrete. The scene has no connection with whether a director is analytical or not.

Criticism of the Theory of Montage

What created this illusion among Japanese cinema theorists was the strong influence of Eisenstien's theory of montage. The fundamentals of his theory are that a single shot in a film does not have much meaning. Meaning is created when the shots are linked. A truly unique cinematic form of expression comes alive only when a series of shots expressing antithetical meanings are brought together to generate conflict. It is at that stage the film achieves the same status as a language. A film is not merely a depiction or a record of something, and it therefore becomes possible to speak of an abstract idea or to put forward an argument.

Eisenstein's theory was successful within a limited framework, i.e. successful when the earlier and later shots were used to make ironic comparisons. However, a film does more than that. It can convey ideas better by using the story, the dialogue, the acting as well as the camerawork. Therefore, in practice, Eisenstein's theory did not have much effect on film-makers. The objections to montage are that it oversimplifies the rich content of each single shot, reducing it to a mere metaphor, and impoverishes the composition.

In his essay, Uryu Tadao criticizes Mizoguchi for ignoring the theory of montage:

> In the course of breaking down a human being into various parts and creating a synthesis at the same time, it is necessary to base the process on a dynamic idea of 'human formation'. A cinematic reality formed on this premise will necessarily demand the bold layering of cuts, even if it sometimes appears excessive, because this layering, by ignoring the reality of place and time, will create a new reality. The question is whether sufficient elements have been prepared or not for one scene.

Mizoguchi packs everything he wants to say into one shot. Uryu Tadao believes that a film is made by linking a series of unrelated fragments and Mizoguchi's way of film-making is therefore incorrect. Mizoguchi also rarely used the close-up. This too, Uryu Tadao sees as reactionary and he makes his position clear:

> Film has a fearsome weapon to get close to a human being – the close-up. The close-up shot is not merely a way to get close to the face, but to any part of a person – the hand or the finger, or even the tip of the nose, to concentrate attention on one point of a person's body. Clearly, there can be similar expectations from the long shot and the full shot, but the two are possible precisely because there is a close-up. These two types

of shots scatter the attention of the viewer and make it difficult to overcome the obstacles of conceptualising the momentum, the scene.

Uryu Tadao believes that each aspect of reality should be expanded with close-up shots, failing which the viewers' attentive powers will be dispersed. However, I have studied how Mizoguchi, in quite the opposite way and without using the close-up, is able to hold the viewer's attention. He does this by including many things in one shot.

The criticism of Mizoguchi from a perspective that saw montage as the ultimate theory now appears ridiculous, even though the argument that attempted to dismiss him as an outdated master was a strong one. Actually, Mizoguchi came across as a great man from the past. He chose his subject matter from the past; but even in films like *The Victory of Women* where the content is new, the work hardly differed from the old *shinpa* theatre. Compared to the younger generation of directors like Kurosawa Akira, Kinoshita Keisuke, Yoshimura Kosaburo and Imai Tadashi, Mizoguchi did appear extremely old-fashioned. But while he did nothing to counter the critical appraisal, it did hurt him and he took it to heart. When any young director became popular, Mizoguchi would berate his staff, telling them they were not working hard enough.

Given his was a competitive spirit, Mizoguchi wanted to keep up with the new breed of talented young directors. But in a contrary sort of way, the more he desired the new, the more tenaciously he clung to the old. The best works of his life – *Life of Oharu, Ugetsu, Sansho the Bailiff* and *A Story from Chikamatsu* – were all based on Japanese classics in his mature period, between 1952 and 1954. These films dealt with human relationships and feelings, with the morality and beliefs of a pre-modern social system. This was a challenging task for Mizoguchi, particularly at a time when it was considered worthwhile to demolish the whole feudal system, if that could take you even a step closer to Western modernity. Mizoguchi, however, always failed when he tried to simply be new. He needed to grapple with the old in order to discover the new, and this engagement with the old world made him really love it, so much so that he sometimes dismantled the original stories, sometimes even changed them completely.

A Passionate Woman

Life of Oharu (1952) was based on Ihara Saikaku's 1686 novelette, *A Passionate Woman*. The title in Japanese – 'Koshoku ichidai onna' – has a special meaning: the word *koshoku* means passionate and erotic, while *ichidai onna* means a woman who has led a full life. It conveys the sense that this is the story of a woman who has spent her life in erotic pleasure. The book is composed of six sections and each section has four stories. Each story treats a different profession, and we see the erotic life of the woman protagonist as she moves through twenty-four jobs.

A Passionate Woman is a recognized masterpiece of pre-modern Japanese literature, but if read as a modern novel, it comes across as unnatural. For one, the female protagonist who is the narrator of the novel, does not have a name. The story starts with her working in the kitchen of the imperial palace. Then, by turns, she becomes a dancer, the mistress of a feudal lord (*daimyo*), a courtesan (*tayu*) in the Shimabara geisha district, a prostitute, a temple page (to serve on the head priest, even as a sexual partner), a priest's mistress (a *daikoku* or god of wealth) on a three-year contract, a private secretary to a calligraphy teacher, a servant to a merchant, a helper in the kitchen (*oku jochu*) of a feudal lord (*daimyo*), a geisha-type prostitute, an assistant to a bride, a dressmaker for a city official, a hair-dresser, a tailor, a tea-helper in a samurai's residence and so on, moving from one profession to another and ending as a Buddhist nun.

More than a realistic portrayal of one woman, the novelette goes through all the possible professions a woman could have, a sort of professional guide. Not satisfied with letting her experience these professions, the writer also has her learn the jobs of the women around her. *A Passionate Woman* is both a novel and a work that reveals the many aspects of women's work – in particular, the various kinds of prostitutes who worked at that time.

That most jobs for women mentioned in the book are related to prostitution mirrors the reality of the times. The female protagonist lives quite happily in this world, working as a prostitute. Even in her 'good' jobs such as a maid, a hairdresser or a tailor, she displays her innate sensuous nature and ends up having sexual relations, and this is why she returns to prostitution. Not for a moment does she regard it as demeaning. On the contrary, she feels that in the so-called 'good' jobs, a woman has to obey the orders of her employer, however unjust they may be, while in prostitution – if a woman is attractive – she can manipulate the man into doing her bidding and derive a sense of satisfaction. However, the working life of a prostitute is short. As she loses her attractiveness, her lot, too, becomes miserable. The pathos of this situation is one of the themes of the book.

Ihara Saikaku does not write of prostitution as a social problem. Ultimately, it is the female protagonist's nature that is passionate, and even when she gets a 'good' job she chooses to return to prostitution. This was not Saikaku's point of view alone; it was a widely prevalent one in the seventeenth century. It is only modern thinking that sees prostitution as rooted in difficult social conditions. Saikaku sympathized with the women who live this erotic life. Since they were born with a love for sex they could never give up prostitution and he felt, therefore, that they could never be free.

Although *Life of Oharu* is based on *A Passionate Woman*, its content is quite different. The protagonist has a name – Oharu – and she goes through only about a third of the jobs mentioned in the story. The bigger difference focuses on the reason why she takes to prostitution. In the original story it is her passionate nature that is the driving force. In the film, however, Oharu does not engage in prostitution because she wants to. Behind it are a few despicable men who think of women as reproductive machines, men of a feudalistic persuasion who feel it natural to exploit women. In the original story, the woman uses the men and enjoys the pleasures of sex; she only regrets that a prostitute has a low position in society. In the film, Oharu is a strong woman with a pure heart who, even while working as a prostitute, holds her head high.

The most significant reason for changing the story was to revise the prejudices of the seventeenth-century writer. But there was another reason as well. In 1952, the year the film was made, people were conscious of the process of democratization, and women's liberation was a crucial issue within the larger framework.

At the start of the film the heroine is a nobleman's helper in the imperial kitchen. She falls in love with a young samurai, the retainer of another nobleman. Under the law this is a crime. She is thrown out and the young samurai is sentenced to death.

In the original work she knows of the death sentence given to the young samurai. For a while her profound sadness makes her contemplate suicide, but she soon gets over it. In Saikaku's opinion, 'There is nothing so fickle as a woman's heart.'

In the film, the young samurai awaiting execution is asked if he has anything he would like to say. He replies: "Why is it wrong, sir, for a man and a woman to love each other? I do not understand why this is adultery. I desire a world where this status system is abolished and where everyone can love freely. Oharu, live with these true memories.'

It is difficult to imagine a seventeenth-century samurai sounding so democratic. I saw the film when it was first released and I felt these lines were unnatural and out of place.

That Mizoguchi rewrote the lines 'Live with these true memories' in the script of the film over and over again is well known. He even had the scriptwriter rewrite the final version. While filming the scene, he called him back and had the lines written yet again (see *Yoshikata Yoda Collection of Scripts*, Eijin-sha, 1978). There are always differences between the published version of a script and the one actually used in the film. In this case, too, the words 'Live with these true memories' were probably added at the very last minute. One can see it is as the defining moment when the shooting finally took place.

The officer at the execution records these last words and sends the message to Oharu. Oharu's mother stops her from committing suicide, and the young samurai's words, 'Live with these true memories', becomes the guiding principle of her life. As a prostitute, she continues to have relationships with many men. But she looks for a partner from whom she can expect to 'live with these true memories'.

When, as a sixty-year-old streetwalker, the heroine in the original work sees a statue of the 500 Buddhas (*arhats*), she thinks that each one resembles one of the men she loved. However, there is no mention of her first love, the young samurai. In the film, Oharu sees the face of her beloved young samurai in the very first statue.

In the next story the heroine is a concubine to a feudal lord (*daimyo*) in eastern Japan. Her job is to provide him with an heir. The samurai who has come to select the concubine tells the broker in detail, and with great humour, of the type of concubine the *daimyo* wants. In this, and in the scenes that show the jealousy of the lord's wife (*okugata*), the film follows the novel. The last half, however, is entirely different. In the original, the lord is impotent but Oharu mentions this 'to anyone, and regrets it constantly'. When he becomes paralysed, his ministers blame it on her sexual vigour and dismiss her from her job.

In the film Oharu gives birth to the lord's son. This is a major departure, made apparently on Mizoguchi's suggestion. It created a wonderful climax, for the son later succeeds the lord to the title, while Oharu ends as a streetwalker. This reworking of the original text highlighted the tragedy of a mother's love for her son, even as it showed the tragi-comedy of Japan's brutal concubine system that regarded a woman only as a procreative instrument.

In the film the lord is not shown as impotent but the reasons for Oharu's dismissal remain the same; the lord is obsessed by her, indulges in too much sex, and ruins his health. It is only in this one case that the heroine's eroticism as described in the original story is retained, for here, as in the literary work, Oharu is dismissed because of her passionate nature.

The original story emphasizes the heroine's miserable character – she has become a prostitute despite her young age. In the film, however, Oharu may be a prostitute, but she is not despicable. Instead, she resists the patrons who buy her. This, too, is a major change from the original.

In the novelette Oharu (even as she works in the houses of merchants or samurai after her indenture with the brothel is over) harasses the master of the house; in the film, she is different. In the original, while she is the respected 'wife (*naigisama*) of the fan-maker', her remonstrations with the customers lead to her divorce. In the film, her husband is killed in a robbery. This not-too-happy change is meant to show that Oharu's happiness is destroyed accidentally, that bad luck is the cause of her sorrow.

Hereafter, she despairs of the world and enters a Buddhist nunnery. The film shows her flirting with the cloth merchant's clerk and incurring the wrath of the head of the nunnery. She is thrown out.

Oharu goes on to work as a maidservant at an inn, at a public bath and at a teashop; she then goes aboard a small ship to work as a prostitute. Each of the many types of prostitution she engages in are little vignettes. The original has many more, each related through an episode. The script reduces this drastically and uses broad strokes to show Oharu falling gradually into a disreputable state.

Mizoguchi also shortens the four scenes from the time she leaves the nunnery and separates from the cloth merchant's clerk. He skips about twenty years to show her sitting in front of a temple outside the city of Nara, playing a *samisen* and begging for food. A feudal lord's procession passes by and the young scion is seen riding in a magnificent palanquin. We later learn that he is her son. Whether she is aware of this or not, she stares fixedly at the procession. This scene is from the film script. The feudal lord's procession was not in the published script but figured in a later addition, and it is a truly scorching scene.

Oharu falls ill in the cold. She is helped by a group of wet nurses, whom she will later join. These nurses – the lowest type of prostitutes, all of them at least over fifty years old – fool clients in the darkness of the night. Oharu does likewise. One customer takes her to a pilgrims' inn and exhibits her, in candlelight, to his young friends, to let them know what prostitutes look like as they get older; that behind their thick make-up they are actually quite grotesque.

This fall to the ranks of the wet nurses is faithful to the original work. It is only in this one incident that they followed the original faithfully and transferred its frightening realism to film. This was not the case with most of the other episodes

FIGURE 19 Tanaka Kinuyo (left) and Sugai Ichiro in *The Life of Oharu* (1952), © Toho Film Co. Ltd.

that Mizoguchi and Yoda rewrote in a bid to turn Oharu from a sensuous to a modest woman.

These episodes were written anew for the film. After the child born to Oharu becomes a lord (*daimyo*), she is recalled to the *daimyo* household. She returns, thinking she has found happiness at last, will wear beautiful clothes and have attendants to serve her. However, at the *daimyo* residence she is imprisoned: if it were revealed that the lord's real mother is a prostitute, it would spell disaster – something she had never imagined would happen. Earlier, she is treated with care and permitted to meet the lord, but not as mother. She can only look at him while kneeling in the garden as he walks down a corridor. Upon seeing him, Oharu breaks through the samurai guarding her and runs after the lord. When they try and stop her, she cries, 'That is my child.'

The samurai bow down and kneel when they hear these words but the *daimyo* walks by without giving any sign of recognition. Once again Oharu runs after him, once again the samurai try to stop her and she says, 'Please return my child.'

Her air of maternal dignity is enough to make the samurai kneel instinctively. This scene – with the *daimyo*, Oharu, the samurai, the chase with its humour, grace and tragedy – is really the climax of the film. The grotesque wet nurses appear to be transformed into noblewomen, playing gracefully in the exquisite garden. The queens of an erotic world have become pure young maidens. In an offensive and ugly world, the heroine who has spent her life bewailing her fate, changes at the end into a dignified noblewoman. This innate dignity, which makes the samurai kneel, is not false or fabricated. Compared to the *daimyo* who has been raised as a nobleman, her dignity is inborn; and it is the *daimyo* who cannot call his real mother 'Mother', that we pity. Oharu is the prisoner in this *daimyo* house, but it is the *daimyo* and the samurai we see running helter-skelter.

In the last scene in this sequence, the palanquin meant to carry away the noble prisoner is placed outside the gate of the *daimyo* residence. Oharu, who is to be taken away, is nowhere to be found. The panic-stricken samurai run about in confusion. How impossible for an old woman guarded by a large group of samurai to suddenly disappear! But disappear she does. Oharu has mysteriously escaped. Equally mysterious is how the old wet nurses reappear as dignified noblewomen in the next scene. With so many strange occurrences, Oharu's disappearance is not so remarkable after all. Entranced by the exquisite direction of this climax, the audience understands and accepts it all.

Image of the Prostitute as Sacred

The climax makes it clear that the real subject of the film is not the freedom to love, but something else, something which does not exist in the original work: the creation of the image of the prostitute as sacred, the attempt to discover a higher spirit in a woman who otherwise lives an appalling life. This image can also be seen in the character of Sonia in Dostoevsky's *Crime and Punishment*, and in Katushya in Tolstoy's *Resurrection*. For Mizoguchi and Yoda, this creation is the culmination of a process of examining women through films such as *Osaka Elegy*, *Sisters of the Gion*, *Straits of Love and Hate* and *Women of the Night*, where they present a highly refined and polished world with realism.

The need to discover a higher spirit within a despised existence is above all a religious impulse. It is not confined to any specific religion such as Christianity or Buddhism, but lies hidden at the root of many religions. But while Saikaku's novelette is extremely irreligious, Mizoguchi's film is a deeply religious work, and this is clear not only in the climax but also in the scene that follows – the last scene where Oharu goes from house to house as if on a pilgrimage, chanting a Buddhist *sutra*. The prayer is set to Western music, while a chorus sings 'The Complete Realisation of a Vow' (*Seiganjoju*), in a very high pitch.

In a recently discovered script of the film, this last scene has Oharu – now the head priestess of a temple outside the capital (Kyoto) – reciting the *sutra* in front of the statue of the Boddhisatva. This scene was changed during the filming. In Saikaku's work, the heroine, after she becomes a nun, offers herself to two men who have come to the temple. The writer's intention in narrating the life of a woman as an austere nun, who offers herself sexually to men, fits into a popular genre of pornographic writing that readers find erotic. Saikaku's novelette is not just a pornographic novelette, it is a wonderfully realistic one. There are other examples of brilliant pornographic novels that have satirised religion sharply.

The idea of a nun recalling her past was rejected from the moment the script was written. Oharu becomes a nun only at the end. The decision to show her as a pilgrim and the addition of devotional music was made during the filming. In both the original work and the film, Oharu becomes a nun in her old age. But there is a world of difference between a nun talking erotically and a nun who leaves the world of desire for the world of religion.

Mizoguchi is more successful than Saikaku in creating a realistic world. Saikaku mistakenly believes that a prostitute has an intrinsically passionate nature and cannot give up her profession. This was a commonly held belief and did not reflect any particular prejudice on Saikaku's part. But it did lead to an inaccurate portrayal of the prostitute's real world. Mizoguchi, on the other hand, by showing that prostitution was evil and the product of a male-dominated society, corrects Saikaku's perception. There is no coquetry in Mizoguchi's Oharu; there is nothing cheap. She does not appear as a woman using sex as a means to earn a living.

This can be explained by referring to the predominant interests of Japanese audiences in the 1950s. They would not have welcomed an adulterous, promiscuous woman as a heroine. A romance would not have worked if the heroine was not the man's first woman. In *A Picture of Madame Yuki*, made two years before *The Life of Oharu*, Mizoguchi narrated the story of an upper-class woman who, while yearning for a pure-hearted man, is bewitched by her brute of a husband. The film was a box-office success, since the strangeness of the heroine stimulated the curiosity of the audience. But it was not the sort of film that one would want to see repeatedly. Oharu was played by Tanaka Kinuyo, who had also played a street-walker in Mizoguchi's *Women of the Night* (1948). She became one of the most popular actresses in the history of Japanese cinema, embodying chaste, healthy, pure, winsome characters – the very models of the 'pink flower of Yamato'. Her role of a streetwalker was a remarkable exception: she would normally play a well-bred, moral woman – the kind of character that would resonate with her audience. Which is why no one objected when Oharu's character in the film turned out to be so completely different from character in the original work.

Changing her character to conform to the audience's moral values was what made *The Life of Oharu* a masterpiece. While basing himself on Saikaku's female protagonist, Mizoguchi depicted a totally different woman – an ideal, sacred woman, a woman who would take on herself all the sins of men, their meanness, weakness and ugliness; a woman who, through her misery would make men ashamed of themselves; a saint of a woman. This is why if you read the original after seeing the film, the novel seems to be a parody written 266 years before the film was made.

Mizoguchi replaced the light and witty style of the original book with some-thing different, something sombre. The cinematography of Hirano Yoshimi, who worked alone on this with Mizoguchi, was marvellous. It showed a wonderful grasp of Mizoguchi's 'one scene-one shot' technique. Hirano Yoshimi's graceful scenes recall old picture scrolls.

The camera movements and the panning shots are much more than just beau-tiful photography – they go beyond the film-maker's characteristic style. The movement of the camera itself exudes power – the same power that skilled dancers exercise with their movements. It leaves you enticed and intoxicated.

There is a scene where Mifune Toshiro plays the noble apprentice, a samurai, who is beheaded for the crime of falling in love with Oharu. The scene starts with a general shot of the execution ground with its bamboo palisade. We then see the bound samurai; in the background is the executioner, holding back a little. When the young samurai cries out, 'I pray for the time when love will not be a crime!' the camera suddenly moves away from his face to a close-up of the executioner's sword. The executioner wets the blade and puts it back in the scabbard. The camera follows the sword, panning up and then stops. The fluidity of the movement is like drawing a line with a brush. You grip the brush tightly, draw it to the point you want to, stop firmly with a sense of satisfaction, and sigh with pleasure. This is the kind of satisfaction that this fleeting camera movement gives. The sword is brought down soundlessly; the camera stops moving and shows just an empty space: a scene meant to induce a gasp of sorrow even from those who would normally be unaffected. In the empty frame we see the sword, having finished the beheading, being brought back up in the executioner's left hand. For a moment it is suspended, like some decoration, almost as if the quickened breathing has slowed down now that the killing is over; and then it is quietly lowered. The camera once again follows the sword, panning down, and the long 'one scene-one shot' ends. In Mizoguchi's films the movement of the camera is subtle; like the hands, feet or neck of a dancer, it moves just a little and stops.

The following scene shows Oharu leaving Kyoto with her parents. It is night. Under the light of the lanterns she and her group are seen on the river embankment taking leave of the people who have come to see her off. The camera, placed on the dry riverbed, shows the group walking in a line and crossing over to the other bank, appearing almost doll-like. At first it is quite stationary; one cannot tell that it is mounted on a carriage. Suddenly it moves under the bridge and looks across, from below a barge to the top of the embankment. By the end of the scene, however, the minimal movement of the camera is almost unnoticeable; and this is so appropriate to the scene.

In a scene of a reluctant farewell, the camera is normally fixed at one point to show the sadness of those who depart and those who have come to bid the group goodbye. It may follow the former from the perspective of the latter. The director may imbue his shots with sympathy and a silent appeal against an unjust exile.

Mizoguchi does not use the shot-reverse-shot even once. His camera, installed at one point, looks fixedly and with detachment at the others. It is an objective look that seems to say: these are unlucky people, resign yourself and go back. In the end, when the line of people has crossed to the other bank and is difficult to see, Mizoguchi moves the camera forward on a carriage, and once again takes a peek at the group from the top of the barge. Although his stance appears to be cold and dispassionate, this movement of the camera suddenly shows that he is gazing at the group with deep sorrow. His use of the barge, from where the line of people appear as small dots, is a good move, foretelling their gloomy fate as they head off into the darkness, and evoking much more than would have been possible through a shot-reverse-shot or any other camera movement.

After her husband, the fan-maker, is murdered in a robbery, Oharu seeks admission in a Buddhist temple. We have a shot of a nun standing quietly with Oharu in the temple garden. A vertical ray of light shining on their two faces seems to bind them together. The entire scene is bathed in these vertical rays that come across like a rain of tears, as if the camera were weeping for Oharu.

Tanaka Kinuyo as Oharu gave one of the best performances of her life in this film. In an early scene in the *arhat* hall (*rakando*), she gazes at the statue of the *arhat*, recalling each of the men she has been intimate with. It is an excellent rendition of a pitiable old prostitute of the lowest order who, though modest and humble, is not coarse or vulgar. An erotic smile flits across her face revealing a hard-to-violate dignity. It's a contradictory impression, and is expressed simultaneously by her pose and expression.

FIGURE 20 Tanaka Kinuyo (left) and Mizoguchi Kenji in Venice.

Another case in point is the scene where Oharu begs for food outside the temple gate. She is hunched over as she tries to protect herself from the cold wind. Then her face slowly awakens to look at the palanquin of the *daimyo*, full of a deep and vibrant feeling and a certain despair.

The Life of Oharu is one of the greatest films made by Mizoguchi Kenji, Yoda Yoshikata and Tanaka Kinuyo. Winner of the best director award at the Venice Film Festival in 1952, it is also one of the finest films in the history of Japanese cinema. This gave Mizoguchi a sense of great confidence. The following year he made *Ugetsu* and the year after, *Sansho the Bailiff*. Both won the Silver Lion at the Venice Film Festival and his name became known internationally.

Cinematization of Form and Subject of Traditional Drama – *Ugetsu*

Ugetsu (1952) was based on an eponymous collection of short mystery stories written by Ueda Akinari in 1776. As with *The Life of Oharu*, in this film, too, Mizoguchi fundamentally changed the classic. He conceived the structure of the story himself and it was under his very strict supervision that Yoda wrote the script. Even while it was being written, the novelist and director on the board of Daiei, Kawaguchi Matsutaro, published it as a novel. It was common practice at that time to get a novelist to write a script as a novel and have it published in a magazine to promote the film.

The original work had nine sections consisting of ghost stories and tales of the grotesque. Mizoguchi selected only *The Inn at the Ford* (Asaji ga yado) and *The Lust of a Snake Character* (Jasei no in) from the collection. To this he first thought of adding the theme of Guy de Maupassant's novel, *I Was Awarded a Medal*. However, he only took the germ of an idea from it, not the whole story.

The original story of *The Inn at the Ford* was borrowed from a Chinese novel, *Jien Deng Xin hua*. Katsushiro, a peasant from Shimofusa, sells his fields, buys some silk and sets off to sell it in the capital, Kyoto. He finds the capital in the throes of a rebellion. He is robbed, falls ill and doesn't return to his village for seven years. When he does, he discovers his wife waiting for him in his dilapidated house. She is overjoyed and they go to sleep together. The next morning, when Katsushiro wakes up, Miyagi, his wife, is missing. He then sees her grave with her dying words written on the gravestone and realizes that his wife had appeared to him as a spirit the night before. He wails and laments.

The Lust of the Snake Character (Jasei no in) is also a translation of a Chinese novel, *Xihou Jiahua*. In the book, Toyoo, the young son of a wealthy man (*chojyo*) of Kishi, seeks shelter from the rain in a poor man's hut. There he meets Manago, a beautiful woman, who says that she, too, is waiting for the rain to stop. When Toyoo returns home he dreams that he is visiting her magnificent house, is received with great hospitality and spends the night with her. The next morning, when he actually visits her house, it appears exactly as he had seen it in his dream, and he is welcomed with the same hospitably. The woman presents Toyoo with a sword, which he takes home. His elder brother is suspicious as it is an extremely valuable sword. Upon investigation, he learns that a minister from the capital had presented the sword as an offering to the Kumano shrine from where it had been stolen. Toyoo goes to the shrine to return the sword but is taken for the thief who had stolen it, and is handed over to the authorities. He pleads his innocence and takes the officers to Manago's house. It turns out to be an abandoned house, home to wild animals.

When Toyoo is released he goes to live at his married sister's home in Yamato. Here Manago visits him again. She says Toyoo is her husband but Toyoo replies that she not a human being, only a ghost. Manago weeps and defends herself. She convinces both Toyokazu and his sister, and at the latter's urging, the two perform the wedding rites.

One day Toyoo takes Manago to a Shinto shrine where they meet an old man who stares at them and reveals that Manago is a ghost. Manago flees. Toyoo is saved from her and returns to his father's house. The father persuades him to marry Tomiko, a girl from a good family. On the second night after the wedding, Tomiko suddenly talks in Manago's voice and shows her frustration. The morning after this frightening night, Toyoo pleads for help from a priest who has come from the capital. The priest comes to their house with a potion. Manago reveals her true form as a huge snake and attacks the priest. He tells her that she can take him wherever she likes but pleads for Tomiko's life. The big snake agrees. Tomiko's father appeals to Priest Hokai, the head priest of the Dojoji temple, and a man of great virtue. He gives Toyoo a sacred shoulder scarf (*kesa*). Toyoo hides it in his bosom, goes to his bedroom and uses it to cover the snake's face, still in the guise of Tomiko. The snake fights back but its body is revealed and he is caught. The priest digs a hole in front of the temple hall in which he buries the snake and Toyoo is saved.

These two stories were combined into one in the film script. The characters of Katsushiro in *The Inn at the Ford* and of Toyoo in *The Lust of the Snake Character* were merged to create the character of Genjuro, a potter from Omi, his wife Miyagi, and the beautiful, young woman, Wakasa, whom he meets on the way to sell his pottery. She combines in herself the spirits of the two women. Wakasa corresponds to the Manago of *The Lust of the Snake Character*. But in the script, instead of a snake in disguise, she has been changed to the spirit of Kuchiki, a princess from a noble house which was ruined during the war.

> Genjuro (Mori Masayuki), the potter from Omi where war has broken out, wants to use the opportunity to make a profit. He quickly makes a large amount of pottery and with his wife, Miyagi (Tanaka Kinuyo), young son Genichi, younger sister Ohama (Mito Mitsuko) and her husband, Tobei (Ozawa Eitaro), sets off for a town on the other side of Lake Biwa to sell his goods. On the way, they realize that the war has become much too dangerous, so Genjuro sends his wife and son back. However, a fugitive samurai spears Miyagi to death for the food she is carrying.
>
> Unaware of this tragedy, Genjuro, Tobei and Ohama sell their pottery and make a profit. Tobei, anxious to make a name for himself and become a samurai, buys a sword with his share of the money and joins the war. His company comes to a town where he visits a brothel with his men and discovers that one of the girls working there is his wife, Ohama. Tobei begs his wife's forgiveness, gives up being a samurai and they return home.
>
> Meanwhile, Genjuro is praised for his skill as a potter by Wakasa, the noble princess in the Kuchiki residence, and is entertained by her. They become intimate and he spends his days as if in a dream. One day a travelling priest stops Genjuro in town. The priest says that he sees the shadow of death on him and gives him a charm to drive away spirits. That evening, Wakasa cannot come close to Genjuro because of the charm; yet she clings to him desperately. Slashing wildly with his sword, Genjuro flees and falls in a faint outside. The next morning when he opens his eyes, he sees that he is in a desolate place, with nothing around him but the burnt remains of a house.
>
> Genjuro returns to his village. It is night and his wife Miyagi, who is putting their son to bed, welcomes him. He heaves a sigh of relief and sleeps peacefully. The next morning Miyagi is nowhere to be seen and Genjuro realizes that Miyagi was a ghost and had stayed back to protect their son till he returned.

The story of Tobei and Ohama was developed from elements in Maupassant's *I Was Awarded a Medal*. This is a story about a man who longs to get a medal. His wife is involved in an adulterous relationship with a member of the Assembly. One day the husband discovers the Assembly member's medal at home and questions his wife about it. She lies, telling him that it has been secretly presented to him. He believes her and is overjoyed. This theme, satirizing a stupid man's desire for fame, is developed in the story of Tobei and Ohama. But the story is completely different from Maupassant's. In it, Mizoguchi introduced his lifelong theme – the

FIGURE 21 Kyo Machiko (left) and Mori Masayuki (right) in *Ugetsu* (1953), ©
Kadokawa Pictures, Inc.

sacrifice of a woman for a foolish man. However, Daiei, the production company,
insisted on a happy ending and so it was changed: Tobei, the fool, who longed for
fame, falls for a prostitute but by chance meets his wife and reforms. He abandons
his desire for the social status that he had wagered his life for, and returns to his
earlier life of a peasant. This unbelievably saccharine resolution was clearly the
result of a compromise with the demands of the company. As Yoda wrote in his
book, *Mizoguchi Kenji: The Man and the Art*, this was not at all what Mizoguchi
had wanted.

As a matter of fact, this happy ending turned the story of Tobei and Ohama into
a most dreary tale. Yet *Ugetsu* was a superb film. The scenes depicting the relationship between Genjuro and the two ghosts are simply exquisite. Wakasa, played
by Kyo Machiko, has a bewitching eroticism, and her appearance in the Kuchiki
mansion is imbued with a mystical beauty. Tanaka Kinuyo as Miyagi plays the role
more as a mother than a wife, and with a boundless love. Of the many women characters that Mizoguchi portrayed in his work, these two ghosts are among his most
powerful depictions of women.

One might well ask why Mizoguchi, who is regarded as a realist in Japanese cinema, and who made films such as *Osaka Elegy* and *Sisters of the Gion*, so zealously depicted ghosts in his last mature years. He had, of course, made *The Passion of a Woman Teacher* in 1926, when he was young. But ghosts *are*, in fact, one of the most important elements in traditional Japanese theatre. In *noh*, particularly, most of the masterpieces have a specific pattern, where a ghost meets a traveller and narrates the problems he had encountered when he was alive and how he had died. Mizoguchi had studied traditional Japanese theatre more thoroughly than most Japanese directors. He used ghost tales because he wanted to bring subjects and forms from traditional Japanese theatre into cinema.

The most attractive parts of *Ugetsu* are those that were heavily influenced by *noh*. The transformation of the snake into human form in *The Lust of the Snake Character* follows a typical *noh* theatrical form. Wakasa, who should have been happy as a princess, appears as a ghost because she had died without knowing love, and her spirit returns to find it. She even wears the costumes of a *noh* play which Mizoguchi borrowed from a *noh* family head (*iemoto*). Her make-up and expressions give the impression of a *noh* mask; her way of walking is derived from *noh*'s theatrical techniques. The scene where she appears in the Kuchiki mansion, with a room at the end of a long corridor and the view seen from the garden, replicates a *noh* stage. In *noh,* a corridor becomes a mystical space as it links this world with the other world. In the film as well, a truly mystical atmosphere is created as the maids go down the dark corridor carrying lanterns to the rooms, with the *noh* flute (a lateral flute that sounds like a strong wail) providing the music.

Mizoguchi was adamant that Hayasaka Fumio, his musical director, who wanted to use Western music, must use the *noh* flute instead. In the music for his previous film, *The Life of Oharu*, he made Saito Ichiro experiment with Japanese instruments and Buddhist music in a Western orchestra. He was successful in creating a unique music, but in *Ugetsu* he made Hayasaka Fumio integrate Japanese and Western music more fully. More than just a masterpiece of film music, it broke new ground through this integration. The composer, Takemitsu Toru, who apprenticed under Hayasaka Fumio, later used this method to write a number of brilliant musical compositions.

When Wakasa begins to perform as in a *noh* play (*shimae*) in the mansion, a suit of armour displayed in one corner of the mansion begins a *noh* chant. This is the voice emerging from the other world of the dead. The music transforms the Kuchiki mansion into something resembling a *noh* stage. It creates a world filled with terror where the dead may appear at any moment; but it is also a world of indefinable grace and elegance, and filled with pathos; a world where the dead who cannot become Buddhas (*Hotoke ni naru* – escape from the cycle of birth and death) wander about. It is more pitiful than terrifying.

This special characteristic of Japanese ghost stories differentiates them from Western or Chinese ghost tales. *Noh* expresses this with great clarity. It is often said that *noh* has mystery (*yugen*), a word with complex overtones and difficult to explain. A number of scenes in *Ugetsu* express this feeling effectively. This film is also one of Mizoguchi's most famous in the West. Perhaps it is this sense of mystery that explains its fame.

In the original work, *The Lust of the Snake Character,* the snake is terrifying in the way it changes its form several times to pursue the man and even kills the priest who tries to exorcise it. In comparison, Wakasa is a very gentle and sad ghost. Mizoguchi shortened the later, more frightening part of the original work, where Manago, the snake, changes herself and appears as Tomiko. *The Lust of the Snake Character* was a sufficiently long story for a film and in 1921 a film of this name was indeed made. However, Mizoguchi threw out the tale's frightening part and incorporated, instead, the more benign sections from *The Inn at the Ford*. He also changed the character of Miyagi, who in the original work appears as a ghost only because she wants to be reunited with her husband. He made her a gentle, loving mother. More than a ghost she should be called a holy mother. It is in this sense that Mizoguchi's film is religious.

Yanagida Kunio argues that ancestor worship, which lies at the core of Japanese beliefs, seems to explain many aspects of these beliefs. We in Japan have faith in both Shinto and Buddhism. To believe in two religions simultaneously may appear impure and irresponsible, but what links them is ancestor worship. In Shinto, it is the *kami* (superior being), the spirit of the distant ancestors of a tribe or an ethnic group (*minzoku*). In Buddhism (and the essence of what we call the Buddha – *hotoke* – is quite different from the teachings of Buddhism), it refers to the spirit of the dead members of the family.

The basis of our religious thoughts and feelings is that the spirits of our near and distant ancestors are our protective deities. Naturally this is not the only thing that forms the religion of the Japanese, but it does lie at its core. That is why, as is in the *Harp of Burma*, the task of collecting the remains of their compatriots who died in war is a deeply religious act. Even now, more than sixty years after the Second World War, the Japanese regard it as their national duty to bring back the remains of their dead soldiers for burial in Japan. The dead, it is thought, will not be able to sleep in peace on foreign soil; their spirit must be returned to their villages and placed in graves under the protection of their family or descendants. But when the Japanese went to collect the remains of their war dead, the countries that had been invaded by Japan began to fear that the Japanese were somehow trying to return. The Japanese could not understand this fear. They felt they were merely performing a sacred duty.

If the soul or spirit of a dead person appears to bear a grudge, it can be quite frightening; as a rule, however, the spirits protect the living and can be turned to for help. A ghost normally refers to malevolent spirits, but in Japanese ghost stories a spirit often protects the family or children. One of the most exquisite expressions of this is the role of Miyagi as played by Tanaka Kinuyo.

When Genjuro escapes from Wakasa's spirit and returns to his village, it is late at night and his house is desolate and in ruins. He enters the house but sees no one. The camera follows him casually as he goes in, and once again the back of the wall comes into the camera frame. The fire dies down and suddenly we see Miyagi. This adds an eerie element to the scene. But Genjuro is not surprised. He treats her with his usual kindness and goes to sleep. Having completed the household work, Miyagi sits beside her peacefully sleeping husband and child, her expression one of contentment, her heart overflowing with happiness. The camera moves extremely slowly.

In this exquisite night scene, the wife is a ghost, yet there is nothing ghostly about her; instead, in what proved to be a brilliant performance by Tanaka Kinuyo – she appears her normal, kind self, waiting for her husband to return.

The next morning, Genjuro is surprised to learn of Miyagi's death from the village headman who has dropped in to see him. The last scene has Genjuro, Ohama and Tobei hard at work on one side of the house, while we hear Miyagi's voice off camera. The audience seems to have become Miyagi the ghost, looking protectively at the actors. The camera, mounted on a crane, moves up as the child runs to the other side of the workshop. The film ends with the solemn scene of Miyagi's grave coming into view and the child standing before it with his hands joined together as if in prayer. As the grave appears under the credits, we get a truly superb camera movement. There is a feeling of gravity, seriousness and a surprising awareness that the Miyagi of the previous evening was really a spirit, a solemnity stemming from the fundamental beliefs of the Japanese religion that the dead from the other world are caring for and protecting the people they love. It is shown here not as just a concept, but as something tangible; it is given a form visible to the naked eye. No other film, at least in my understanding, has depicted the idea of Japanese religion so clearly and completely. Ueda Akinari's translation of the Chinese original was thus rewritten and transformed into a very Japanese story.

An Experiment with a Historical Film: *Sansho the Bailiff*

Sansho the Bailiff (1954) was based on Mori Ogai's eponymous novel written in 1941. Ogai in turn based it on a well-known traditional tale, which may have originally been sung as a song by wandering outcasts in medieval times, as they went around begging for food. This kind of narrative poetry is called a Buddhist folk tale (*sekkyobus*). Many famous examples of such poetry can be found – 'Thatching a Roof' (*Karukaya*), 'The Ship Shintoku' (*Shintoku maru*), 'Oguri' (*Oguri hangan*) among many others, and they all happen to be tragic tales. Since these poems are part of an oral performing tradition, there are no authoritative texts, and they continue to be transmitted orally even today by a few blind women, mainly travelling artists (*goze*), their original form known only to a few professionals. Nevertheless, most people are still familiar with them as children's stories. Mori Ogai's novel is one of the most famous retellings of the original Buddhist folk tales.

Unfortunately, the popular transmission of oral traditions often gloss over the cruel portions of these stories and transform them into sweet tales. *Sansho the Bailiff* is a classic example of this transformation. The original Buddhist folk tale tells the following story:

> Masauji, the judge of Iwaki in the country of Ou (Mutsu), is exiled to distant Chikushi. His wife, daughter Anju and son Zushiomaru, who are left behind, set out on the long trip to Chikushi with one female attendant. On the way they are tricked and sold as slaves in the Bay of Naoe, then separated and put on different ships. The mother and the attendant are sold to a ship going to Ezo (modern Hokkaido). In Ezo they are put to work to shoo away birds from the fields. The muscles of their arms and legs are severed to prevent them from escasping.

> Zushiomaru and Anju are sold to Sansho, the bailiff of the country of Tango, to work at his manor (*shoen*). The elder sister, Anju, is made to pump seawater, while the brother is sent to the mountains to cut wood. They are still children and this is hard work for them. Anju's character strengthens under these adverse circumstances and she encourages her younger brother, even taking on herself the punishments meted out to him. One day, Saburo, Sansho's son, overhears the brother and sister talk about escaping. As a punishment, the two youngsters are branded with a hot iron. Then Zushiomaru prays to an image of a Buddhist saint (*jizo bosatsu*) given to him by his father, the marks on their faces disappear and appear instead on the image of the Buddhist saint.

> The sixteen-year-old Anju helps Zushiomaru escape, but is caught and tortured to death by Saburo. Zushiomaru escapes to a temple where he is helped by a travelling priest, Hijiri. Hijiri hides him in a leather basket and, without arousing suspicion, carries him on his back all the way to Kyoto. When they arrive there, the cramped Zushiomaru finds he cannot stand or walk. With the help of several people, he begs his way to the temple of Nanboku Tennoji. Little by little, movement is restored to his legs and he begins working at the temple.

> In Kyoto, a minister who is childless wants to adopt a child. One night the goddess Kannon appears in his dreams and commands him to go on a pilgrimage to the Nanboku Tennoji Temple. The minister travels there and from among the hundreds of orphans, adopts Zushiomaru. Zushiomaru discloses that he is the son of Masauji, the judge of Iwaki. Later, he is made governor (*kokushu*) of Tango by the emperor.

> As Zushiomaru proceeds to his appointment in Tango, he learns that his elder sister Anju has been killed. He has Sansho arrested and buried in the ground up to his neck. His son Saburo's neck is cut with a bamboo saw. Saburo's retainers who had tortured Anju are also disposed of. Having avenged himself, Zushiomaru divides the estate between Sansho's two remaining sons, Ichiro and Jiro who had treated him well during his imprisonment.

Finally, Zushio crosses over to the island of Ezo to look for his mother. He finds her working in a millet field shooing away birds. She is completely blind, but recovers her sight miraculously when Zushiomaru puts the image of the Buddhist saint to her eyes. Next, Zushiomaru goes to the Bay of Naoe to take revenge on Yamaoka, the bailiff, who had sold them all as slaves. He then proceeds to the capital with his mother. At long last, his father, Masauji, who had been exiled to Chikushi, is allowed to return, where the three meet in a tearful reunion.

The father and son build a temple in the country of Tango to pray for the repose of Anju's spirit, and enshrine their charm (the image of the Buddhist saint) there. They then return to Ou where they had ruled earlier and regain their wealth and possessions.

This is the story of *Sansho the Bailiff* as it was sung in medieval times. The anthropologist Yanagida Kunio reckons that the word 'Sansho' means a 'place of dispersal'. In classical Japanese it meant a place where outcasts, who served as slaves to the governor of a manor (*shoen*), lived. The historian Hayashiya Tatsusaburo says that *Sansho the Bailiff* was the headman of this zone, where he exercised strict authority over his people. Mizoguchi found this explanation helpful while making the film, since the original story had been forgotten. He reintroduced it, emphasizing that Mori Ogai had changed the original and shortened it considerably. The original, based on the harsh lives of those who suffered discrimination, may have been a cruel story, but it was a cry for their liberation. Hayashiya's essay, 'The Original Image of "Sansho the Bailiff"', is an important piece of research on the life and culture of the people during the late ancient and medieval periods, and has had a significant influence on young scholars.

FIGURE 22 *Sansho the Baliff* (1954), © Kadokawa Pictures, Inc.

Until Japan's defeat in the Second World War, questioning the notion that the Imperial house had descended from the gods in an unbroken lineage of 2,600 years, was taboo. This theory, transmitted through popular tradition and regarded as indisputable, had severely shackled historical research. If ancient history was to be studied scientifically, historians would have to deal with the mythology of the Imperial house and face the contradictions within the real history of the court. Scholars who questioned the myths and histories collected by the Imperial court, were often attacked by the right wing; consequently, the empirical study of ancient and medieval history remained undeveloped in Japan. Kinugasa Teinosuke's film, *The Sun* (1925), was attacked because it argued that the myths differed from the true facts of ancient history. Only when this taboo was broken after Japan's defeat, could historians actively ask such questions. In making *Sansho the Bailiff*, which described the slave society of medieval Japan, Mizoguchi found Hayashiya's historical study to be of enormous help.

Mori Ogai's novel is similar to the Buddhist narrative poem, but it does erase the cruelty of the original story. The biggest difference is Zushiomaru's behaviour when he becomes the governor of Tango. He does not seek revenge on Sansho, but issues an order prohibiting the sale of human beings, forcing Sansho to free the slaves working in his manor. He now has to give them a wage, but because of this he prospers.

Why did Mori Ogai modify the original story? Keeping in mind Hayashiya's interpretation, he can be criticized for removing the anger and the desires of the people of medieval times, something that was integral to the oral tradition. Did he wish to temper the story's cruelty? Or was it in response to the prevailing climate when a section of the intelligentsia had already come under the influence of socialism and the idea of class war? On its part, the ruling class, in its desire to diffuse the impact of socialism, tried to appropriate the idea of people's liberation and acted progressively to address the problem of ensuring prosperity for all. How quickly this could have been achieved in those days is a matter of debate, but worth thinking about nonetheless.

A major change in the story is that Anju is not tortured and killed, but commits suicide in a swamp after she helps Zushio to escape. The part where Zushio cannot stand on his feet after emerging from the leather basket, and has to beg his way to Nanboku Tennoji temple with the help of strangers, is also shortened. The charm that Zushio carries is used to cure the daughter of the Regent (*kanpaku*), and this gives him an opportunity to rise in the world. His father dies during this time.

It is the introduction of the father's death that makes the new version sadder than the original. On all other points the revision sanitizes and glosses over the cruelty of the old story. Interestingly, Buddhist narrative poems were originally transmitted by groups of beggars who gathered around shrines, many of them with injuries or deformities. Today, however, traditional tales transmitted to children are 'cleaned up' and the horror of original Buddhist narrative poems eliminated; what is stressed, on the other hand, is the miracles that happen through the use of the image of the Buddhist saint that Zushio carries with him.

Mizoguchi first requested Yahiro Fuji to write the script for *Sansho the Bailiff.* This script was faithful to Mori Ogai's novel, but the director was unhappy with it. He decided that it should be rewritten by Yoda because he believed that while it was fine to have Anju and Zushio as ten-year-old children in the first half of the film, they had to be young adults in the latter half. Although the original was a well-known tragic tale of abused children, to have children become governors, take revenge on Sansho and free the slaves would turn it into a nursery story with no realism. I believe that Mizoguchi wanted to craft a more realistic and credible story.

Both the Buddhist narrative poem and Mori Ogai's novel are silent on why the father, Masauji, is exiled from the country of Ou to Chikushi. What Mizoguchi does is to stress that Masauji's sympathetic policies towards the people aroused the anger of the authorities and led to his exile. These changes make it clear that Mizoguchi's purpose in revising the original was to handle this traditional tale in a more realistic way. He also drastically reduced the many miracles brought about by the image of the Buddhist saint and the image is used more as a symbolic proof of Zushio's identity.

The story is also changed to allow Anju and Zushio to become adults in the latter half of the film. They are shown to have worked for some ten years after

FIGURE 23 Tanaka Kinuyo in *Sansho the Baliff* (1954), © Kadokawa Pictures, Inc.

being sold to the Sansho manor. The mother, who sold Sado as a prostitute, suffers abuse and has her leg muscles severed when she tries to escape, is an old woman when she meets Zushio. This change considerably expands the role of Tanaka Kinuyo as the mother. At the beginning of the film, where she is seen travelling with her children across the plains of the pampas grass (*susuki*), she is a noble and refined beauty. The scene in Sado, where she is used as a prostitute and is shown gazing longingly from the beach, across to the distant mainland, crying 'Anju! … Zushio!' is one of profound grief. And in the last scene where, as a blind old woman, squatting on the beach in tattered clothes, she finally meets Zushio, she gives a performance that evokes heart-wrenching pity for her wretched condition.

The greater change is that Anju is made the younger sister and Zushio the elder brother, quite the reverse of the original story. This was done to suit the actors. It had been decided from the outset that Hanayagi Kisho would play the adult Zushio and Kagawa Kyoko, the grown-up Anju. Given their ages, Zushio would have to be the elder brother. Hanayagi had acted in *The Story of the Late Chrysanthemums*, and was the son of the famous *shinpa* actor, Hanayagi Shotaro, who was himself a friend of both Mizoguchi Kenji and Kawaguchi Matsutaro.

Mizoguchi wanted Hanayagi Kisho in the film. But this choice of actors created a problem with the original story of a strong, healthy, elder sister who sacrifices herself to save her weak, defenceless, younger brother. It showed the latent sense of noble motherhood that has moved people ever since medieval times. To alter this and show a strong younger brother allowing a weak elder sister to sacrifice herself for him would just not be acceptable. So they thought of showing Zushio helping one of his old female slave friends by carrying her on his back in a bid to help her escape. In the story Anju encourages Zushio to escape without her, admitting that while she, too, would like to flee, her legs will not carry her. This seemed an unconvincing reason for Zushio to leave her behind; his image as a hero would have considerably weakened. Although everyone knew that *Sansho the Bailiff* was a story of an elder sister and a younger brother, Mizoguchi was not particularly bothered by the confusion he would create by changing the story around.

The episode of Anju and Zushio being branded and tortured by the cruel Saburo was dropped. In its place Zushio, now a grown man, is forced on Sansho's orders to brand an old slave who has tried to run away. The innocent young man's character has begun to change with the long years of slavery and his friends start disliking him. Anju finds this painful and advises Zushio to escape. This change was inspired by a desire to make a more realistic human tragedy in a way that the episode in which the branded face is miraculously cured by the Buddha image could be dropped. So, too, were the cruelty and violence of the original narrative that stirred feelings of revenge in the abused. So we have Anju dying – not of torture as in Mori Ogai's novel – but of drowning, as she wades into a swamp of her own volition.

The Buddhist oral tradition in which Zushio becomes physically disabled and turns to begging is also changed. He is shown going to the capital alone to plead directly with the Regent (*kanpaku*) and being appointed Governor of Tango. These scenes are flat and hard to believe – they were nowhere near as interesting as the stories of the miracles and the begging in the original epic poem.

In Mori Ogai's novel, Zushio's father is already dead in Chikushi when he (Zushio) becomes a success at the Imperial court. This means that Zushio has to go to Chikushi to visit his father's grave. He learns that the people always regarded his father as a deeply compassionate and upright man.

Zushio hears of Anju's death after he takes up his appointment in Tango, and declares the freedom of all slaves. Sansho, who refuses to recognize this declaration, is exiled. This places the film somewhere between the traditional narrative and Mori Ogai's novel. Mori Ogai writes as though the freedom of the slaves happened effortlessly. But in fact the lands of the manor belonged to the nobility at the Imperial court; the authority of the local administrators, such as the governor, did not extend to it. Zushio uses his soldiers to achieve the liberation of the slaves, even as he sends his resignation to the Imperial court and leaves for the island of Sado to find his mother. When he is finally reunited with her he tells her that he is perpetuating his dead father's tradition of compassion to the people.

As the summary indicates, the film is marked strongly by the way Mizoguchi transforms a mystical tradition into a historical reality. Most historical films of those years were of the absurd 'superman' variety, and only a handful could be described as genuinely historical. The move to make historical films began just before the war years, and some great works that were faithful to the past – such as Mizoguchi's *Chushingura* – were, indeed, produced. But in general they were no more than works in support of the Emperor system without any real historical vision. That is why *Chushingura* contains some unbelievable elements such as Oishi Kuranosuke's anxiety about the reaction of the Imperial court as he wreaks his revenge.

A movement in the early 1950s sought once again to make real historical films. In 1951 came Yoshimura Kozaburo's *The Tale of Genji*; in 1952 Mizoguchi's *The Life of Oharu*; in 1953 Yoshimura Kozaburo's *Before the Dawn,* a film about the Meiji restoration (*ishin*) from the perspective of the people in the provinces; and in 1955 Shibuya Minoru's *Bronze Christians*, on the persecution of Christians in the seventeenth century, and Mizoguchi's *Taira Clan Saga*. In 1954 Kurosawa Akira made *Seven Samurai*, again a film that painted a realistic picture of the plight of farmers during war (*sengoku*). *Sansho the Bailiff* was one of the works that emerged from this new trend of historical cinema.

Does *Sansho the Bailiff* succeed as a historical film? It is difficult to say. True, it deals with a sparsely documented period, but the real problem is that the slaves on Sansho's estate come across as products of the imagination rather than real people. The images lack cinematic power, and the ideas of compassion that Masauji, a provincial official, propounds seem like mere propaganda for democracy. It is incredible that a provincial official of that time utter such words. Equally unnatural for a historical film was to show that the high-born Zushio, who was brought up as a slave, is suddenly appointed Governor of Tango when he appears in court. This may be part of the traditional story, but it does lack credibility.

For all that, the film is a rare masterpiece in its portrayal of the strength of a woman's love within a larger love for the sacred. The camerawork of the famous cinematographer Miyagawa Kazuo gives us a magnificent depiction of Tanaka Kinuyo (as the mother) and Kagawa Keiko (as Anju), as goddesses.

Several conclusions can be drawn about Mizoguchi from his portrayal of the three characters – the detestable Sansho (played by Shindo Eitaro), the ill-treated mother and the self-sacrificing Anju: that Mizoguchi did not respect his father; that he felt deeply about the unfortunate life his mother led; and that, in his youth, his firmest supporter was his elder sister. His film can thus be seen as partly autobiographical, with mythical and abstract overtones. Zushio is not the pure and incorruptible spirit of tradition. He perpetrates great cruelty on his fellow slaves and does not forgive Sansho, as in Mori Ogai's novel. But he is not as vengeful as in the traditional Buddhist folk tale either. In fact it may just be possible to see Mizoguchi in Zushio's character.

Of course the film is not Mizoguchi's autobiography, but in Japan's patriarchal society, many children regard it as all right for a woman to sacrifice her life for her husband. Popular stories with such themes abound. It is out of compassion for this unhappy mother figure and out of a yearning for her love that the trend to deify her emerges. This deification has become a fundamental element in the moral sensibilities of the Japanese.

Sansho the Bailiff is one of the best expressions of the Japanese tradition of stories of sons and daughters reuniting after a long separation. In the climactic scene where Zushio finally meets his mother on the coast of Sado, their very movements express their joy and amazement – desperately clasping each other, as if with a pent-up, uncontrollable energy, moving slowly closer and then apart with surprise, running their hands over each other, groping, their conversation muffled, almost a groan. The performance is like that of puppets and even has the tempo of a chant. Perhaps Mizoguchi's instruction to the actor who played Zushio in this scene was to bring out the real solemnity of *noh* or *bunraku*. It was important for the role to be enacted as an adult and not as a child, and Hanayagi Kisho's high-energy performance was exactly what he desired.

Mizoguchi extracted history from an old tale. Not only was it an appropriate story for a traditional narrative performance, it was one through which he discovered 'his' story, as it were, and discovered, too, a superb cinematic language. Through Tanaka Kinuyo and Hanayagi Kisho, he created some of the most exquisite scenes in the history of film: the fear in the scene where mother and children, having been sold as slaves, are sent off on different ships; the ethereal beauty of the scene where Anju takes a dip in the water; and then again in the scene I just described, where Zushio and his mother are reunited.

A Western Romance: *A Story from Chikamatsu*

Mizoguchi cast some of the most beautiful heroines in his films but rarely did he make romantic films where a beautiful woman and a handsome man meet and fall in love. The men who fall in love with his heroines are either unworthy, weak or immature. But films such as *Cascading White Threads*, *The Story of the Late Chrysanthemums* and *Lady Yu* are true Japanese-style romances. The only Western-style romance Mizoguchi ever made was *A Story from Chikamatsu* (1954).

The original puppet play (*sewa joruri*) of Chikamatsu Monzaemon is a love story, but one which does glorify love. The love it portrays is actually adulterous, and while it has a certain beauty, it is also marked by an underlying fear. The original play, *The Old Calendar Maker* (Daikyoji mukashi Goyomi) was performed for the first time in 1717. Based on an actual incident that took place in 1683, this performance on the thirty-third anniversary of the incident, was in the nature of a Buddhist ceremonial entertainment, aimed at pacifying the spirits of the executed protagonists. Many plays have been performed upon the unnatural death of actors and noted figures at such Buddhist ceremonies, a practice that continues even today on a *tatami* mat stage. The belief is that the spirit of a person who has killed, been executed, or has died unnaturally, will not leave for the other world but will wander about here and now, and foment trouble until it is pacified. And that called for a holding of a ceremony. It is, therefore, necessary to have a performance to pacify its spirit. These ideas grew out of older and uniquely Japanese beliefs.

The model for the original work, the real story of Osan and Mohei was as follows:

Isyun is a calendar-maker who lives in the fourth ward on Karasuma Road in Kyoto. His wife, Osan, is having an adulterous affair with Mohei, the clerk. With the help of the maid Tama, they run away and hide in Yamada village, Hikami county, in Tanba. They are caught and brought back to the capital, Kyoto, on 22 September 1683, and executed at Awataguchi. Osan and Mohei are crucified and Tama is jailed. (*Collection of Japanese Classical Literature*, vol. 47, Saikaku Collection, introduction, Iwanami Publishing House) (Nihon koten bungaku taikei 47 Saikaku shu jo kaisetsu, Iwanami Shoten)

Subsequently another version, *A Shinto Funeral Prayer for the Calendar-Maker Osan* (Daikyoji osan uta saimon) became popular. This was its story:

The maid, Tama, is asked by Mohei to carry a love letter to Osan in which he says that if he cannot fulfil his love for her, he will die. Osan's heart is moved and she agrees to meet him one night. Having fulfilled his desire and afraid he may be accused of adultery, Mohei wants to have nothing to do with her any more. But Osan does not comply, and their relations continue till she becomes pregnant. Osan and Mohei escape to hide in Tanba but their notorious story spreads like wildfire. Osan's husband, who is in Edo, discovers their whereabouts and the three are found and executed at the Kurodaguchi.

Adultery may be considered to be immoral, but in a feudal society, it assumed an absolutely frightening dimension. People could be executed for even a minor act like carrying love letters.

Even before *The Old Calendar-Maker*, Saikaku used this material for a three-volume novel, *Five Women who Loved Love* (Koshoku gonin onna), the story of the passionate love between Osan, the wife of an upper-class man, who was a calendar-maker. It should be pointed out that in those days a paperhanger, with his monopoly on publishing calendars, had considerable wealth.

The calendar-maker goes to Edo, and during his absence the honest Moemon (Mohei) comes to work there from Osan's parental home. Rin, the woman working for this noble family, falls in love with him. Since she is illiterate, she has a love letter written on her behalf by Osan and gives it to Moemon. Moemon, partly in jest, writes a smug reply. Rin asks Osan to read the note to her. Osan, irritated by Moemon's sense of himself as a ladies man, decides to send a fitting reply, and hatches a plan. She writes a beautiful love letter and asks Moemon to come to Rin's room secretly at night. She plans to be there in place of Rin, raise an alarm when Rin arrives, call the servants and make a laughing stock of him.

Osan wears Rin's night-clothes and falls asleep in her room. Moemon enters secretly, and unknowingly gets into bed with Osan. Once the two realize they are in a compromising position and likely to be accused of adultery, they decide to leave the house and drown themselves in Lake Biwa. Then they change their minds, stage a drowning and escape over the mountains of Tanba. They are helped by a mountain dweller who has treated Moemon like a son. This implicates him as well, so he too hides with them in Tango. The Buddha appears to them in a dream and says, 'You have committed adultery and will suffer but if you separate and live apart, perhaps the world will let you live.' 'It doesn't matter what happens to us,' they answer, 'but you, the Buddha, cannot understand love.' They decide not to renounce their love for each other.

After some time, Moemon goes back to Kyoto but, frightened by the rumours circulating about him and Osan, he returns to Tango. Meanwhile a chestnut seller from Tanba travels to Kyoto and talks of a couple exactly like Osan and Moemon in Tango. The calendar-maker pursues them. The two and and their go-between (and not Rin), are executed.

Saikaku shows that Osan and Moemon's love is born of a purely accidental encounter: since Osan wants to be free to experience the happiness of love, she sets out to mock Moemon and substitutes herself for the maid. But once she has slept with him, she feels she has loved him all her life. Osan and Moemon are people who have forsaken the morality of the world and abandoned the Buddha's teachings for the joy of sex. Even when they have been condemned to death, they write,

'Finally, we feel we have done nothing wrong and have nothing to apologize for.' Saikaku, it must be added, did not approve of adultery. He felt it was morally wrong, but accepted that it did happen.

Chikamatsu Monzaemon's puppet play is far more moral than Saikaku's novel in which the husband Isyun is presented sympathetically as a simple merchant. Chikamatsu shows him as a man whose affairs set the stage for Osan's tragedy. Far more than in Saikaku's novel, Osan and Mohei are portrayed as moral individuals and not as people moved by their passions.

The puppet play shows that the love between a man and a woman may lead to tragedy and not turn into something beautiful. Osan, the wife of an upper-class merchant, is at no point a lover of the clerk, Mohei. Their adulterous relationship stems only from a series of accidents. Osan's family needs a loan. Since it is difficult for Osan to ask Isyun, her husband, she requests Mohei to find the right opportunity to talk to her husband. As Osan is the wife of the master, Mohei does not think he is committing a crime and he writes out a money order using Isyun's seal. He is seen by a crafty clerk, Sukeemon, who informs on him. Isyun demands to know what the money is for and before Osan or Mohei can defend themselves, Tama, the maid, who had earlier fallen in love with Mohei, tries to help him by saying that she was in a difficult situation and has asked Mohei to loan her the money to help her family.

When Osan questions Tama, she learns that her husband had been quietly visiting Tama's room every night. Osan is angry and that night changes places with Tama. When her husband steals into the room, she keeps silent and sleeps with him. However, afterwards she is ashamed of what she has done. The same night Mohei, who has been confined in another room, feels that Tama has taken on his crime because she has fallen in love with him. He escapes and goes quietly to Tama's room, and thinking that it is Tama, he gets into her bed. At this point Isyun enters and sees that Osan and Mohei are sleeping together.

Osan and Mohei are not really in love. They flee only to escape death for adultery, and even then they do not become lovers. Mohei is convinced he is guilty of a great crime, while Osan is angry with her husband for his affair. Yet she does not think that gives her the right to take a lover. Since theirs is a journey of penitence for an unfortunate act, they are saved in the end by the benevolence of a virtuous priest.

Osan and Mohei are decent people in an ill-fated situation, but because they cannot change their fate of their own volition, their appeal as tragic individuals is limited. The really tragic figure in this play is the maid, Tama, who, because of her love for Mohei, lies and informs the master's wife about the master seducing her. She takes the initiative and acts of her own free will. The result is that Mohei, whom she loves, and Osan, whom she respects, are driven to a tragic end. Though Tama weeps with regret, she is vocal in her declration that Isyun's adultery and Sukeemon's guile are the real cause of the tragedy. She accepts her responsibility and is killed by her uncle, the storyteller Akamatsu Bairyu. It is Tama who is the main protagonist of the play.

The head of Daiei Studios, Nagata Masaikazu, agreed to have Mizoguchi direct this film provided the role of Mohei was given to Hasegawa Kazuo. This was the first time that Mizoguchi had worked with Hasegawa. Hasegawa came from the western Japan (Kansai) kabuki stage, which had maintained the authenticity of the puppet play tradition. From being a Japanese-style (*wagoto*) matinee idol he had become a film star. Both Mizoguchi and Hasegawa were later to become directors in Daiei.

An aggressive Mizoguchi said he would not tolerate any foolishness. He rejected the script written by Kawaguchi Matsutaro, not only because it was overly faithful to Chikamatsu's original story, but because it put Tama in the main role. He demanded that elements from the third volume of Ihara Saikaku's *Five Women who Loved Love* be included. Saikaku, as I have said earlier, had used the same incident, but had concentrated on Osan and Mohei's life after their escape – the time when they actually fell in love. Finally, Mizoguchi suggested that, given the formal status of the family of the calendar-maker, his adulterous act should at least lead to the confiscation of his estate.

It was decided that Yoda write another script expanding Mohei's role in the way Mizoguchi wanted. He was also told that he should write more concretely of how love was judged within a feudal, social and family system. This had not been dealt with in the original.

The script is more or less faithful to the original up to the point when Osan and Mohei commit adultery and flee. It departs from both Chikamatsu's and Saikaku's version, from the time they decide to throw themselves into Lake Biwa. Mohei admits that he has been in love with Osan from the start. On hearing this, Osan 'decided that she did not want to die'. For the first time the two, aware of their love for each other, resolve to live.

When Yoda wrote the lines 'She decided that she did not want to die', Mizoguchi, shaking with excitement, cried out, 'With just this, the film is complete.'

With these elements from the Chikamatsu and Saikaku's stories, the film took on an altogether different colour – a sort of Western love story of Osan and Mohei, who do not see their adultery as immoral and are not ashamed to declare their love openly in front of the gods. Even when they are tied back to back, mounted on a horse, and taken through the town to their execution, they are satisfied. They smile and hold hands.

Changing the story from a Japanese tale of the dark and difficult road of a forbidden love, to a Western story of the triumph of love, meant changing Mohei's character as well. In the first half of the film, he is a weak but handsome man, unable to fight his fate. In the latter half, Hasegawa Kazuo plays the role in the classic manner of the matinee idol (*nimaime*), taking the initiative and deciding that he will live for his love. He becomes the hero of a Western romance, ready to battle fate if necessary.

Mizoguchi hated the character of the weak matinee idol. In this film, however – made at the peak of his maturity – he turned him into a courageous hero.

By refuting the idea that the couple are a pair of criminals, the film becomes a series of incomparably beautiful scenes, filled with brightness, quite unlike the bitterly sorrowful *bunraku* or kabuki stories. Kagawa Kyoko, who was not a particularly great actress, played Osan. She was among the prominent stars known for her youth and grace, and proved to be the right actress for the role of a young noblewoman whom Mohei treats with respect. Adding to the delightful performance by Hasegawa Kazuo and Kagawa Kyoko is the great camerawork by Miyagawa Kazuo. Music director Hayasaka Fumio's brilliant use of Japanese instruments in certain scenes (where Mohei carries Osan on his back across the dry Kamogawa river bed; where they plan to commit suicide but decide against it; where Mohei comes secretly to Osan, who has been taken back to her parental home; where Osan argues with her mother (Naniwa Chieko) who urges her to leave him; and where they are taken back) is quite simply perfect. These scenes are counted among the most memorable in the history of Japanese film. *A Story from Chikamatsu* is entirely Mizoguchi's work – not Chikamatsu's or Saikaku's.

FIGURE 24 Naniwa Chieko (left), Hasegawa Kazuo (centre) and Kagawa Kyoko (right) in *A Story from Chikamatsu* (1954), © Kadokawa Pictures, Inc.

The film does more than present the nature of feudalism through a paper-hanger's family. The status of this paperhanger is based on the monopoly of his profession. He mixes with the nobility in the capital and has considerable standing in society. Any scandal, any hint of adultery can easily destroy him and his family. He is aware that his professional colleagues, who know about this affair, are plotting to snatch his commercial rights even as they call him a gem of a man. This is Yoda bringing out the reality of feudal society, not Chikamatsu or Saikaku. Also, Sukeemon is not the evil character he is in Chikamatsu. When he discloses Mohei's failed plan, the master is reluctant to single out one person, and makes it the responsibility of all the managers. This act of showing Sukeemon in a realistic light rather than casting him an innately evil person is essentially a rejection of feudalism.

In Chikamatsu, the climax in the middle of the story is the tragic scene when the three positive characters, Tama's uncle, Akamatsu Bairyu, the professional sto-ryteller, and Osan's upright parents, come together and lament at what fate has done to them. Yoda however, threw this scene out of the script and replaced it with the character of Osan's younger brother, played by Tanaka Haruo. In the gallery of really detestable characters that Mizoguchi created, this one is surely among the worst, an extreme example of his disparaging view of the man.

As the tragedy moves inexorably to its conclusion, Sukeemon, who has failed in business, comes to borrow money from his elder sister, and quite coolly calls in a music teacher to relieve his depression through music. He then goes off to fawn over his brother-in-law Isyun, leaving his sister in a miserable state. When she and Mohei escape, he has no hesitation in calling them fools, but when the money that he has asked them for arrives, he grovels and thanks them obsequiously for saving him from jail. In keeping with his character, when Osan is confined to his house and Mohei secretly comes to see her, he believes that by informing Isyun he will safeguard his position, and runs out of the house looking quite cheerful. Interestingly, despite his odious nature, he never displays his meanness. Even while crying, he appears to be merely cunning. His actions are always portrayed as natural, and he is happy and unworried as he carries out his plans, humming as he impudently pours tea just as he is about to inform on Mohei. Tanaka Haruo gives a lively performance with these touches, in keeping with his many other fine per-formances he has given.

Many of Mizoguchi's characters treated women badly, but Mohei is the only one who seems happy to be mean. It added a particularly cruel twist to his lifelong depiction of the privations forced on sisters by worthless brothers. He assailed the paternalistic family system where, for the sake of safeguarding the sole inheritor, all the sisters and younger brothers are made to suffer; and was grimly amused by the total lack of awareness of this injustice to Japan's patriarchal society.

–10–

The Last Works

Gion Festival Music

Gion Festival Music, made in 1953, can be viewed as Mizoguchi's post-war version of his film *Sisters of the Gion* made seventeen years before. The story is similar – that of an elderly geisha who tries to live like the geisha of an earlier day, as against a younger geisha who does not hesitate to fight feudal oppression. But the word 'oppression' is perhaps a misnomer since the post-war period was actually quite accommodating. Hence, the resistance of the younger geisha to a system which had none of the cruelty of the old, is transformed into something humorous. Mizoguchi was not a young geisha burning with the zeal inspired by post-war reforms – he was a successful and reputed director, and his interests had moved from making a film that approached the problem directly to narrating a story skilfully, and *Gion Festival Music* is indeed a skilfully told story.

A young woman, Eiko, played by Wakao Ayako, wants to become a geisha and goes to Miyoharu (Kogure Michiyo). Miyoharu is a geisha who (Shindo Eitaro) had once been helped by Eiko's father. The father is now facing problems. This film is unusual in that Mizoguchi contrasts Eiko practising to become a geisha or going to a Shinto shrine dressed as a *maiko* (an apprentice geisha) with the way she was in school. Her education reflects the new democratic atmosphere, when forced prostitution was banned. The scenes are light-hearted, humorous and fresh. Eiko has no regrets about becoming a geisha, in fact she is overjoyed. The world, however, is not so accepting.

As always in Mizoguchi's films, there is a lecherous, greedy, shameless, middle-aged man who molests these two women. Miyoharu gently rebukes him but Eiko creates a scene by biting his tongue when he tries to kiss her. These lascivious, middle-aged men use the boss (Naniwa Chieko) of a *machiai* (meeting place), a big power in the Gion district, as a cat's paw with which to persecute Eiko. All it takes is to let it be known that she is a ferocious kind of woman, and contracts for Eiko and Miyoharu are cancelled one after another. There is nothing to be done. Miyoharu submits, while Eiko for the first time understands the cruelty of the geisha world.

In the last scene of the earlier *Sisters of the Gion*, Mizoguchi had the spirited young geisha cry out, 'A geisha is for sale … is it all right if there is no work?' In

FIGURE 25 *Gion Festival Music* (1953), © Kadokawa Pictures, Inc.

this film he stopped short of making such cold statements. Instead, he has the sad, melancholy air of defeat; he has, in places, gone back to his earlier days and used elements of *shinpa* drama.

One of the highlights of this film – apart from the way in which Mizoguchi shows the suppression of women in Gion – is the shocking but funny scene when Wakao Ayako, a new actress who plays the fearless young *maiko*, bites the tongue of the salacious, middle-aged man. Surprisingly, Naniwa Chieko as the boss of the *machiai*, gives a brilliant performance. Another highlight is the way in which the suppression of women in Gion is portrayed.

The Woman in the Rumour

The Woman in the Rumour (1954) is a traditional comedy set in the Shimabara brothel district of Kyoto.

> The film centres on a widow (Tanaka Kinuyo), the head of a large old brothel. She looks upon her work as a vocation and puts her heart into it. The film shows the behaviour of men and women in Shimabara, Japan's most famous red-light district. Her daughter (Kuga Yoshiko) has been to university in Tokyo and, following an abortive attempt at suicide because of an unfortunate love affair, has returned to Shimabara. She is ashamed of her mother's profession. But while looking after the prostitutes who work

FIGURE 26 Kuga Yoshiko (left) in *The Woman in the Rumour* (1954), © Kadokawa Pictures, Inc.

there, she begins to sympathize with their plight. Her mother falls ill and the daughter, quite naturally, takes over from her and manages the brothel.

There is also a comic element in the story – the mother's jealousy over a young doctor (Otani Tomoemon) whom she loves. During her illness the doctor begins to fall in love with the daughter. Mother and daughter fight over the young doctor but when they discover how awful he is, both throw him out of the house.

Mizoguchi's demonstrates his truly skilful directorial technique, and Tanaka Kinuyo puts in a superb performance, especially in the scene where she is mad with jealousy on learning about the doctor's betrayal. Yet Mizoguchi could do nothing about the stale, worn-out story – surprising, indeed, that the man who had earlier made combative films in support of the fundamental rights of poor women, was now making a light-hearted film that barely touched upon the problems of prostitution. *Gion Festival Music* and *The Woman in the Rumour* are like a holiday he took from the great works of his last years. They are full of contradictions that were born out of his own position: a critic of prostitution as well as a man of the *demi-monde*.

Princess Yang Kwei-fei

After *Gion Festival Music* and *The Woman in the Rumour* – films made with prac-
tised skill on familiar subjects but devoid of ambition – Mizoguchi went to the
other extreme and made two films on an unfamiliar theme: *Princess Yang Kwei-fei*
and *Taira Clan Saga*.

Princess Yang Kwei-fei is a story of the Imperial court in ancient China.
Emperor Xuan Zong (Mori Masayuki) has lost the beautiful princess he loved.
In a bid to gain influence with the Emperor, An Lushan (Yamamura So), a
warrior, introduces him to the daughter (Kyo Machiko) of the house of Yang.
The Emperor calls her Kwei-fei and makes her a princess.

This is the story of Yang Kwei-fei, the most beautiful woman in Chinese history.
Kwei-fei's eldest cousin, Yang Kuo-chung is made Prime Minister and her three
sisters are also given important positions. They all live in luxury. But Yang Kuo-
chung is a bad Prime Minister and the people are outraged. An Lushan is
unhappy about being the ruler's representative and he informs Kwei-fei of this.
The Emperor is suspicious of the relationship between Kwei-fei and An Lushan.
He returns Kwei-fei to the house of Yang, but finding he cannot live without her,
summons her back. Meanwhile the people's resentment against the arbitrary

FIGURE 27 Kyo Machiko (left) in *The Princess Yang Kwei-fei* (1955), © Kadokawa
Pictures, Inc.

rule of Yang Kuo-chung and his family builds up, and this anger is turned against Kwei-fei. An Lushan takes advantage of this discontent to lead a rebellion against the Emperor. The capital falls into the hands of rebel troops and the Emperor and Kwei-fei are caught. The people demand that the Emperor kill Kwei-fei but he is unwilling to do so. Instead, Kwei-fei commits suicide. The Emperor, who has lost his throne, dies yearning for a glimpse of his princess.

This film is an excellent example of Mizoguchi's understanding of the traditional arts. However, since he had insufficient historical material, the recreation of ancient Chinese customs is not just imaginary, it comes across like an unreal painting. Though Mizoguchi took the help of a Chinese in writing the script and making corrections to suit the times, the film still lacked a Chinese ambience.

Mizoguchi put all his strength into the love story of the Emperor and Kwei-fei. Scenes like the one when the Emperor and Kwei-fei walk in disguise among the people during a festival are most romantically shot; but the story never goes beyond a syrupy, sentimental melodrama. Japanese critics judged it as completely lacking in the intensity that had been the hallmark of Mizoguchi's other films.

Princess Yang Kwei-fei was not rated highly in Japan, but film-makers and critics in Europe and America saw it as a work of great importance. Since we in Japan are familiar with Eastern clothes, objects and rich colours, we don't see them as particularly striking, but this exoticism might have held an appeal for others.

Around the time this film was made, Nagata Masakazu, the president of Daiei, began to nurse hopes of building up an export market for Japanese films. Interest had already been created by the Grand Prix won by *Rashomon* and *Gate of Hell*. Nagata advocated the idea of participating in Asian film festivals, and made concrete plans for exporting to Asian markets. The collaboration with the Hong Kong producer Run Run Shaw was an important first step. Nagata felt that exoticism was Japan's best tool for increasing its film export.

Mizoguchi agreed with Nagata. He chose for his film his much-loved theme of lovers' devotion and clothed it in the exotic. However, the rejection of history for the sake of a pure love story turned it into a hackneyed exercise.

Taira Clan Saga

I believe Mizoguchi brought a burning passion to his film *Taira Clan Saga*. The original work, a very long novel by Yoshikawa Eiji, was then a best-seller. Daiei thought of turning it into a series and Mizoguchi directed the first film. In the magazine, *Asahi Weekly* (Shukan asahi), where the original work was serialized, Mizoguchi wrote:

> I have been happy looking at art and am the sort who enjoys looking up historical events. This is not the difficult part. Making the film according to what has been

planned is. Particularly if all the members of the team do not bring the same passion and interest to it, for it is a cooperative team effort. The first concern is to din this into the heads of the crew.

Reflections on *Taira Clan Saga* (10 August 1955)

Mizoguchi put all his energy into rediscovering twelfth-century Japan, which is when the film is set. That period was a turning point, a time when political authority was transferred from the ancient Imperial court to samurai leadership. Earlier, the nobility itself would lead troops into battle, a practice that was soon discontinued. Noblemen turned to social matters, leaving the fighting to their subordinates, the samurai. The samurai gradually increased their control and by the twelfth century they had seized political power from their rulers.

The first samurai to establish their political authority was the leader of the house of the Heike, Taira Kiyomori (Ichikawa Raizo). The film shows Kiyomori's early years – how

FIGURE 28 Ichikawa Raizo in *Taira Clan Saga* (1955), © Kadokawa Pictures, Inc.

the nobility despised him as a samurai and how he built up his self-confidence. With military power in samurai hands, it should have been easy for them to seize political power from the nobility, who were well versed only in the literary arts and social graces. However, the samurai had first to rid themselves of the notion that they were lower and meaner human beings than the nobility. Taira Kiyomori was the first samurai to succeed in this.

One day Kiyomori learns that his mother, an entertainer (*shirabyoshi*) of Gion (Kogure Michiyo), had been made pregnant by the retired Emperor, Go Shirakawa, who had given her away as a wife to Tadamori (Oya Ichijiro). Kiyomori respects his father, the loyal Tadamori who has quietly carried out his duties as a leader of the samurai, in spite of the poor award he has received. When Kiyomori is told by his mother, 'You are Go Shirakawa's son,' he replies evenly, 'I am Taira Tadamori's son.' Kiyomori's heart is filled with greater pride at being a samurai (a despised lot though they are), than at being told that he is the Emperor's secret child.

It was customary for the monks of Hieizan to make an ostentation of the religious privileges they had been given by the Imperial court. Sometimes they would come out in a group and use violence to get what they wanted. To keep their opponents at bay, they would carry a *mikoshi* (palanquin of a Shinto god) with their sacred image. In a fight between these monks and the samurai of the Heike house, Kiyomori stands boldly in front of the *mikoshi* the monks are carrying, strings an arrow into his bow and before the surprised monks and samurai, shoots it through the divine mirror (*goshintai* – the divine image). With one stroke he destroys the mystical power of the *mikoshi* and levels the special powers of the monks. After that it is was a general rout.

The nobility has no idea that their power is declining rapidly. In one scene they are shown sporting elegantly in an open field bathed in a serene light. Kiyomori's mother is with them and the nobles flirt with her. Looking down on this scene, Kiyomori is confident that the samurai's time will soon come.

In the climactic scene where Kiyomori fires an arrow into the *mikoshi*, Ichikawa Raizo gives a truly brilliant performance. It is his role and its cold demeanour that gives this work the feel of a Mizoguchi film. On the whole, though, *Taira Clan Saga* is fairly boring. Mizoguchi kept postponing the shooting of the climax even though several hundred extras, all ready and dressed, were milling around or being forced to wait on Hieizan. He would just not give the order to begin shooting. Instead, he asked Yoda to decide whether the scene should be shot or not, saying jokingly, 'Since you wrote the script for this please give the order for shooting.' It seems he was apprehensive that the film would be criticized for posing a challenge to the authority of the Emperor system (the mirror – *goshintai* – in the *mikoshi* is the symbol of the religious authority of the Imperial house). Yoda argued that the entire story was structured to work up to this climax, and it was impossible now to suddenly change it and substitute it with another. In the end, Mizoguchi shot the scene.

Mizoguchi's apprehensions proved baseless. No one raised any objections when the film was released. Yoshikawa Eiji, the writer of the original work, was a well-known, conservative writer but because he was writing in the environment of post-war democracy, he brought in, even if to a small degree, a progressive historical vision. There was no question of any problem as no one ever imagined that the book could be construed as a challenge to the authority of the Emperor system, and neither was this scene considered a challenge.

Nevertheless, this episode shows how deeply the authority of the Emperor system had percolated into the hearts of the Japanese; it is an indication of Mizoguchi's diffident nature which surfaced occasionally. At times he could be a pitiless tyrant, at other times extraordinarily timid. When he made *Metropolitan Symphony* (1929), a radical proletarian film, he was worried it would anger the censors. It is said he was actually scared about going to the censor's office alone. And yet, he made a number of anti-establishment films and contributed to the development of Japanese cinema. He even went on a reconnaissance trip to China during the Second World War to make a propaganda film for the Army, though in the end it was not made. Some works, such as *The Story of the Late Chrysanthemums* and *Chushingura*, were close to being classified as conservative, but he never made an outright reactionary film. At first, he was too timid to make a film that would challenge the authority of the Emperor system, but he did end up overcoming his diffidence by constantly battling with himself.

Taira Clan Saga was the first Japanese film to show the Emperor as a character (of course he is a retired Emperor) and this caused a scandal. Oya Ichijiro, who plays Kiyomori's father, Tadamori, the old, industrious samurai who goes quietly to his death, performs with great zest in the scene before Kiyomori shoots the *mikoshi*. Natsume Shunji, who plays the retired Emperor, Toba, a supporter of Kiyomori, also gives a very spirited performance in the few scenes in which he appears. There are other memorable sequences in the film as well. Made on the scale of an epic poem, *Taira Clan Saga* is a much finer film than *Princess Yang Kwei-fei*, but it is still not one of Mizoguchi's best. It is more in the class of *Princess Yang Kwei-fei* for, taken as whole, its artistic style never crystallizes as it did in *Chushingura* or *The Life of Oharu*.

In a period film, action and battle scenes are what normally attract the viewer. But in all his period films Mizoguchi hardly ever shot any action or battle scenes, with the exception of *Miyamoto Musashi* (1944). He made a sloppy job of it, perhaps because he shot it during the tumultuous, end-of-the-war days. He is reported to have said while filming *Chushingura* that making scenes of killing in a realistic way was a useless exercise.

Taira Clan Saga is based on the samurai class's assumption of power. Even here, Mizoguchi did not shoot any battle scenes. He seems to have let down his viewers who had expected to see a grand spectacle. Perhaps he was far more interested in the conflict of ideas rather than in action and battle.

The film was made at a time when the Japanese film industry was in good financial health. Mizoguchi could have had any kind of sets he wanted. There was an abundant supply of extras, so smooth-flowing shots were extensively used in the crowd scenes. But he was never able to bring out the beauty inherent in the actions of a brave and heroic figure. This did not bother him, though; he was a director who excelled in portraying the resistance of the weak.

Street of Shame

With the making of *Street of Shame* (1956), Mizoguchi once again returned to the world of prostitutes. Scripted by Narusawa Masashige, Mizoguchi's childhood friend, the film's story was set in the days before Yoshiwara, the red-light district in Tokyo, was closed down and prostitution was legally abolished. Narusawa, who used to share a place with Mizoguchi, had followed him into films and learned a great deal from him. He was the son of a merchant from Ueda in Shinshu, the old fief of Mizoguchi's elder sister's husband, the Viscount Matsudaira's family. His father had business with the Matsudairas and he visited their home frequently. When Narusawa decided that he wanted to enter the film world, he was placed in Mizoguchi's care. He became an assistant director for *Chushingura*. In 1947 he became a scriptwriter, and in 1953 was noticed for his script of Toyoda Shiro's *Wild Goose*. Narusawa assisted Yoda with the scripts of *The Woman in the Rumour*, *Princess Yang Kwei-fei* and *Taira Clan Saga*. Mizoguchi wanted Narusawa to help Yoda with the script of *Street of Shame* as well, but Yoda refused. He explained why:

> Before I was asked to write the script, I was told by some people to please be patient about *Street of Shame*. The reason is that the script for *Princess Yang Kwei-fei* had not been liked in Tokyo. Prior to that, I had also done *Women of the Night*, but even though I tried my best, it did not make for a good film. (*Mizoguchi Kenji no hito to geijutsu*)

After this, Yoda plunged into the script of *Osaka Story*, based on Ihara Saikaku's novel which Mizoguchi subsequently brought to the screen.

Narusawa finally wrote the script for *Street of Shame* alone. He borrowed a part of it from the novel *The Susaki Paradise* (Susaki paradisu) by Shibaki Yoshiko. As Mizoguchi's disciple, he was particularly suited to write the scripts for women-based films. He was in his element writing emotional works. In *Street of Shame* he followed Mizoguchi's instructions and aimed at making it realistic. It contained a severe social indictment as well. According to Yoda, Mizoguchi had, of late, become a relaxed, fairly uncritical old granddad, but Narusawa says that working on *Street of Shame* was a hellish experience. He was always on the sets during the shoot, with Mizoguchi constantly ordering him to make changes in the script.

FIGURE 29 *Street of Shame* (1956), © Kadokawa Pictures, Inc.

The film is about women in a brothel, 'Village of Dreams' (Yume no sato), in the Yoshiwara red-light district of Tokyo, when the anti-prostitution draft bill was raised in the Diet and voted down. The couple who run the place (Shindo Eitaro and Sawamura Sadako) are always fighting about what they will do when the law is passed and they have to shut shop. They are adamant in their belief that their profession does not in any way oppress women. Rather, they argue, it supports poor women who would not be able to survive in any other way.

Hanae (Kogure Michiko), a middle-aged woman who suffers from pulmonary tuber-culosis, comes to this brothel while her unemployed husband looks after their child. The husband praises Hanae's friend, Yorie (Machida Hiroko), who wants to give up prostitution. Unthinkingly, he says, 'Prostitutes are the dregs of mankind.' Listening quietly, Hanae is filled with complex emotions. Her husband, she knows, has given up hope and tried to commit suicide; she herself has been supporting this weak, worthless hanger-on. But she is determined to survive. She wonders what will happen to a society that crucifies honest people like her.

The story's fierce spirit captures the spineless character of a weak-willed man, and the will to live of a tyrannized woman who ultimately transcends him. It is comparable to the wonderful climax we saw in *The Straits of Love and Hate* and *And Yet They Go*.

Mikki (Kyo Machiko) is the sensuous daughter of a bourgeois. She becomes a pros-titute following a fight with her father who has been grieving over the death of her mother. When her father comes to see her, she says, 'Try holding me, I am a very sensual woman.' Her father is shocked out of his mind.

After he fails in business, Oharu's father in Saikaku's *The Life of Oharu* quite shamelessly asks his daughter to become a prostitute. *Osaka Elegy* also has a despicable father. The theme of the abject father is an important one in Mizoguchi's work.

Yasumi (Wakao Ayako), sacrifices herself for the sake of her father, a corrupt Diet member, and becomes a prostitute in order to get the money for her father's bail. She believes she is justified in tricking men and making money in a materialistic and patriarchal society. She entices a stockbroker, cheats him, then throws him out. The angry stockbroker plans to kill her but is arrested. With her savings, Yasumi buys a clothes shop. Her character resembles the heroines of *Osaka Elegy* and *Sisters of the Gion*.

Yumeko (Mimasu Aiko), a mature, beautiful woman has left middle school and is working. She has a grown-up son and her one dream is to live with him. One day the son, who has come from the village, is shocked to see her talking obscenely with a client. Ashamed, he leaves her and the crushed Yumeko loses her mind.

This sad and depressing story of the ugly world of prostitutes is very different from the colourful world of *The Life of Oharu*; it is a world that survives till today. The film came as a shock for most people for they knew that around this time Chieko, Mizoguchi's wife, had lost her mental balance and was confined to an institution.

A number of motifs that Mizoguchi had used earlier reappear briefly in *Street of Shame*. Among the memorable ones is a scene at the end where, in the dreary wasteland of an industrial town, Yumeko is called by her son and repeatedly insulted, and the bond between mother and child is broken. Another is the scene when the young girl (Kawakami Yasuko), who has newly arrived from the village to become a prostitute, tries to solicit a customer for the first time. She stands in front of a shop, mortified. The last scene shows her at the sink, letting the water run over her head. All these are expressions of Mizoguchi's unique style of presenting a cruel world without resorting to overt brutality, yet leaving an indelible impact.

Mizoguchi's women, no matter how terrible their situation, live with great courage; the men, on the contrary are low and contemptible. In *Street of Shame* Mizoguchi deals in an unforgettable way with the themes that obsessed him all his life.

The film was completed and released in March 1956. Two months later, in May, the law abolishing prostitution was passed in the Diet. It came into effect the following year.

Death of Mizoguchi

Immediately after *Street of Shame* Mizoguchi began preparing for *Osaka Story*. Yoda first wrote the complete script and, as usual, Mizoguchi began by whittling it down. This time the criticism was severe and even Yoda, who was used the director's censure, was reduced to tears. However, during the many discussions that took place while revising the script, it suddenly struck Yoda that Mizoguchi's intensity never lasted more than three hours. Soon, Mizoguchi had to be hospitalized. He was not told, but he had been diagnosed with incurable leukaemia. Many of his friends and disciples, who knew of this, came to visit him. Yoda, who had gone to see him in the hospital, writes:

> He would become feverish every evening, and when he was told that this is how his illness was, he came close to tears and he said, 'I can't bear it, it's hell.'
>
> I was startled, thinking he was talking about fighting his fear of death and said, 'There is nothing to worry about.'
>
> 'You are saying that, but it isn't like that,' he replied.
>
> 'If there is anything we can do, don't hesitate, just ask,' I said, my heart tightening, restraining the tears welling up in my eyes. Mizoguchi, who was seated cross-legged on a mat on the floor, sat up, folded his knees under him and, putting his hands on his knees, he said, 'Thank you for everything.' I was so surprised that without thinking I drew back my legs that were resting on a chair. I never knew what he meant by the statement – was it that he was preparing to die? Were these parting words of regret to me? Or was he thanking me for doing a good job over the years? Or only for what I had done since he was admitted to hospital? (*Mizoguchi Kenji no hito to geijutsu*)

Mizoguchi Kenji died in the Kyoto Municipal Hospital on 24 August 1956. His wife, Chieko, who had exerted a great influence on his films, and who matched him in their explosive fights which sometimes resembled mortal hand-to-hand combat, died much later, in 1975.

Mizoguchi's elder sister, Matsudaira Suzu, died in 1981, at the age of eighty-five, her husband Matsudaira Tadamasa having passed away in 1963. She spent the last years of her life with her daughter, Kawakatsu Kyoko. She lived a happy life, surrounded by her grandchildren and great-grandchildren. Two months before her death, I had presented an NHK programme, 'The Cinematic Expression of the Masters: Mizoguchi Kenji'. She saw it and she said, 'I don't like this because I am always discussed whenever they discuss Ken-chan.'

During the difficult days after the war, when the Matsudaira house was collapsing, Suzu once asked Mizoguchi for financial help. He refused, writing in a letter, 'Respected Elder Sister – Man originally came with nothing, these are the words of the Buddhist priest.' All Suzu said was, 'Is that so?' She had spent her whole life helping her parents, her younger brothers and the children, working in a Nihonbashi geisha house, attending to the physically disabled, going so far as to care for them in her own house, always thinking about others, never about herself.

–11–

The Dialectic of Camera and Performance

'One Scene-One Shot'

The technique known as the 'one scene-one shot' is a distinctive characteristic of Mizoguchi's direction. He eschewed, as far as he could, the close-up, and mainly used the long or the full shot.

'One scene-one shot' meant that the scene is filmed in one take, without interruption. A normal one-and-a-half to two-hour film has between 100 and 120 scenes, each scene being composed of a number of shots. A film normally has between 500 and 800 shots. If two people are in a conversation, for instance, each is shot alternately, and where the camera pulls back, a long shot is used to give a sense of the whole scene. At an important moment, a close-up is used to show the expression of the speaker or the listener. This is a normal technique in film-making.

When Mizoguchi joined the Nikkatsu Mukojima Studio as an assistant director, Japanese films were at their formative stage and had just begun to experiment with these techniques. The 'one scene-one shot' approach did not seem strange – it was like shooting a play by letting a fixed camera run continuously. However, in a few years – mainly because of the influence of American films – shots began to be finely divided. Film technology also developed rapidly so that by the latter half of the 1920s, it was not unusual to find a one-and-a-half-hour film composed of about 1,000 shots. In silent films, because complex expressions were limited by what could be put in the inter-titles, it was necessary to exaggerate every expression and movement. If there were several shots, it was easier to bring out a rhythmic flow while editing.

The theory of montage, developed by Sergei Eisenstein, became a significant cinema aesthetic towards the end of the 1920s, and montage attained the status of a dogma among a section of influential critics. This meant that the artistic uniqueness of a film was now seen in the way a number of different shots were linked.

In the 1920s, Mizoguchi, too, worked within this general trend. His oldest existing work consists of fragments of the 1929 *Tokyo March,* which has a scene of a middle-class house on a hill with a tennis court. Below the walls of the house is a poor man's hut. The son of the bourgeois hits the ball over the wall and the poor man's daughter throws it back. Mizoguchi uses the shot-reverse-shot to contrast the lives of the bourgeois and the poor.

FIGURE 30 *Tokyo March* (1929).

However, somewhere along the way, he began to dislike both the shot-reverse-shot and the close-up, and began favouring the 'one scene-one shot' where he moved the camera back from the object being photographed.

In an article, 'The Art of Mizoguchi Kenji' (Mizoguchi Kenji no geijutsu) in *A Personal History of Film* (Watashi no eigashi 1955, Ikeda publishers), Kishi Matsuo quotes from an interview done during the filming of *The Life of Oharu*, where he questions Mizoguchi about his methods:

Kishi: This time also it is very much in the Mizoguchi style of 'one scene-one shot'. When did you start filming in this way? It is really overdone in *Sisters of the Gion*
…
Mizoguchi: Is that so? But I have been using it for a long time, since *Okichi the Foreigner* in which Umemura Yoko appeared. At that time Ikenaga's father (the studio chief) got angry with me. (*Laughs*)
Kishi: Really? But when *Sisters of the Gion* was made, wasn't it popular to use a long shot with a moving camera? It was the influence of King Vidor.
Mizoguchi: That is so, but a friend of mine, Naito Kojiro, influenced me. Kojiro is the son of Professor Naito Konan (historian) who is probably still a professor in some university. Kojiro, who studied psychology, was an extraordinary man. He was trying to see how to use touch and smell as forms of expression in films. It was he who led me to think about some of these things. The 'psychological weight' on the viewer varies, depending on how many 'one scene-one shot' type of shots are

repeated in quick succession, or how they are divided into a number of shot-reverse-shots. If you use a succession of quick cuts, then somehow there will always be a cut that you didn't want. It is a huge mistake to think that just because it is short it is good. Perhaps I haven't explained it properly but ... it is my way of replying ... In any case, it was around that time that I began to study the 'one scene-one shot' method. There are quite a few problems with this method as well. It can be quite a disaster to rattle along, filming without any shot-reverse-shots.

Just as Ozu Yasujiro has given no satisfactory explanation for his famous use of low-angle shots Mizoguchi, too, has left no real explanation about why he uses the 'one scene-one shot' method. Nor has Yoda Yoshikata, who wrote scripts for Mizoguchi for so many years. With regard to *Chushingura*, Yoda writes that on one occasion while they were having a meal together, he asked Mizoguchi about it and Mizoguchi replied, 'I don't know. Never thought about it like that,' but he looked like he had been cornered.

Yoda thought the one scene-one shot made it possible, even in a long scene, to keep a person moving towards the camera, to keep him in the frame. The camera could move towards the person, and if there was a slight change of direction, it could pan. By moving with the person it would add speed to his movement, all within that one shot. Similarly, with a group of people, the camera could move into the group, or away from it or, depending on their positions, could attempt more complex ways of shooting. A variety of shots could be sustained within one shot – the full body, medium shot (half the body) and a tilt-up. By weaving these shots together, one could show changes in speed and rhythm even for slow and monotonous movements. During this shot, the camera is kept at a slight angle and both it and the person coming towards the camera, move. This is what Miyagawa Kazuo, the cinematographer for all of Mizoguchi's films after 1953, said he consciously tried to do. As director of photography, he made Hirano Yoshimi, the cameraman for *The Life of Oharu*, use them as well. From Yoda's writing it is clear that Mizoguchi had carefully considered the effects of the camera's movements, but he offered no other explanation apart from the interview with Kishi.

At this point we may consider the meaning of the statement 'the length of the shot has an emotional weight'. If a scene changes very frequently, say every few seconds, it can appear frivolous. On the other hand, if it is shot continuously over a length of time, it risks becoming heavy. This has to do with the nature of the drama unfolding in the film as well. In films such as Alfred Hitchcock's *Rope*, there is no sense of heaviness even though the entire film, from start to finish, is shot without a cut. Others, like Eisenstein's *Battleship Potemkin*, is divided into many detailed shots, yet leaves us with a feeling of solemnity. Undoubtedly, if the same object is being shot continuously, then greater concentration is demanded of the viewer.

In *Osaka Elegy* (1936), the one scene-one shot method is already fully developed and extensively used. More interesting is the fact that the film was almost exclusively made up of long shots. The close-up is used only when the female pro-tagonist, Ayako, who is frustrated with her family, leaves home. This is shot with the camera moving back as she crosses the bridge towards the town. At first she is fully visible, but as she approaches the camera only her upper body is seen. This is the only close-up among the film's long shots.

Normally, a close-up is used to show highly charged emotions. Mizoguchi could have used it in the scene where Ayako plots to cheat the stockbroker and threatens him, or at some other emotionally laden moments. But he does not. Instead, he pulls the camera far back to show the complete scene. The camera looks down dis-passionately at Ayako and the figure of the angry stockbroker sitting next to her with his back to the camera. Again, in scenes when the used and discarded heroine has fallen into despair, other film-makers would have moved the camera back to show her face getting gradually smaller, as if to symbolize the big world swal-lowing her up, as if to bring out the general hopelessness of the situation. But the only time Mizoguchi uses the close-up is when he wants to confirm the protago-nist's determination to exercise her will.

Mizoguchi depicts in a cool and composed way the predicament in which an unthinking young woman finds herself – a woman who works single-mindedly for her family, but owing to her carelessness does something unimaginably stupid. At the very moment when she leaves her home, declaring that she will become a pros-titute, Mizoguchi uses a tilt-up to show his heroine's face. For all her outrageous use of language, what really propels her is this great determination to become independent. Far from showing her in a dissolute state, Mizoguchi brings out the beauty of her cheerful countenance.

The Straits of Love and Hate (1937) has a number of 'one-scene one-shot' scenes. Take, for instance, the scene where the heroine, who has joined a travelling theatre group, is practising in a small village theatre. The poor condition of the stage bespeaks their poverty. The camera is to the side of the stage where the dancers are rehearsing in a somewhat half-hearted way. It shows the hall, with a few viewers seated in old-fashioned chairs. The one scene-one shot is used beau-tifully to bring out – through the movement of the camera – the highs and lows of the travelling theatre group as they practise.

A moving shot is one that builds up expectations of what is to come into view. But it can also temper our expectations of the performers as they move about without arousing any excitement, and thus create a strong air of pathos.

As a stylistic method, the one shot-one scene was perfected in *The Story of the Late Chrysanthemums*, and used with the most stunning results. For instance, the long dialogue in the course of which Otoku declares that Kikunosuke has matured as an artist, is shown with the two of them strolling together along the edge of the moat at night. As they wander in front of the eaves of the houses, discussing, the long moving shot is taken from a camera placed, not on the road, but in the moat. It looks up at them from an angle. There is no semblance of a romantic ambience in the man and a woman walking in the city at night, arms linked, because the woman belongs to a low class and is criticizing her employer's son, and naturally the man is objecting to this. They stroll along aimlessly and the moving camera follows them at the same speed, getting the viewer to focus his attention on the two. And just as Otoku's words penetrate Kikunosuke's heart, so too, do they penetrate the viewer's.

Picturization Style

In *Chushingura* (1941–2), Mizoguchi makes a comprehensive use of the one scene- one shot and the long shot. The film's two parts taken together make up a very long three-hour, thirty-five-minute film. Yet the entire film has only about 160 shots. This means that on an average, one shot is about one minute, twenty seconds long. Usually, an average shot lasts about ten seconds, but Mizoguchi's shots are unusually long. There are many scenes of small rooms, as in *Street of Shame*, where even though it was difficult to move the camera, the 80-plus minute film has just 139 shots.

The one single shot in Alfred Hitchcock's *Rope*, is supposed to be the longest recorded shot. But because it was technically impossible to roll a film for more than ten minutes, the camera was moved to a dark corner of the room and covered to change the film. It was then moved back to its original place and the shot was continued as if the camera had not been moved at all. The next longest shot is in Jerzy Skolimovski's film, *Walkover*, which had thirty-five shots. Oshima Nagisa's *Night and Fog in Japan* used forty-three shots. There are also onescene-one shot films made by film-makers like Andy Warhol, who used a fixed camera to shoot a subject that did not move for many hours. He changed the film several times without once moving the camera. Therefore, there is nothing special about the length of Mizoguchi's shots. He has set no records. The way in which he used the long shot was essential in bringing all the aspects of a scene together: the tension of the actors, the set, the brilliance of the light, etc. The skilful movement of the camera gathers it all into a harmonious whole. No one has so far surpassed him in his uniquely individualistic use of the camera. In *Chushingura* this works particularly well.

Chushingura is the famous story of the revenge of the forty-seven *ronin* (master-less warriors). Sundry films have been made on this subject, but Mizoguchi chose the great play *Chusingura of the Genroku Period*, by Mayama Seika, as his base. He made the film intermittently between 1931 and 1941, and was far more historically faithful to the original story than others. Oishi Kuranosuke, the leader of the forty-seven *ronin*, hesitates to take revenge because in a feudal society taking revenge for the sake of one's lord (*daimyo*) is tantamount to being disloyal to the Emperor. This is a new interpretation. One of the high points of the story is that Oishi is secretly told of the Emperor's approval. Overjoyed, he is now determined to act on his decision. Mizoguchi's attempt to ingratiate himself with the militarists through this new twist to the story was quite pathetic.

Throughout his life Mizoguchi pursued the theme of the woman's sanctity, her suppression and her subsequent inner transformation; the man, all the while, remained his own insufferable self. But *Chushingura*, with its theme of a warrior's loyalty, is very different. As one of the top directors in the world, Mizoguchi seemed to have been compelled to make propaganda films on the war. He tried, but as an artist, he could not bring himself to churn out a run-of-the-mill film. Hence his decision to make a film that was something of a compromise with the militarist policies of the wartime government, and to use the story based on Mayama Seika's version. While glorifying loyalty, revenge and the spirit of honourable death, Seika had added an episode showing Oishi Kuranosuke's distress caused by his fervent loyalty to the Imperial house.

Mizoguchi did not film the raid, which is the well-known climax of the story of the forty-seven *ronin*. Even while he supported the policies of the state, he was careful to eliminate any hint of advocacy. One can see this work as a small artistic compromise. The amount of money spent in making it was unprecedented. Huge sets were constructed and shooting continued for long periods with no thought

FIGURE 31 *The Forty-seven Ronin* (1941).

given to the expense. There was only one aim: to achieve the desired effect. Yet, its enormous budget notwithstanding, the film failed both at the box office and as a propaganda film. My mother took me to see it when I was in primary school and I still remember how disappointed she was that it did not have the scene of the raid. Mizoguchi may have left this out because he did not feel confident enough to make it. In fact it was planned, but even as the sets for the Kira mansion were being made, it seems he remarked, 'I will not film a lie,' and stopped the work. After the war, directors such as Kurosawa Akira in *Rashomon* and *Seven Samurai*, or Yoshimura Kozaburo in *Waltz at Noon*, found ways to film realistic fight scenes. But when Mizoguchi filmed *Chushingura*, the fight scenes were always one-sided, unrealistic and artificial, and hence his decision not to shoot them.

It was not just a simple compromise that led him to create this masterpiece. Mizoguchi had given considerable thought to developing his cinematic style. If the subject here is relatively weak, the style is unsurpassed. Usually, films with plenty of style and little content are dismissed as failures. *Chushingura* was irrefutably Mizoguchi's greatest failure. Many of its aspects – subject, characters, action – fail to evoke any interest. And yet, you cannot but laud the exquisite beauty of the style, particularly the camerawork which, for its haunting elegance, is unequalled in the history of cinema. There are not many examples of films that can move people with just their style. *Chushingura*, I believe, is definitely one.

This was a time when period sets were constructed to actual size, and the term 'Actual Size-ism' (*gensunshugi*) was coined, a word that Mizoguchi used to suit his own purpose. Since he did not understand the 'way of the warrior' (*bushido*), he focused his attention on investigating customs and manners and became passionately involved in shaping the forms through which they were represented.

There is no denying that 'shaping the form' is everything in this work. If the 'way of the warrior' is perceived as loyalty to the shogun, then clearly Mizoguchi did not 'grasp' this in *Chushingura*. But if we were to change our perspective slightly, we would understand that the 'way of the warrior' also means doing one's daily work with great care and attention to detail. If we accept this premise, then *Chushingura,* in my view, exquisitely captures this 'way'. Mizoguchi's inability to grasp its ideological aspects and instead focus single-mindedly on 'arranging the form', allowed him to capture the manners and behaviour of warriors, and show them with solemn precision, better than in any other period film. The beauty of the warrior who lives and acts with great attention to the correct way of doing things was masterfully conveyed. But as far as the subject of this story was concerned – loyalty and revenge – Mizoguchi failed to evoke a response. In fact, the audience was bored.

For those who saw this work as merely stressing the outward form through its 'Actual Size-ism', *Chushingura* was an outright failure. It was a failure in the 1940s, when it was easy to move people through the theme of loyalty; and it is even more of a failure today, when loyalty is viewed as an old-fashioned sentiment.

But 'arranging the form' is not just formalism, even if it appears to be so. The fact is that when 'something to live for' is given a human face through 'arranging the form', the beauty of the style itself affects people emotionally. This can be used to show not just warriors, but merchants, peasants and geisha as well. Each in his own way has a specific way of being and behaving, ways that are regulated and transmitted over generations. This is what Mizoguchi brought out beautifully in his later years in a series of masterpieces: *The Life of Oharu, Ugetsu, Sansho the Bailiff* and *A Story from Chikamatsu.*

The concept of loyalty in *Chushingura,* as complex as the concept of democracy, became the theme of a series of masterpieces made in post-war Japan. For instance in *The Life of Oharu,* sensuality – the subject of the original work – is changed to women's freedom. *Ugetsu,* where the motif in the original work is the relationship with the world of death, adds an anti-war theme, at complete variance with the original. In *Sansho the Bailiff,* the Buddhist worldview of the original story, which had survived in Mori Ogai's novel, was erased and replaced with the new ideology of people's liberation. And where the original story of *A Story from Chikamatsu* is an ill-fated tragedy, in the adaptation it is interpreted as a modern story on the supremacy of love.

In all these films such subjects have been dealt with because post-war Japan saw the rise of democratic thought. Twenty years after they were made, they continue to be powerful works, despite their naïve, if well-intentioned objectives, and despite the fact that the additions of contemporary elements to the original story are occasionally inconsistent, even too ideological. *A Story from Chikamatsu* is an excellent example. In *The Life of Oharu,* though, it is not easy to accept that the heroine willingly sacrifices herself to the desires of a man when in fact she is not a passionate woman at all in the original. For all that, one can hardly call *The Life of Oharu* a failure and *A Story from Chikamatsu* a success. *The Life of Oharu* is a timeless work of art.

How can a work be a masterpiece when its subject has not been properly integrated into the story? Because by 'arranging the form', these films have reached the highest level of art. They represent a series of moments of sublime beauty.

One of the highlights in *Sansho the Bailiff* is the scene of Anju with the pitcher. The young Anju has decided that she is willing to die to help Zushio escape – a wonderful example of respect for behavioural propriety. Yet another masterly scene is when Zushio is reunited with his blind mother in Sado. Zushio has fulfilled his dead father's and Anju's wishes by freeing the slaves. Forsaking the great success he has enjoyed in life, he returns to look for his mother. His act epitomizes the right way of living and carrying forward a tradition. There are other similar scenes as well, but in these two instances, Mizoguchi – from what I can remember – has maintained a very slow tempo and succeeded in endowing the notion of 'arranging the form' with the majestic beauty of a religious ceremony. If his film has a scene of suicide, that scene is not merely shocking, if it has a reunion of mother and son, it is not just deeply emotional. There is something more. Slowly, very slowly, he arranges the movements of the actors with immense grace to prove how an individual can control the most important moments of his life.

The female protagonist in *The Life of Oharu* falls from her position of a maid in the Imperial Palace to that of a streetwalker (lit. nighthawk). To the outside world her life appears wretched, but she refuses to surrender her sense of pride and human dignity. Pride, perhaps, is a modern idea that may not be quite appropriate for those times; but if pride is interpreted to mean will, then it is definitely appropriate. The protagonist faces a string of problems, yet typically retains her composure; nor does she place herself at the mercy of fate and weep; rather, she puts her problems behind her and moves on. Mizoguchi puts a great deal of effort into 'arranging the form' through the way he shows her face at such moments. The beauty of *The Life of Oharu* goes beyond the subject of the equality between the sexes (unimaginable in the feudal period); it is partly influenced by the post-war democratic climate.

'Arranging the form' was fundamental to Mizoguchi's film-making. Even when he failed to 'grasp' the subject, this 'arrangement of the form' transcended external beauty to convey something else.

Artistry of Mizutani Hiroshi's Sets

A major element in 'arranging the form' is the art of set construction. Mizutani Hiroshi made most of the sets for Mizoguchi's masterpieces. He was only twenty-seven when he worked on *Sisters of the Gion*, going on to make the sets for *The Jinpu Gang*, *The Straits of Love and Hate*, *The Story of the Late Chrysanthemums*, *Osaka Elegy*, *Chushingura*, *Women of the Night*, *Lady Yu*, *The Life of Oharu*, *The Woman in the Rumour*, *Princess Yang Kwei-fei*, *Taira Clan Saga*, *A Story from Chikamatsu*, *Street of Shame* and others.

Ito Kisaku was the artistic director for Mizoguchi's films from *Ugetsu* to *Sansho the Bailiff*. They had a good deal of trouble while shooting *The Life of Oharu*. Hirakata Park, the building in Osaka's Hirakata district that they used, was in a terrible state. Mizoguchi was upset and blamed Mizutani, saying he had 'cheated' him. But, unable to do without Mizutani, he brought him back for *Woman in the Rumour*. Mizutani's sets were made like theatrical stages, posing problems for cameraman Miyagawa Kazuo. *Sansho the Bailiff* had an open set and Sansho's mansion showed the slaves at work in the 18,000 sq ft garden. A rail to move the camera was laid in front of this garden and the camera pointed to the far side so that later, whether they shot from the left or the right, it was obvious that it was a set. We are told that Mizutani would be smiling as he sat next to the cameraman who would be shouting with rage as he moved the camera along the rail.

A director needs to hold a discussion with the artistic director before beginning his shoot. Mizoguchi would neither take a prior look at the plans, nor make a preliminary inspection of the sets. Once he arrived on the sets he would make utterly unreasonable demands. Not wanting to face any problems, the artistic director, too, tried to fashion the sets in keeping with Mizoguchi's expectations. Mizutani Hiroshi, in particular, put up with the director's style of working and after reading the script, would come up with an unimaginably beautiful set. So, either way, it worked to Mizoguchi's advantage.

It is the artistic director who arranges the plans of what action takes place and where, where the camera will be placed, etc. He explains all this in detail to the director. This is what happened with Mizoguchi too. In all three films – *The Story of the Late Chrysanthemums*, *Women of the Night* and *The Life of Oharu* – there is a moat, a rock and an embankment. The actors perform while standing on them; the camera is placed below, tilting upwards – a position I feel was typical of Mizoguchi. However, Mizoguchi himself never positioned the camera. Since it was used differently in all three films, who was it who decided the camera position? Perhaps it was Mizutani Hiroshi, but we do not know for sure.

There is a famous scene in *The Story of the Late Chrysanthemums* where the camera is in the moat, pointing upwards to the road where Kikunosuke and Otoku, who have come close to each other for the first time, are walking and talking. There is endless movement on one side, but on the other side of the road the upper portions of eight houses are visible while the lower portions have been deliberately cut out of the scene. This distortion was deliberate, since from the bottom of the moat the road would appear widened and the foreground would become lower. Mizutani Hiroshi's artistry is built on such detailed planning, which enabled him to give Mizoguchi exactly what he wanted.

Mizutani Hiroshi also designed the sets of *Chushingura*. The war made conditions difficult, but Mizutani and Shindo Kaneto, the person responsible for the construction under him, were determined to do a good job. So when Professor Oguma Hisakuni, the advisor on historical architecture, brought in the designs for the pine corridor, the stage equipment department was ordered to build it, with Mizoguchi's approval. But when construction started, the manager and the company director were dismayed at the colossal size. No one was willing to tell Mizoguchi that it could not be done. Ultimately, the director of photography took the responsibility for exceeding the budget and was promptly fired. Shindo Kaneto writes about this incident in the above-mentioned essay, 'Mizoguchi Theory of Actual Size-ism' (Mizoguchi Kenji no gensunshugi).

> Mizoguchi came and inspected the pine corridor, walked around and looked at it. This was the time when he was using his 'one-shot' theory with a vengeance. As I secretly watched him walking around the corridor, I chuckled, thinking that Mizoguchi he may well be, but there was no way he could use his 'one-shot' method here when Kira

Kozunosuke fights with Asano Takuminokami and there is great confusion all around. I thought this is not a scene that can be shot in one shot.

However, Mizoguchi did precisely that. There is a supplementary scene, but the scene where Kira suffers a sword wound can be called a 'one shot'. It is short and everything seems to happen very fast. Even the large open set of the pine corridor was set up very quickly.

The scene in the pine corridor was actually filmed in five cuts. The first is the full shot of the pine corridor from the front. In the second, the camera faces the garden looking out from inside the corridor, slowly moving from the right till Kira Kozukinosuke (Mimasu Mantoya) comes into view on the right edge of the screen. Kira is vehemently criticizing Asano in front of another samurai, giving the impression of an emotional and irritated old man. The camera pans to the right and shows the pine corridor running up. At its far end, Asano (Arashi Yoshisaburo) can be seen, trembling with rage as he listens to Kira's criticism. Asano's expression suddenly changes and he runs towards Kira. The camera pans, following him as he stabs Kira in the back. In the third shot, the camera turns to face a stunned Kira, and the alarmed samurai who grab Asano.

The change from the second to the third shot, even though the camera is placed at a vertical angle to the corridor, is achieved merely by turning the camera 180 degrees in the same place. The result is that there is no real shift in the distance between the camera and the characters. The structure of the frame appears almost unchanged and the viewer hardly registers the change which occurs in a flash at the very moment when Asano kills Kira. We are caught up in the action and completely fooled into thinking that it is a continuous shot.

The fourth shot shows the samurai and the attendants running helter-skelter in confusion in the corridor. Finally, in the fifth, in the same confused atmosphere, some attendants and samurai hurriedly carry Kira into a room.

The pine corridor scene may not strictly be a 'one scene-one shot', but Mizoguchi clearly Mizoguchi wanted to film the movement of a large group of people in as few shots as possible. Normally, if an incident had to be shown in a crowd scene a long shot would show the whole crowd. The camera would then zoom in, or a close-up would be used to show the actions of the main figure. Characteristically, Mizoguchi does not do this; he prefers, instead, to use a long shot for everything. No mid-shots frame Kira or Asano, which is why we miss the transition from the second to the third, and third to the fourth shots.

Although this style of filming does give a general picture of the commotion, the actions of the main character get buried in the crowd and are difficult to follow. Mizoguchi may have wanted the main character's performance to stand out in the midst of this melee; perhaps he felt he could extract such a performance. Whatever his reasoning, his direction did bring out each character's meaningful and specific action in the midst of a scene where several people are milling around.

The usual method of a long shot for the crowd and a close-up for the main character might be easy to follow, but it does weaken the strength of the conflict between the individual and the group. Mizoguchi repeatedly asked his actors to give careful thought to the actions of the other characters. Each individual, he believed, needed to react to the actions of the group. This would not have been possible in a film with many cuts.

Moving the Crane

This technique of one scene-one shot, using long shots but not the close-up, served two other very important purposes as well. Here, let me quote a number of successful examples from *Chushingura*. First, the scene where Asano, who has been ordered to commit *hara kiri*, turns to face the site of the execution. A long shot is used and the camera starts from a commanding view of Asano as he is guided along the outer road of the execution grounds till he comes before the seated retainer, Kataoka Gengoeimon. As Asano and Kataoka exchange farewells, the crane is used to lower the camera to the level of the seated Kataoka. Asano seems to steel himself and then walks through the gate into the execution ground. The crane lifts up the camera and shows the execution ground from the outside, surrounded by a low fence. The camera has not entered the ground; it appears to place itself where Kataoka sits. It is as though Kataoka has bid Asano goodbye outside, but wants to take a look at the execution ground. There is almost a feeling of his having climbed over the fence to look at the scene.

His work in the castle over, Oishi (played by Kawarazaki Chojuro) goes off by himself to carry out his revenge. He plans to have his compatriots join him. However, a *ronin* and his son enter at that moment and commit *hara kiri*. As they struggle to breathe, Oishi cries out, 'No, no, not yet!' and rushes to help them. It is a wrenching scene. The dying man, an old friend of Oishi's, pleads that their true feelings be made known and Oishi confidently replies, 'I am going to confront the shogun.' Satisfied with the answer, the man succumbs. This long scene keeps the castle gate in the far background throughout. The camera gives the appearance of following Oishi's movements, when in fact, it does not move at all. It follows the dying man and stops short at the body of the dead son. It matches the different movements that Oishi, played by Kawarazaki Chojuro, makes. These grief-filled movements also match the mood of the men as they slowly come to a decision. The most powerful expression of that decision can be action, an expression, or a word. The exaggerated performance is in keeping with the camera's movement as it anticipates the reaction and brilliantly stops at the very moment when the right pose is struck.

There is the scene of Oishi's wife and child leaving for home. Oishi stands in front of an elegant, thatched-roof house that looks like a teahouse, seeing off his wife (Yamagishi Shizue) and their two young children before they set out on their journey. Mounted on a crane, the camera looks over the hedge and follows them as they come out. Oishi and Chikara, the older son, are saying their goodbyes. An inconsolable Chikara follows his mother. At this point the camera moves once again, then stops, showing the single road running vertically through the bamboo grove. This long shot is not just about the camera running continuously. The calm beauty of the composition conveys the feelings of separation. The camera moves only twice with Chikara and then stops. Oishi and Chikara are torn by the contradictory feelings of wanting to go together as far as possible, and knowing they cannot. They run and stop; stop and long to run. The positioning of the camera changes three times, and each time (the composition of the house, the garden, the fields and the bamboo grove, and then the single road running through the grove) it is like a beautiful painting. The second time, the camera moves to a fixed position, which shows the scene at its best. This open set was carefully thought out, designed with scrupulous care and the superb camerawork used it with great skill.

The scene where Asano turns towards the execution grounds and the scene on the mountain slope were also used effectively because a Japanese house allows this kind of camera movement.

If the sliding screens are left open, the camera can look into large parts of the room. Normally the hedge is low, so if the camera is mounted on a crane and lifted slightly, the composition resembles the classical painted scrolls (*emaki mono*) that show a panoramic view of the inside of the house. If a crane-mounted camera is used with skill, it would not appear unnatural even if it were to move right into the house. Mizoguchi's camera fully exploited this aspect of Japanese architecture. It entered castles and samurai mansions, following the actors uninterruptedly and with total freedom even at the most tense moments of the performance. Sometimes the camera would heighten dramatic tension by showing a scene before the entry of the actor.

Mizoguchi used the characteristics of the Japanese house adroitly in other films as well, moving the camera from outside the door to the hedge; from the garden into the corridor; from the corridor into the room; and then letting it roam freely from room to room, sometimes in a 'one scene-one shot', and at other times in a ' three scenes-one cut' technique.

The most ambitious example of this is the Ohama Goten palace scene at the beginning of the second part of *Chushingura*. The crane-mounted camera gives us a brief glimpse of the elegant roof of the *noh* stage in the inner garden of a large *daimyo* mansion. After creating a heightened expectation of something wonderful, it seems to slide down at an angle and show the stage. It then travels past the court to the rooms at the far end of the corridor in front of the stage and shows a proper, dignified assembly of samurai. This elegant scene is visually captivating. Mounted on a gigantic scale, it nonetheless imbues every small movement of the characters with gravitas. The scale also represents the grace of the shogun's government, the strength and stability of the authority that Oishi and the *ronin* seek to attack. No matter where the camera moves, the buildings and the lines of samurai seem to go on endlessly. The 'one shot-one scene' was useful in conveying the right sense of pomp and majesty. Only the composition changes as the camera slides smoothly through this space. It is one of the cinematic high points of the film.

The last scene when Oishi and his band commit ritual suicide (*hara kiri*) in the Hosokawa mansion is a tribute to the beauty of the sets. The expression on the face of each samurai as he is called on to commit *hara kiri* is reflected in the voice of the one calling him. When the samurai who have helped Oishi call him, they are shown from the corridor. They enter Oishi's room and exchange parting words while the camera pans, giving a full view of the scene to show the waiting Oishi. The moment his name is called, Oishi leaps up smiling, and starts walking down the corridor. The camera moves with him. At the end it is raised a little, bringing into view the expanse of the execution grounds across the hedge. The stark atmosphere is also built up through the solemn way he walks. The movement of the crane-operated camera creates a sense of foreboding in the scene of the execution ground where they wait, as if for a sacred ceremony. The ground seems to recede into the background as the camera focuses on Oishi, showing him taut and controlled.

The several examples of the superb camerawork bring the whole film together like an exquisitely choreographed dance. The decisiveness of the characters is sustained by the way the camera is handled. The scene is permeated with a terrible pathos inherent in the formality that tradition demands of the moment, and superbly conveyed and almost given life to by the camera.

The subject of *Chushingura* (loyalty to the shogun) had an outmoded and boring air to it, even in wartime Japan when loyalty was proclaimed a high principle. In making this unfashionable subject coincide with wartime Japan's Emperor system, Mizoguchi feared that loyalty to the shogun would be interpreted as disloyalty to the Emperor. He had also to deal with the conflict faced by the retainers: that in seeking to avenge their lord (*daimyo*), they were being disloyal to the shogun's authorities. In fact, questions of disloyalty to the Emperor had no connection with the essence of the story. All they did was to provide Mizoguchi with an opportunity to ingratiate himself with the wartime authorities. This ridiculous interpretation added another layer of gloom and oppressiveness to the story. The film failed, and even today it seems absurdly outdated and reactionary because it was so excessively grave and dark, and very different from the popular *Chushingura*.

And yet, *Chushingura* is beautiful because it brings out the pathos of people acting in a determined way, and with exquisitely proper ceremonial correctness. What moves us is the purity of a powerful and unstoppable impulse to seek the beauty of the form.

The film's basic form is undoubtedly derived from Mayama Seika's *kabuki* play, but it is questionable whether these forms work realistically. Mizoguchi's concern with exploring the embodiment of a person's will is seen in all his films, even in the *shinpa* style *Story of the Late Chrysanthemums*, *The Life of Oharu* and *Sansho the Bailiff*. But it is in *Chushingura* that we see one of the most skilful manifestations of film form.

The Long Shot

The answer to why Mizoguchi thought the long shot necessary or why he rejected the close-up and persisted in showing the full body, lies in his working method. He was extremely demanding. There was always tension on the sets because he expected the best, and hated shortcuts or compromises. For him, close-ups were meaningless. The expression on the face could be seen, but the hands and feet which also reflect the state of mind remained invisible. He felt it was not really acting when an actor faced the camera alone, and when scenes of the co-actors playing opposite him were added later through the shot-reverse-shot. Considering it absolutely necessary for actors to face each other while acting, he rejected the close-up and the bust shot. As against this, he used the long shot to perfection.

On the day of shooting, Mizoguchi would bring a blackboard to the completed sets and have the lines of the scene written on it. After studying them carefully, he would have the scriptwriter or the producer make revisions if the lines did not sound good or if they needed to be changed to suit the atmosphere of the set. If the artistic director had built a larger set than planned, Mizoguchi would call for stronger lines in the script.

Mizoguchi told the scriptwriter or the producer exactly what changes he wanted and where. He was also concerned about the reaction of the whole film crew. This generated great tension on the sets for, while the crew carried on with their preparations, they would be worrying about the revisions. Only when the changes struck the right chord with Mizoguchi would they heave a collective sigh of relief. Mizoguchi's approval would raise everyone's spirits.

Even as he kept the crew on their toes, he was himself in a perpetual state of tension, even though he planned well. He loved using the crane-mounted camera and the ease with which it could be manipulated in any direction. Once during a shoot, Miyagawa Kazuo noticed the crane swaying slightly. He saw Mizoguchi sitting next to him in the camera seat, so wrapped up in watching the performance that in his excitement he had gripped the handrail and was shaking it. Later he asked Mizoguchi not to sit with him in the crane. Such deep involvement only served to heighten the tension further.

A characteristic of Mizoguchi's style was the way he created a flow by using a long shot taken from a crane. In most cases his approach was to leave the cameraman to his own devices; his discussion was limited to where to begin a shot and where to end it. The cameraman would then decide on how to get the best angles while the actors rehearsed.

There are basically two kinds of directors: those who base their work on the camera and those who build it around the performance. Ozu Yasujiro belonged to the former class and Mizoguchi to the latter. The director normally decides on the shots to be taken in a scene: a long shot for this part, a medium shot for that, a close-up for these lines, here a shot-reverse-shot, there a camera movement and so on. The actors and crew plan their moves accordingly.

In the performance-based style, the performance was first viewed, and then the decisions were made about the length of the shots or the best positions for the camera. Generally, camera-based direction is preferred; even if the acting is not up to the mark or if the actors cannot emote with their entire bodies, a close-up can at least capture the expression on the face. If the delivery of the lines is not right in one shot, the shot can be divided into three and, by moving the camera slightly after each take, can mask the small jerkiness that occurs when shots of unequal lengths are spliced together. When the actors are not particularly proficient, such techniques are inevitably used. But Mizoguchi was an exacting director, summarily dismissing those who could not match his expectations. Since his rehearsals were far more rigorous than those of other directors, he found no reason at all to use camera techniques to cover up bad acting. And since he ensured that the actors did their work, he left the cameraman free to concentrate his energies on looking for the proper background, the timing of the interaction between the actors, and the proper angle; in short, he could become an active participant in the scene.

How did Mizoguchi behave with his actors? He always wanted them to be realistic. By asking questions like 'How does one understand this psychologically?' or 'Have you thought about on this?' or 'Are you reflecting on that?' he was actually pushing the actors to analyse the psychology of the character in a particular scene, to reflect on how they perceived the scene and whether their lines stimulated an appropriate feeling in the actor playing opposite them. He believed that an actor works within an environment created by the director and crew, and it is within this environment that he creates the character and evokes the desired response. He did not criticize sternly or give concrete suggestions. He merely said that it would be good to do it this way or that.

Mizoguchi was involved in the entire production process. The completed film always had his recognizable stamp. This was because his crew and actors had to concentrate fully on extracting from his scattered words what he really wanted. Everyone's energies would be totally focused on his every move. Mizoguchi's direction was marked by an ability to draw on the ideas of his crew members and crystallize them into his own composite vision. Those who could not build on his suggestions were unceremoniously dismissed.

Mizoguchi's tyrannical behaviour was legendary. He would make even well-established actors shoot scenes repeatedly till he was satisfied. On some days, only one shot would be completed. Film-makers such as Ozu Ysujiro would give definite directions from the slightest movement of the hand to the line of vision. Others like Kinugasa Teinosuke, would themselves act out the performance they wanted from their actors. Mizoguchi felt that the actor must devise his own performance. He gave suggestions only when they made a fundamental error in understanding the character. For instance, in *Street of Shame* he did not like the way Mimasu Aiko walked. He made her correct it. But his only suggestion was, 'You are not walking on stage,' meaning that her style belonged to the stage, that it lacked cinematic rhythm. He made her repeat the shot till he got out of it what he wanted.

A performance that did not meet his approval made him incensed. Sugai Ichiro recounts his experience while working in *My Love Burns* where he played Oi Kentaro, the people's rights activist during the Meiji period:

> It was on the second day of shooting. About two hundred extras playing Socialist Party members are assembled in a large hall below a wide staircase leading to the meeting room upstairs, eagerly awaiting the results of the meeting on the second floor.
>
> The camera follows the president, Senda Koreya, jumping over the chairs and running up the stairs just as I come out of the meeting room. We meet in the middle of the staircase. I catch his sleeve and shout out in excitement, 'Please sir, wait.' This 'one cut' was a little long and we were stuck at this point.
>
> There was always something wrong. Shooting continued from ten in the morning to eight in the evening, but Mizoguchi refused to approve the shot. He said that I needed to express the tension of the meeting in the way I rushed, in the way I caught Senda's sleeve and in the speed with which I ran up the stairs. He felt that I was giving no sign that I had thought about the situation. ('Are you reflecting?' This was an expression that Mizoguchi used when he was directing. He often said that if there was no reaction to the others' emotions then the acting was dead. It is easy to understand the sentiment, but taken out of context it can be confusing. Mizoguchi was very firm and would not put up with compromises. If one did not follow what he really wanted, it could get tough. If, let us say, the way the hair was dishevelled was not realistic, he would raise hell).
>
> Because my performance did not come up to his expectations, about two hundred extras, other actors and crew had to wait while the same shot was done repeatedly for ten hours. (Sugai Ichiro, 'Random Memories' (Tsurezure no oboegaki) in *Films are Difficult* (Eiga wazurai)).

This was the norm in Mizoguchi's films, and even Sugai Ichiro, with his long experience of working with the director felt likewise. 'I couldn't get it right. Mizoguchi then told his assistant director, "When you get it right call me!" and went off to his office. It was only because of the assistant director's sympathetic understanding that we stopped shooting after ten hours.'

Many directors will shoot till they get the right performance. Some devise solutions such as changing the distance between the actor and the camera to get a somewhat different shot. This is easier on the actor and usually turns out well. Other techniques include a slight reduction in the time between shots to quicken the tempo. In the language of the sets, this is known, as 'stealing time'.

Mizoguchi had done this occasionally. In *Lady Yu,* Tanaka Kinuyo's perform-ance faltered slightly in the middle of a long shot. She apologized and asked to do it again. Mizoguchi, unlike his usual self, was kind enough to approve what had been shot up to that point. He changed the position of the camera for the remainder of the performance. The staff was surprised at this extraordinary exception and put it down to the fact that he was in love with her. Normally he would order retakes till he was thoroughly satisfied. This incident was widely discussed because it was really an exception. Retakes were difficult because Mizoguchi would get angrier and angrier, and the actor would be openly insulted and humiliated. Sugai Ichiro writes in his memoirs:

> As soon as the order to stop was given, I composed myself, ran to his office and pros-trated myself in front of Mizoguchi to apologise sincerely.
>
> When I did this, he suddenly took off his slipper and hit me on the head, shouting, 'You should be sent to the mental department of the university hospital.'
>
> Everyone in the office was shocked at Mizoguchi's violent behaviour and rushed to separate us.
>
> I cried in my hotel room.
>
> Mizutani Hiroshi heard me crying. He came and calmed me down. If he had not been in the same hotel I don't know what I would have done.

Suagi Ichiro was not the only one to be hit with a slipper. Such things happened often and someone or other would be reduced to resentful tears. Little wonder then that the sets were always so tense. The actors would nearly be driven insane before they received Mizoguchi's approval and Mizoguchi maintained this tension till he got what he wanted.

Like Mizoguchi, Kurosawa Akira, too, could get violently angry if the shooting did not go the way he wanted. He also wanted his actors to be in a constant state of extreme tension. Kurosawa came up with the idea of using three cameras simul-taneously, taking three different shots – a long shot, a bust shot and a tilt-up – so as not to stop shooting when this tension had been adequately built up. Such tension is much easier to maintain on stage because it lasts thirty minutes or an hour, and even contributes to an increased audience involvement. In a film, however, a shot takes just a few minutes so the tension is continuously interrupted. These breaks are compensated for by using the angle of the camera, its movement, editing the flow of the visuals, modulation or the rhythm. Kurosawa used a multi-camera system to achieve this. Mizoguchi mainly used the crane.

The result is that Mizoguchi's camerawork is an excellent combination of inten-tion and passion. How far he planned this consciously is an unanswered question. He rarely gave detailed instructions, largely following what was technically nec-essary. But ultimately it was he himself who found the solutions to problems and his was the last word of rejection or approval. The drama he extracted after squeezing the script and the actors dry was the fruit of putting the right pieces together as in a painting. He achieved this because he determined the position of the camera, but the end result came across as though he had set out from the very beginning to achieve exactly that.

–12–

Looking Up, Looking Down

Ozu Yasujiro's Low-Angle Shots

Mizoguchi loved using the crane so much that, according to Tanaka Kinuyo, actors would jokingly say that a crane would even be part of his funeral cortege! Kuroda Kyomi, assistant cameraman on *The Life of Oharu*, told me that Mizoguchi used the crane even for a normal moving shot. Hirano Yoshimi, the cameraman, explained to Kuroda that the crane gave the feeling that the camera was floating in the air. But while it was certainly required for the moving shot, Kuroda saw no point in using it for normal shots since the camera still had to be moved up and

FIGURE 32 Mizoguchi Kenji (left) and Ozu Yasujiro at the Association of Japanese Film Directors, 1948.

down in the usual way. I think Mizoguchi loved using the crane for its own sake – it was not necessarily a question of artistic technique.

By and large the crane is used for tilt-down or high-angle shots as it can take the camera up to a height, usually mounted on a carriage, from where it can be moved up and down. This technology was not fully developed during the silent era or in the early period of the talkies. In *Osaka Elegy* and *Sisters of the Gion*, Mizoguchi's prime concern was to accurately and realistically examine the lives of urban people; he did not, therefore, use the crane in these films. Films made during the war, such as *The Story of the Late Chrysanthemums* and *Chushingura*, have wonderful crane shots, particularly in the second part of the latter film, where – even though we do not sympathize with the film's main theme (the glorification of feudal loyalty) – the camerawork and the use of the crane are superb.

This skill is also evident in post-war films like *Women of the Night* and *Lady Musashino*. *The Life of Oharu* has an exquisite, quite unforgettable use of the crane shot. In *Ugetsu*, *Sansho the Bailiff*, *A Story from Chikamatsu* and *Taira Clan Saga*, crane shots have been used for most of the famous scenes. Honed to a fine skill through repeated use and long study, Mizoguchi's handling of the crane is a lesson in the aesthetics of this shot.

One approach to the question of what a crane shot is would be to consider the work of another great master, Ozu Yasujiro, who never used it. Ozu was famous for his characteristic placement of the camera just a few inches above the ground – a style he used throughout his life. He did not find it necessary to resort to a crane for a high angle. However, in one scene where Hara Setsuko and Miyake Kuniko are walking quietly among the sand dunes, a crane *is* used, although it is not obvious to the viewer. Had the camera remained fixed, the faces of the two characters would have remained hidden. But so imperceptibly is it raised that the viewer does not notice it. As its position changes completely in a crane shot, so does the composition of the scene. In *Late Autumn*, Ozu used the crane in a way that did not change the composition of the scene, even though the characters were moving.

In abiding by his principle of not employing a crane for high-angle shots, Ozu Yasujiro often ended up using unnecessary shots. For instance, in *The Hen in the Wind*, a wife who waits impatiently for her demobilized husband to return from war is shown leaving the house with her child, and then returning to her rented room on the second floor. The landlord's elderly wife, who lives below, is waiting outside her door. She tells the wife that her husband has already returned.

Usually, in such a scene, the husband's shoes would be shown outside the entrance and the shot would show how moved the wife is at seeing them. In this way, continuity would be established. This, however, is not Ozu's style. The wife does not notice the shoes but her expression brightens as she runs up the stairs the moment she hears that her husband is home. Perhaps Ozu did not show the shoes because he would have needed a crane to take a wider shot!

The wife enters the room to find her husband fast asleep on the *tatami* floor, exhausted from a long journey in a packed train. Had Ozu tried to film the husband sleeping on the floor, he would have needed to raise the camera. This would have been the most natural shot, whether broken up or not. But Ozu is careful to avoid it. As the wife enters the room, he first shoots her from a low angle from the front. Next, he lowers the camera to show the sleeping husband. In this way, the same shot shows the sleeping husband in front of the camera with the wife's face looking down at him from the other side. Ozu had to make adjustments in the composition of the scene, as the face of the sleeping husband would otherwise have been out of proportion and the full body would not have appeared in the frame. To show the husband lying down, he has the wife quickly sit beside him and look at him protectively. For this, the camera is kept very low, which appears quite natural. So we see how Ozu manages with just a low-angle shot when a pan would have been natural.

Ozu did not explain his preference for the low-angle shot. Kawashima Yuzo has an interesting story about Ozu's influence on him. Kawashima was a junior member at the Ofuna Shochiku Studios where Ozu made most of his films. From the time he was in secondary school, he had held Ozu in high esteem. Though he had never worked with him, he had imbibed the fundamentals of film-making by watching his films. When Kawashima's assistant, Urayama Kirio, became a director and made *A Town with a Cupola*, Kawashima praised the film highly, but was somewhat critical of a few high-angle shots. 'You have to have some reason for taking high-angle shots of people,' he observed.

The theme and style of Kawashima's films were quite different from Ozu's, but there is a surprising resemblance to Ozu's style; or Kawashima may have simply thought that Urayama's high-angle shots were artistically wanting. Or again, he may have couched his criticism as a moral problem in order to reduce its harshness. What he was saying in essence, though, was that a tilt-down shot looks down on a person and is therefore ethically unacceptable.

Maybe Kawashima did not, after all, get his ideas directly from Ozu. Nor was there any direct assertion by Ozu himself stating that his shooting style was based on an ethical perspective. Ozu simply did not like the high-angle shot because he did not want to disturb the balance of the composition for even a second. This explanation seems to make sense, even though critics try and construct different meanings of what they perceive as his aesthetic style. But given his emotional depth, it is quite likely that his shooting style was closely connected to his ethical values.

I also think that his preference for the low-angle shot was marked by a dislike of the moving shot. This, he felt was akin to casting a sweeping, contemptuous glance at people of a lower status, like a shogun giving an audience to his lords (*narabi daimyo o nagameru*), like a figure of authority looking down on his subordinates. Ozu felt strongly that a director's use of the camera reflected his ethical ideas, and Kawashima imbibed this from watching his films.

To imagine that every shot reflects a director's ethical ideas would be a major mistake. The relationship with belief is more complex, and it would be risky to over-simplify it. This is precisely what we would be in danger of doing if we were to regard the high-angle shot as authoritarian merely because it looks 'down' on people, and the low-angle shot as humble and respectful because it looks 'up' to people.

Historical and war films normally use high-angle shots for their many spectacular scenes and for creating a sense of large crowds. Here, it is essential to take a long shot and move the camera back. High-angle shots show the grandeur of the large, specially constructed sets. On the other hand, in family dramas, which have very few sequences of crowds, and where most scenes are confined to small rooms, there is little justification for such shots.

Mizoguchi, who made many historical films, loved using the crane for the tilt-down while Ozu, who made family dramas, disliked them intensely. It is entirely likely, then, that the differences in their techniques were the outcome of their different subject matter, and did not necessarily reflect any intrinsic difference in their thinking.

Panorama and Aesthetics: Angle of Elevation

It is important to note that *Chushingura*, *The Life of Oharu*, and *Taira Clan Saga* are all historical films using crowd scenes and large sets, and the crane helped Mizoguchi in high-angle shots. In *Ugetsu* and *A Story from Chikamatsu* (both love stories), the many tilt-downs were most effectively used, although they were not always wide-angle shots using the crane.

Examples of such shots can be found in the love scenes between Genjuro (Mori Masayuki), the potter, and Wakasa (Kyo Machiko), the princess (actually a vengeful ghost). Mizoguchi took a number of such shots in the scene where the potter realizes that the princess is a ghost and scrambles backwards – still seated on the *tatami* mat – to escape as the ghost advances. The scene is shot from over the ghost's shoulder. Then the shot-reverse-shots, taken from Genjuro's level and looking up at her, are spliced together.

You have here a relationship in which the potter has been bewitched by the princess. Her higher status and her behaviour make her the more aggressive of the two. The scene is conceived from the perspective of an upper-class woman, furious at the very idea of a socially inferior man trying to evade her. To underline this inequality, a tilt-down is mixed with shot-reverse-shots taken from an angle. It conveys the pressure exerted by the upper-class woman as she bears down on the socially inferior man, while the low-angle shot looks up from the potter's position at Wakasa's weirdly beautiful face. The mix of the two together produces a very real feeling of terror.

Mizoguchi's lifelong concern was to show the problems in a man-woman relationship. He directed love scenes in a way that brought out the social differences between the protagonists, and this, in turn, had a profound relationship with the use of the tilt-down or the angle of the camera. For instance, in the love scene between Shiraito (Irie Takako) and Kinya (Okada Okihiko) in *Cascading White Threads*, there is a long shot that pulls back, showing a bridge at night. The shot is taken at a slight angle, with the bridge in the middle of the upper half of the frame and Kinya crouching at the top of it. Shiraito notices him as she passes by and stops to talk. The camera moves over the bridge and captures Shiraito standing and talking to the huddled Kinya.

Shiraito is the star of the Mizugei Ichiza Group. Kinya is a poor cart-driver who had damaged his cart that afternoon and had been thrown out of his job. Now, with no place to go, he is sleeping on the bridge. They had met for the first time that afternoon and become friendly, and now they meet again. Shiraito, the richer of the two, thinks of Kinya as a poor student and plays the role of the patron. This inequality is shown with her standing and looking down at him, while he crouches, looking up at her. Her superior position is brought out with great skill in the first shot. The camera looks up from the riverbed at the bridge, which comes into the top of the frame, and then above that you have the slim figure of Shiraito walking on the bridge.

In a surviving copy of the script the scene starts this way:

A small closed shop.
Below the Boshin bridge, Shiraito walking alone gazing at the moon.
Shiraito: 'What a lovely moon, it will be difficult to sleep.'
She comes to the bridge.
Shiraito: 'It's a little depressing, here I am twenty-four and have never managed to get my hair done by Taka Shimada.'
Then, putting Shimada out of her mind, she twirls her hair, looks up at the bridge and realizes that there is someone there.
Shiraito: 'Who is there? Aren't you a retainer of the Mito domain?'
She climbs up. A man is lying at the top of the bridge. She comes up behind him.
Shiraito: 'How amazing, he is really fast asleep.'
She comes close and peers down at him, and is surprised to see Kinya.
Shiraito: 'Why it's Kin-san!'

The scriptwriter first has Shiraito look up to Kinya as she walks up the bridge, but as she steps towards Kinya, she is shown not looking down but 'peering at him'. Mizoguchi's direction follows this with a long shot of Shiraito looking up at the bridge so that the expression on her face is unclear. Then Shiraito walks up the bridge and sees Kinya lying there, and we have a truly beautiful shot-reverse-shot of her looking down at him and him looking up at her.

After this the two stroll down the riverbed, talking to each other. Kinya says he wants to go to Tokyo and study law. Shiraito replies that if this is what he wants, she will support him and pay his tuition fees. They go to Shiraito's hotel room and continue their conversation. The scene in the script is as follows:

> *Kinya*: 'I will never, in all my life, forget this great debt.'
> *Kinya*: 'Whatever I achieve in the future, I will make every effort to repay you. Tell me what is it that you desire?'
> *Shiraito*: 'I am quite satisfied if I can help you achieve your ambitions.'
> *Kinya*: 'No, that won't do. I am obliged to you but you as my benefactor are not obliged to me.'
> *Shiraito*: 'All right then, should I tell you? I would like …' she says and hides her face.
> *Shiraito*: 'There is no need for an old woman like me to feel embarrassed like some young girl,' she says bashfully and hides behind a screen.
> *Shiraito*: 'What I want, you know, is to be loved by you.' Kinya goes to her.

Mizoguchi filmed Shiraito mostly from the front, but did use a few long shots that had a high-angle feel to them. In this scene their positions are reversed, for it is Kinya now who is of samurai status (he could even become a professor or a minister in the future) while Shiraito is a geisha who hopes that after 'he succeeds in life', he will love her. To portray this reversal of positions, Shiraito's manner, which on the bridge was to 'peer at him', has now changed into a more submissive demeanour. Ire Takako conveys this change brilliantly when she hides behind the screen after saying that she wants Kinya to love her.

To send Kinya money, Shiraito borrows from a moneylender. The evil moneylender gets a henchman to rob her of the money he has just lent her. Shiraito finds out, confronts him and demands that he return the money. The moneylender turns vicious, grabs her by the hair and drags her around the room. A high-angle shot is used to film this sadistic scene.

Angered by the moneylender's violence, Shiraito kills him. She is arrested and produced in court where the judge is Kinya, who has graduated from the university and been appointed to this post. In the court scene the judge's seat is naturally placed at a higher level and the defendant is seated at a lower level. Thus Kinya looks down at Shiraito while talking to her, while Shiraito looks up at him, with an expression that seems resigned to the fact that her whole future depends on his judgement.

Whatever Mizoguchi's personal ideas may have been about the way the characters should have been positioned, in the last court scene these positions were determined simply by the way the courtroom is organized. But the film taken as a whole showed that Mizoguchi's direction brought out the changes in Shiraito's and Kinya's positions by the way he placed them in the scene, or through their situation, so that they are either being looked down at or looked up to.

Standing and Sitting

The Japanese style of sitting and moving about a room is different from the way it is in the West. The Japanese use *tatami* mats and most directors find shooting in a *tatami* mat room difficult. Consider an example of filming a conversation in such a room. The movements would be like this: first the person in the corridor outside the room sits and opens the sliding doors. Then he stands and enters the room and sits and closes the doors. Once again he stands up and moves to the appointed place in the room, sits down and bows. Only then can the conversation begin. Inevitably, the tempo will drag. Unlike in Western films, the characters cannot walk about the room once the conversation begins; you cannot, therefore, have movement and change. During the conversation, if one of the characters stands, the appropriate frame of the person sitting will show the standing person only from the chest downwards, which makes for an awkward composition. In Western films if you have one person sitting on a chair while the other stands, it is still possible to maintain a balance in the frame. This is difficult to do in a *tatami* mat room.

Ozu Yasujiro resolved the problem of how to film the rhythm and tempo of life in a Japanese-style home in his own unique way. He placed the camera at a very low level, had an almost geometrical composition and used fine, subtle editing. Mizoguchi used a different technique. In a Japanese house, if you remove the chairs and leave the sliding doors open, the whole house is one large open space. Mizoguchi was able to create very subtle meanings by the way his characters walked, stood or sat.

Take the example of *Lady Yu* – a story about a beautiful, young, upper-class, married woman, Oyu, who is in love with a young merchant. As she cannot marry him, she persuades her younger sister, who worships her, to do so. The younger sister reasons that if she marries the merchant, he would be her elder sister's brother-in-law, and it would not be strange for them to meet occasionally. On the night of their marriage, she tells her new husband why she has married him and why they must not have physical relations. Although she has planned this for her adored elder sister, she is nevertheless somewhat saddened, and her husband shocked.

In this scene, Mizoguchi uses a long moving shot to connect the rooms in a Japanese house, alternately stopping and moving, sometimes taking the shot from above and sometimes from below. During this particular shot, Oshizu (Otowa Nobuko), the bride, and Shinnosuke (Hori Yuji), the groom, move around in various ways: sitting on the *tatami* mat, rising, bowing, walking, sitting, and then rising and walking again. The rhythm of their movements bring out the psychology of the scene.

In the script, this scene is 'Scene 31 Afternoon – Shinnosuke's room', while the stage direction notes that they will be walking, standing and sitting. It is imperative to study the script to understand the movement of the camera and the actors.

FIGURE 33 *Lady Yu* (1951), © Kadokawa Pictures, Inc.

Scene 31 Afternoon – Shinnosuke's room

Night.

Shinnosuke raises a glass to the marriage broker and Oshizu and says, 'To your good health.'

The go-between moves back. [In the film, the go-between takes Oshizu's hand and walks about three mat lengths across the room and shows her the bedroom, sits down, bows and leaves. The camera pans to follow Oshizu and the go-between. Then a cut to a full shot of Oshizu.]

Shinnosuke and Oshizu come face to face for the first time. (Shinnosuke comes and stands beside Oshizu and then sits down).

Shinnosuke: 'There is something I must say as the breadwinner of this family.'

Hearing this, Oshizu's hands tremble.

Shinnosuke looks at her suspiciously. (In the first part of this scene Shinnosuke is shown looking steadily at Oshizu and after that the roles are reversed.)

Oshizu is shown for a while, looking as if she wants to say something and then:

Oshizu: 'You surprised me by suddenly saying something like this but if I don't ask you now, then …'

Shinnosuke: 'What is it?'

Oshizu: 'Actually, I came here after taking a decision.'

Oshizu: 'Please accept me as a wife in form only.'

(Oshizu gets up as if to run, crosses about three mats across the room and then sits down. Shinnosuke also gets up, runs after her and sits behind her.

Shinnosuke: 'What are you saying?'

Oshizu: 'I know what I am saying. My elder sister never wanted me to marry till now. She herself would reject all the proposals that came for me. Till now.'

Shinnosuke: '…?'

Oshizu: 'This time because it was *you*, she did not want to stop this marriage. She said it felt as if she was getting a new member of the family …'

Shinnosuke: '…?'

(Oshizu is standing. The camera has followed her. Shinnosuke stands up and the two talk.)

Oshizu: 'It's not just that. When she saw you her face suddenly began to glow.'

Shinnosuke: (He seems to be peering at Oshizu's face) 'I think you are just imagining this.'

Oshizu: 'No.' (She sits. The camera tilts down. Shinnosuke follows her and sits down).

Shinnosuke: 'Now that you have become a wife it won't do for you not to fulfil your vows, even if you find it difficult. This puts me in a difficult position.'

Oshizu: '…?'

Shinnosuke: 'You may be right about your elder sister but that doesn't justify your doing this to me … Really … I mean, she couldn't be expecting you to do something like this …'

Oshizu: 'Perhaps you, too, actually like her. Even though you have married me I am sure it was because you wanted to be close to her always.'

Shinnosuke is flustered and gazes at the sky.

Shinnosuke: 'No … not at all …'

Oshizu: 'You can speak freely, I will not tell anyone.'

She walks around Shinnosuke. (He stands up and leans against the pillar. Oshizu also stands up after him.)

Shinnosuke: 'I am fond of her, I will not conceal that, but I think of her as a relative … what have you gone and done? There is nothing that can be done about it…' (Shinnosuke sits with his back to her. Oshizu, after looking down at him comes and stands in front of him.

Shinnosuke: '…?'

Oshizu: 'I thought I would bring the two of you together. It was I who came with the hope that you would make me your sister.'

Shinnosuke: 'Did you think that you could bury yourself for the rest of your life for the sake of your sister?'

Oshizu: 'No, my elder sister will always be with me. Of course life doesn't always turn out the way you want and you have to follow the law.'

Shinnosuke looks questioningly.

Oshizu: 'Please make my elder sister happy. If you think of her as an elder sister, then do just as I would …'

Shinnosuke: 'Oshizu, you don't mind living like a nun?'

Oshizu: 'No, not at all. It is all right with me.' (Oshizu breaks down and cries. Shinnosuke springs up and looks down at her for a moment and then, distraught, turns around and takes a couple of steps back.)

This scene was shot in two long shots, the first of one minute and ten seconds and the second of six minutes and fifty-seven seconds. The conversation continues as Oshizu and Shinnosuke move around, the changing camera angles capturing their mental turmoil. Grief acquires a greater vividness when the man looks down at the seated, anguished woman. Her spirit appears to break when she gets up and moves around to shake off her despair, then sits down again. The man looks confused and indecisive as he stands beside the seated woman. But when he, too, sits down to

FIGURE 34 Katayama Akihiko (left) and Tanaka Kinuyo in *Lady Musashino* (1951), © Toho Film Co. Ltd.

persuade her, he suddenly appears to lose all confidence. Then it is the woman who looks down at him. The moving camera gives an emotional charge to these oscillations between the standing and sitting figures, reflecting their alternating feelings of hope and despair.

Another movement common to Asians but not to Westerners is to squat when resting in the open. It is used with great skill in *Lady Musashino*. A beautiful married woman and her younger cousin are in love. One day, as they walk around Musashino amidst the fields, they come upon a swamp. Reflecting that love is an abyss, they fall into a romantic mood. The man sits down on the hollow trunk of a fallen tree alongside the stream and the girl stands to one side. The man is positioned at a lower and the woman at a higher level. In that position the two laugh and talk. After a while he stands up and they walk towards the left of the frame where he squats in the grass. The woman also walks to the left but the camera stops and looks down on the squatting man. Then the man looks in the direction of the woman, gets up and follows her. The camera follows him as he walks up to her but the figure of the woman appears troubled and she sits down.

The woman is a respectable, married person. Both know that their love is forbidden. They are contemptuous of her husband's vulgarity and proud of their lineage as noble families of Musashino. They cannot speak of their love, and when the conversation does turn to questions of love, chaste and modest feelings well up within her. The man is aware of this and wants to play on her feelings. Their heightened awareness is portrayed through their restless movements of standing and sitting as they walk along the riverside path. This is one long shot without a cut. The two never look directly at each other; they are shown in full, looking down or looking up. They move naturally, sometimes turning their backs to the camera, sometimes hunching their shoulders as if stopped by some outside force. The camera moves and occasionally stops as if it had remembered something, or had changed its mind. At other times it speeds up, as if worried. Hayazaka Funio's theme melody, a brisk pastoral song, heightens this mood and lingers with you.

This, like an earlier scene in *Lady Yu*, is an illustration of how Mizoguchi conveys the delicate changes in the feelings of a man and a woman through their movements. The movements are linked and seem to rise and fall like ocean waves. In one moving shot of dazzling brilliance, Mizoguchi choreographs the movement of the actors as if they were indeed waves.

Lady Yu and *Lady Musashino* are normally regarded as among Mizoguchi's failures. I, too, feel that they are not among his finest films, but they are worth seeing several times just for these scenes. Miyagawa Kazuo was the cinematographer for *Lady Yu* and Tamai Masao for *Lady Musashino*. Their individual styles were very different, but the camera movements and the pan shots reflecting the changing feelings of the characters are similar.

In *The Life of Oharu* there is a sequence where Oharu, a geisha in the Shimabara district of Kyoto, meets a rich man who makes counterfeit money.

When the man scatters his fake money, people happily pick it up. Oharu, however, loathes such people, and will not pick up the money. The proprietor of the shop calls her to the bottom of the stairs and berates her. He is furious that she will not listen to him and tells her to leave. Oharu, who till that moment has worn a determined expression, suddenly changes and, turning towards the owner, bows deeply, begging forgiveness. The proprietor holds his head up haughtily. The rich man says he is attracted to Oharu's strength of character and wants to become her patron. Now the proprietor's face changes. Smiling widely, he bows to Oharu obsequiously.

This sequence has the flavour of a comedy. The owner's swiftly changing attitude when he sees an opportunity to make money is reflected in the way he holds his head, or bows to Oharu and by their lower or higher positions within the frame. Mizoguchi viewed these two movements of looking up or looking down at someone as fundamental to human consciousness.

Drama of Posture/Position

The film that boasts this aesthetic of direction is *A Story from Chikamatsu* , one of the most mature and beautiful films of Mizoguchi's last years. It shows the love that Osan, the wife of a paperhanger in Kyoto, has for her husband's assistant Mohei. The woman is the mistress, the man a servant and the drama starts with the woman in a superior position. At first the two are not aware they are in love. They just happen to come together through a number of coincidences. Finally, they commit adultery, a crime under the law, and flee when they realize they are in love.

Mizoguchi's direction brings out this dawning awareness in them. He begins by showing Osan in an upright stance, very much the owner's wife. The employee is shown with his head bent, almost servile in his humility. Considering their respective positions, this was as it should be. Other directors would also have directed the scene in the same way. But once you see how their attitudes change, you realize that this style was no accident.

So as not to create suspicion among the neighbours, the two pretend they are leaving the house at the same time, quite by chance. Then, with an air of resignation, they board a small boat, intending to drown themselves in Lake Biwa.

The script by Yoda Yoshikata has the following dialogue:

Sunset on the lake, the small boat carrying Osan and Mohei is being rowed out. When they reach a place out of sight, behind a clump of weeds, they stop the boat.
Mohei: 'Mrs Osan …'
Osan, her face distorted, nods.
Mohei, having made up his mind, is calm and holds Osan's hand.
Mohei: 'Keep a hold on yourself. Hold on to Mohei and come.'
Osan clutches Mohei. The two come out of the grass.

Osan: 'Please forgive me … for my sake you have to kill yourself.'
Mohei looks out with Osan.
Mohei: 'I have always adored you and will happily accompany you, if you allow me to.'
Osan is stunned by what Mohei says. Her bosom heaves, her eyes widen and she stares at him.
Mohei urges her.
Mohei: 'Mrs Osan what's the matter?'
Osan: '…'
Mohei: 'Are you angry? Have I done something?'
Osan: 'I do not want to die after what you have said.'
Mohei: 'Now! What are you saying?'
Osan: 'I don't want to die. I want to live.'
Their eyes are steely with determination and they embrace each other passionately.

This love scene in small boat rocked by the waves is like a skilfully choreographed duet of two dancers showing their changing positions. The camera is moved back to show the full scene and there are no extreme close-ups. Initially, Osan sits in front in the boat and Mohei stands at the back holding a pole. It is an exquisite, painterly composition. Mohei's head is higher than Osan's to begin with since he is holding the pole; it is not that he is looking down at her. Next, Mohei talks to Osan as he moves towards her on his knees and ties her legs together with a rope. It was customary to bind a woman's legs before throwing her into the water so that when the body was discovered the legs would not be apart. Simultaneously, as was written in the script, rather than the two just taking off their sandals, it was done to provide Mohei with an opportunity to kneel before Osan. It is in this position that he declares his love for her. As it is the love of a male servant for his mistress, it is a most appropriate posture.

However, unlike Western chivalric romances, Mohei does not declare his love looking up, with his chest thrown back. In chivalric love, the knight may bend his knee in front of the noble lady, but his heart is brimming with confidence. He knows that once he is given permission to stand by her, he will spring up to master her. A knight who lacks this confidence cannot possibly love a noblewoman. When he looks up, therefore, he has a confident air. In Japanese feudal society, for a servant to love his mistress was a crime. So even as he kneels and professes his love for Osan, Hasegawa Kazuo who plays Mohei, bends his head as he clutches her legs beseechingly. He prostrates himself and speaks in a tearful voice and then – so that the two can jump into the water – he binds Osan and the two stand up.

When Osan says, 'Your words have made me want to live,' Mohei sits down once again. It is ingrained in him by custom to bow down when he is talking to his master. But now that he has declared his love for her and Osan has also realized her love for him, she sits down submissively. Her posture changes as she cries, 'I don't want to die, I want to live,' and clasps Mohei. If this had been a Western chivalric romance the man would have stood, clasped the woman and assumed a posture of protection. But Mohei, like a grown child, throws his head back and allows Osan to hold him.

Among Mizoguchi's well-known works, *A Story from Chikamatsu* is not as well regarded in Europe or America as it is in Japan. Praised it is, but not as highly as *Ugetsu*, *The Life of Oharu* and *Sansho the Bailiff*, because Hasegawa Kazuo's style of playing Mohei comes across as very different from a masculine, Western, chivalric, romantic hero. As he falls in love with Osan, Mohei is often hesitant and timid, and his behaviour just evokes laughter among European and American audiences. Far from appearing manly, he comes across as a clown.

In traditional Japanese performing arts like *kabuki*, or those influenced by tradition such as *shinpa* theatre, an actor who plays what is called a 'masculine' (*tachiyaku*) role, does not normally play love scenes. These are played by a 'matinee idol' (*nimaime*), a type of actor often portrayed as weak and shallow. Hasegawa Kazuo, a historical drama actor who played both 'masculine' and 'matinee idol' roles, was never as popular as his fellow actors in period films, such Bando Tsumasaburo and Okochi Denjiro, who played only 'masculine' roles. He was, however, the most popular matinee idol star in period films and had a large fan following among women. In *A Story from Chikamatsu* he performs a pure matinee idol role, not displaying any macho posturing towards women, but assuming masculine poses just before the last scene. Mizoguchi's intention was to slowly and gradually bring out the true feelings of this matinee idol character.

After the two abandon their plans for a double suicide in Lake Biwa, they cross the mountains and escape to Mohei's village. On the way, they rest in a small teahouse. Mohei decides that he will help Osan by surrendering himself, and goes back. When Osan learns of this, she runs after him and finally falls, fainting from the strain. Mohei, who had hidden himself from her, runs to her side and falls to his knees to soothe her hurt leg, kissing it gently. Lying on the ground they hold each other but it is the woman who is on top.

In the end, Osan is caught and forcibly taken back to her parents' home. One night, Mohei steals into the garden to meet her as her mother keeps watch and the two hug, hidden by an open door. This time it is Mohei whose back is straight and Osan who nestles in his arms. He has assumed the posture of the superior person. The mother quickly lets both of them into the room and once they are seated, urges them to separate. Here, too, Mohei sits with his back straight, deaf to her pleas. Osan looks admiringly at this transformed man. Their positions, as revealed by their postures, are reversed. Their physical stances bespeak a mental state: the lower-class servant has now been transformed into a heroic lover, while the haughty upper-class mistress assumes a subdued pose and gazes upon her hero.

Miyagawa, the cinematographer, later recalled that his intention was to film Mohei in a way that would make him appear larger in the latter half of the film. It is not clear how far Mizoguchi deliberately planned the changes in their postures.

Yoda's script of the scene was just a description of what occurs when they come back down the valley and clasp each other.

> Osan, held in Mohei's arms, cries.
> Mohei, overcome with tenderness, holds her firmly.
> Osan gazes up at Mohei, bravely smiling, tears running down her face.

The script does not have detailed notes on their positions. In the earlier scene of the small boat where Mohei hugs Osan, the stage directions are straightforward: 'The two look at each other intensely and clasp each other with great strength.' There is no mention of the woman being in a superior position. However, in the love scene at the bottom of the valley, the script says, 'Osan looks up at Mohei.' Yoda had, indeed, thought about placing the man in a higher position. Before shooting, Mizoguchi had asked Tsuji Kyuichi, the producer, what Hasegawa Kazuo thought of the scene. Tsuji, in turn, asked Hasegawa who replied that he was thinking of kissing Osan's feet. When Mizoguchi heard this, he gave a broad, satisfied grin and directed it in just that way. It would appear, then, that the positioning of the characters was Hasegawa's idea and not Mizoguchi's.

I believe that Mizoguchi tried to depict the man-woman relationship on screen through the notions of status and through the psychological relationships of dominance and subordination, by positioning his characters lower or higher. Alternatively, he translated it through specific camera techniques such as a tilt-up or an angled shot, and these techniques were used in the other films with different crews and cast. Mizoguchi gave few concrete suggestions while directing; but he was in the habit of making the scriptwriters, the art directors and the actors revise endlessly till he had drawn out what he wanted from them. This process of revision would often reveal what Mizoguchi himself had not visualized. It was only then that he realized this was what he wanted all along. By linking the ones he liked from the many variations that the constant revisions produced, Mizoguchi bound the film together with his own underlying logic.

What was Mizoguchi's intuitive focus? He repeatedly returned to the question of the liberation of women and the problem of equality between the sexes. In that sense he was a democrat. Did this mean that he absolutely rejected unequal relations among people? After all, his several period films did contain scenes showing the arrogance of the upper classes and the humility of the lower.

Mizoguchi believed that men and women were wholly under the spell of their social positions until they fell in love. For him, the highest form an expression of love took was the image of an arrogant person prostrating himself before a social inferior. Such an image denotes Mizoguchi's disposition towards a feudalistic way of thinking: even in love, he believes, human relations were determined by who would be the superior and who the subordinate. This is not to slander him. The theme of his art was a constant battle against feudal instincts, and in the very ferocity of this battle lay the source of his tremendous creative power.

Mizoguchi, who loved using the crane for tilt-ups, would have the camera placed low in a ditch, or in a moat and shoot upwards at an embankment. In *Cascading White Threads* and *The Life of Oharu* he placed the camera on the riverbed and showed a brilliant, angled shot of the embankment and the bridge. The long and unforgettable 'one scene-one shot' in *The Story of the Late Chrysanthemums*, where Hanayagi and Mori walk along the side of the moat talking, is taken at an angle from below the level of the moat. I have stated earlier that in general the high angle was often used in historical films and spectacles, where the lavish sets are on display. While Mizoguchi loved the high angle in this kind of film, his striking inclusion of angled shots also shows his brilliant individuality.

The climactic scene of *Women of the Night* is typical of Mizoguchi's use of the camera. This film paints a realistic picture of the tragic life of prostitutes (*panpan*) hanging around the busy streets in the ruins of post-war Osaka. At the start of the last sequence we see a concrete precipice. The camera, placed at the bottom of the cliff, observes a group of prostitutes positioned at the top. It moves downwards, following them as they descend the cliff, chattering. We see a burnt-out church in the lower corner, where they beat up some women from outside their group who are trying to ply their trade without asking their permission. Tanaka Kinuyo, playing the leader of the prostitutes, realizes that among the 'outsider' women is her younger sister-in-law. When she tries to protect her she, too, is beaten up. The two hug each other and vow to change their lives. The camera pulls back for a wide-angle shot looking down at these two holding each other like mother and child, below the stained-glass window of the destroyed church.

This scene, composed along the lines of the Madonna and child in front of a church, appeared contrived and cheap, and was a failure. However, what leaves a powerful impression is the depth of Mizoguchi's imagination, expressed in the way he alternates between 'looking up' and 'looking down' – looking up to the woman as a sacred being and 'looking down' on the pitiful.

The Script: Yoda Yoshikata

Yoda Yoshikata was among the many people who worked with Mizoguchi and was his most important scriptwriter. His father worked in a company called Yuzen Dyes but he later set up his own independent factory. From the time he was in primary school, Yoda and his mother helped in the factory right up to the time of his father's death in 1919. Life was difficult during the depression that followed the First World War. His mother, the only daughter of one of the thirteen mistresses of a famous restaurant owner in Kyoto, and a tough woman in her own right, started a small confectionery shop to support the family, and Yoshikata would help with deliveries for the shop after school. As a young woman she was employed in many places and it was while working as an assistant in a restaurant that specialized in chicken dishes, that she met Yoda's father and married him. She went on to play a major role in bringing Yoda into films with Mizoguchi. Mizoguchi's films themselves have many strong-willed women who live a difficult life. They reflect in part the character of some of the women he had himself admired. Some, possibly, are modelled on Yoda's mother who he respected deeply.

Within a year of being appointed scriptwriter by Mizoguchi, Yoda Yoshikata wrote the script for *Osaka Elegy*. His mother saw the film on the opening night and was very touched.

Mizoguchi had frequent and fierce fights with the women in his life. Yoda, on the other hand, grew up protected by his mother, elder sister and wife. What the two men shared was a strong love for their mothers. Mizoguchi knew many women who had resolutely fought men. Yoda, too, was aware of women's willpower but for him their real strength lay in their ability to bear suffering. The female characters the two depicted in their films were created through the intertwining of their respective views of women. Whereas Mizoguchi – based on what he saw of his sister – constructed a strong image of a gentle woman protecting a man, it was

FIGURE 35 Mizoguchi Kenji (left) and scriptwriter Yoda Yoshikata (1951).

Yoda who fleshed it out wonderfully and made the image real. Mizoguchi's initial reason for appointing Yoda was that he was born in Kyoto and therefore understood the characters, customs and language of the people of Kansai (Osaka-Kyoto area). But the reason why he never parted from Yoda was because he shared his view of women and their innate desire to nurture.

Mizoguchi would make Yoda revise his script several times till he had the characters he was satisfied with. On this he was unrelenting. However, Yoda was not the only one to work under Mizoguchi's direction. Mizoguchi's individuality and tenacity pushed the entire crew in the direction he wanted them to go. Since the people who worked with him also shared his sense of self-worth, they would add their own touches even as they followed Mizoguchi's directions.

A society where men use women is also a society where men use each other. A man who crushes women is not a man to be admired. Portraying such men is a way of portraying a society where men cannot be men. The structure of a patriarchal social order is unquestionably based on violence. Yoda wrote his scripts for Mizoguchi from this understanding of Japanese society. He rarely wrote what is called social drama, where people trample over each other to get ahead. By presenting the very core of society realistically, he provided us with a social analysis that was far sharper and more accurate than ideological works with their direct approach to social problems.

List of Illustrations

1. Mizoguchi Kenji   3
2. Left to right: Mizoguchi Kenji at twenty-eight, actress Sakai Yoneko and distributor Kawakita Nagamasa. Photograph taken at the Nikkatsu Kyoto Studio in 1926.   5
3. Natsukawa Shizue (left) and Kosugi Isamu in *Metropolitan Symphony* (1929).   43
4. Yamada Isuzu (left) and Hara Komako in *Oyuki, the Madonna* (1935).   46
5. Ohkura Chiyoko (left) and Miyake Kuniko in *Poppy* (1935).   47
6. Yamada Isuzu (left) in *Sisters of the Gion* (1936).   62
7. Yamada Isuzu in *Osaka Elegy* (1936).   64
8. Simizu Masao (left) and Yamaji Fumiko in *The Straits of Love and Hate* (1937).   66
9. Kogule Michiyo (left) and Kuga Yoshiko (right) in *A Picture of Madame Yuki* (1950), © Toho Film Co. Ltd.   70
10. Yamada Isuzu and Natsukawa Daijiro in *The Downfall of Osen* (1935).   73
11. Mori Kakuko (lcft) and Hanayagi Syotaro in *The Story of the Late Chrysanthemums* (1938).   79
12. Mizoguchi Kenji in his capacity as the President of the Association of Japanese Film Directors, and as Film Commissioner of the Cabinet, at a ceremony held by the Japanese Government in 1940.   85
13. Yamada Isuzu in *The Sword* (1945).   86
14. Kuwano Michiko (left), Tanaka Kinuyo (centre) and Miura Mitsuko (in front of Tanaka) in *The Victory of Women* (1946).   87
15. Tanaka Kinuyo (left) and Miyake Kuniko in *My Love Burns* (1949).   90
16. Tanaka Kinuyo (left) and Yamamura So in *The Love of Sumako the Actress* (1947).   93
17. Bando Minosuke (right) in *Five Women around Utamaro* (1946).   94
18. Tanaka Kinuyo (left) and Takasugi Sanae in *Women of the Night* (1948).   95
19. Tanaka Kinuyo (left) and Sugai Ichiro in *The Life of Oharu* (1952), © Toho Film Co. Ltd.   105
20. Tanaka Kinuyo (left) and Mizoguchi Kenji in Venice.   110

21. Kyo Machiko (left) and Mori Masayuki (right) in *Ugetsu* (1953), © Kadokawa Pictures, Inc.   113
22. *Sansho the Baliff* (1954), © Kadokawa Pictures, Inc.   118
23. Tanaka Kinuyo in *Sansho the Baliff* (1954), © Kadokawa Pictures, Inc.   120
24. Naniwa Chieko (left), Hasegawa Kazuo (centre) and Kagawa Kyoko (right) in *A Story from Chikamatsu* (1954), © Kadokawa Pictures, Inc.   128
25. *Gion Festival Music* (1953), © Kadokawa Pictures, Inc.   132
26. Kuga Yoshiko (left) in *The Woman in the Rumour* (1954), © Kadokawa Pictures, Inc.   133
27. Kyo Machiko (left) in *The Princess Yang Kwei-fei* (1955), © Kadokawa Pictures, Inc.   134
28. Ichikawa Raizo in *Taira Clan Saga* (1955), © Kadokawa Pictures, Inc.   136
29. *Street of Shame* (1956), © Kadokawa Pictures, Inc.   140
30. *Tokyo March* (1929).   144
31. *The Forty-seven Ronin* (1941).   148
32. Mizoguchi Kenji (left) and Ozu Yasujiro at the Association of Japanese Film Directors, 1948.   163
33. *Lady Yu* (1951), © Kadokawa Pictures, Inc.   170
34. Katayama Akihiko (left) and Tanaka Kinuyo in *Lady Musashino* (1951), © Toho Film Co. Ltd.   172
35. Mizoguchi Kenji (left) and scriptwriter Yoda Yoshikata (1951).   179

Mizoguchi's Filmography

1956
Street of Shame – Akasen chitai

1955
Taira Clan Saga – Shin heike monogatari
Princess Yang Kwei-fei – Yôkihi

1954
A Story from Chikamatsu – Chikamatsu monogatari
The Woman in the Rumour – Uwasa no onna
Sansho the Bailiff – Sanshô dayû

1953
Ugetsu – Ugetsu monogatari
Gion Festival Music – Gion bayashi

1952
The Life of Oharu – Saikaku ichidai onna

1951
Lady Musashino – Musashino fujin
Lady Yu – Oyû-sama

1950
A Picture of Madame Yuki – Yuki fujin ezu

1949
My Love Burns – Waga koi wa moenu (1949)

1948
Women of the Night – Yoru no onnatachi

1947
The Love of Sumako the Actress – Joyû Sumako no koi

1946
Five Women Around Utamaro – Utamaro o meguru gonin no onna
The Victory of Women – Josei no shôri

1945
Victory Song – Hisshoka
The Sword – Meito bijomaru

1944
Musashi Miyamoto – Miyamoto Musashi
Three Generations of Danjuro – Danjuro sandai

1942
The Forty-Seven Ronin: Part II – Genroku Chûshingura

1941
The Forty-Seven Ronin – Genroku Chûshingura
The Life of an Actor – Geido ichidai otoko

1940
A Woman of Osaka – Naniwa onna

1939
The Story of the Late Chrysanthemums – Zangiku monogatari

1938
Ah, My Home Town – Aa kokyo
The Song of the Camp – Roei no uta

1937
The Straits of Love and Hate – Aien kyo

1936
Sisters of the Gion – Gion no shimai
Osaka Elegy – Naniwa erejî

1935
Poppy – Gubijinsô
Oyuki, the Madonna – Maria no Oyuki
The Downfall of Osen – Orizuru Osen

1934
The Mountain Pass of Love and Hate – Aizo toge
The Jinpu Gang – Jinpu-ren

1933
Gion Festival – Gion matsuri
Cascading White Threads – Taki no shiraito

1932
Dawn in Manchuria – Manmo kenkoku no reimei
Man of the Moment – Toki no ujigami

1931
And Yet They Go – Shikamo karera wa yuku

1930
Home Town – Fujiwara Yoshie no furusato
Mistress of a Foreigner – Tojin Okichi

1929
Metropolitan Symphony – Tokai kokyogaku
Tokyo March – Tokyo koshin-kyoku
The Rising Sun Brightens – Asahi wa kagayaku
The Nihon Bridge – Nihon bashi

1928
My Lovely Daughter – Musume kawaiya
A Man's Life: Part III – Hito no issho
A Man's Life: Part II – Hito no issho
A Man's Life – Hito no issho

1927
The Cuckoo – Jihi shincho
Imperial Favour – Ko-on

1926

Money – Kane
Children of the Sea – Kaikoku danji
The Love-Mad Tutoress – Kyôren no onna shishô
My Fault, New Version – Shin onoga tsumi
A Paper Doll's Whisper of Spring – Kaminingyo haru no sasayaki
The Copper Coin King – Dôka-ô

1925

General Nogi and Kumasan – Nogi taisho to Kumasan
The Song of Home – Furusato no uta
The Man – Ningen
Street Scenes – Gaijo no suketchi
Shining in the Red Sunset – Akai yuhi ni terasarete
The White Lily Laments – Shirayuri wa nageku
The Earth Smiles – Daichi wa hohoemu (Part 1)
Out of College – Gakuso o idete
No Money, No Fight – Uchen-Puchan

1924

Queen of the Circus – Kyokubadan no joô
A Woman of Pleasure – Kanraku no onna
A Chronicle of the May Rain – Samidare zoshi
The Trace of a Turkey – Shichimencho no yukue
This Dusty World – Jin kyo
Women Are Strong – Josei wa tsuyoshi
The Queen of Modern Times – Gendai no jo-o
Death at Dawn – Akatsuki no shi
The Sad Idiot – Kanashiki hakuchi

1923

The Song of the Mountain Pass – Toge no uta
Blood and Soul – Chi to rei
The Night – Yoru
Among the Ruins – Haikyo no naka
Foggy Harbour – Kiri no minato
813
The Song of Failure – Haizan no uta wa kanashi
City of Desire – Joen no chimata
Dream of Youth – Seishun no yumeji
Hometown – Kokyo
The Resurrection of Love – Ai ni yomigaeru hi

English and Original Titles of Films of Other Directors Cited in the Book

Baggage of Life, The (Jinsei no onimotsu)
Baptism by Fire (Chi no senrei)
Battleship Potemkin (Bronenosets Potyomkin)
Before the Dawn (Yoakemae)
Beheading of a Hundred in Yoshiwara, The (Hana no Yoshihara Hyakunigiri)
Blood of a Big Snake, The (Orochi)
Blue Mountain Range, The (Aoi sammyaku)
Bronze Christians (Seido no kiristo)
Day Our Lives Brightened, The (Waga shougai no kagayakeru hi)
Drops of Blood on the Snow (Beni yuki funpun)
Duty and Duty (Giri to giri)
Far Away Palanquin (Oboro kago)
Fight Without Arms (Buki naki tatakai)
Five Scouts (Gonin no sckkohei)
Foreigner Okichi, The (Tojin Okichi)
Forsaken Mother, The (Suterareta Haha)
Forty-Seven Ronin, The (Chushingura-Ninjo-hen; Fukushu-hen)
Gate of Hell (Jigokumon)
Half-Brother (Ibokyodai)
Harp of Burma (Biruma no Tategoto)
Hen in the Wind, The (Kaze no naka no mendori)
Instigation (Sendo)
It's My Life (Vivre sa vie)
Just Take it Out (Chuji Uridasu)
Killing Sword, The (Zanjin zanuma ken)
Late Autumn (Akibiyori)
Life of a Man, The (Hito no issho. Ningen banji kane no maki)
Living Dolls (Ikeru ningyo)
Look at this Mother (Kono haha o miyo)
Man's Pain (Ningen ku)
Morning for the Osone Family (Osone ke no asa)
Mother Caught in a Storm, The (Arashi no naka no haha)

My Love Burns (Waga Koi wa moenu)
My Name is Woman (Watashi no na wa Onna)
Navy Bomber Party, The (Kaigun Bakugekitai)
Night and Fog in Japan (Nihon no yoru to kiri)
No Regrets for Our Youth (Waga seishun ni kuyinashi)
Okichi the Foreigner (Tojin Okichi)
Osaka Story, An (Osaka monogatari)
Page of Madness, A (Kurutta ippeji)
Passion of a Woman Teacher, The (Kyoren no onna shisho)
Portrait of a Bride (Onna Keizu)
Predicament (Itabasami)
Quiet Two, The (Futari shizuka)
Rain of Tears (Namida no Ame)
Rashomon (Rashomon)
Regarding Desire (Sei ni kanjite)
Resurrection of Love, The (Ai ni yomigaeru hi)
Rickshaw Man, The (Muhomatsu no issho)
Rope (Rope)
Seven Samurai (Shichinin no samurai)
Song of My Village, The (Furusato no uta)
Song of the Baggage Car, The (Niguruma no uta)
Sun (Nichiren)
Tale of Genji, The (Genji monogatari)
To the Land of Snow out of Desire and Duty (Giri to ichi kara ukiguni e)
Tokyo Hotel, The (Tokyo no shuku)
Town with a Cupola, A (Kyupolra no aru machi)
Tree of Love, The (Aizen Katsura)
Village Tattooed Man, The (Machi no Irezumimono)
Walkower (Walkower)
Waltz at Noon (Mahilu no Enbukyoku)
What Made Her Do It? (Nani ga kanojo o so saseta ka)
What's Your Name? (Kimi no na wa?)
Wild Goose (Gan)
Wonderful Sunday (Subarashiki nichiyobi)
Worrying about Mother (Haha no shinpai)
Yae-chan, The Next Door Girl (Tonori no Yae-chan)
Youth Across the River (Kawa muko no seishun)

Index

813 41, 186

Age of Films, The 56
Akasaka Royal Hall 4
Akimoto Matsuyo 18, 19
And Yet They Go 36–37, 45, 58, 140, 185
Anthropology of the Gods, The 34
Aoibashi Western Painting Research Institute 3
Aoyama Hiroshi 96
Arai Jun 23
Araki Shinobu 23
Arashi Yoshisaburo 153
'Arsene Lupin' series 41
Art of Mizoguchi Kenji, The 144
Asahi Weekly 135
Asakusa Opera 4
Asakusa Sanyukan 29
Asakusa Tagawa Primary School 1
Association of Japanese Film Directors 86–87, 163, 181–182
'Avenue of Life, The' 34

Baggage of Life, The 65, 74, 187
Baishoku kamo nanban 70
Bando Kotaro 82
Bando Minosuke 94, 181
Bando Tsumasaburo 9, 58, 176
Baptism by Fire 27–30, 187
Battleship Potemkin 145, 187
Before the Dawn 122, 187
Blood and Spirit 41

Blood of a Big Snake, The 25, 187
Blue Mountain Range, The 67, 91, 187
Bronze Christians 122, 187
'Brother Do Not Give Your Life' 34
Buddhism 1, 16, 19, 75, 107, 115
Bungeikurabu 2
Bunrakuza 82
Bygone Friends 39, 59

Cabinet of Dr Caligari, The 9, 41
Cascading White Threads 21–22, 35, 38, 41, 47, 61, 74–75, 80, 88, 124, 167, 178, 185
Chaplin, Charlie 9
Chikamatsu Monzaemon 61, 124, 126
Chuo University 9
Chushingura 46, 55–56, 122, 138–139, 145, 148–152, 154-157, 164, 166
Chusingura of the Genroku Period 147
Cinematic Expression of the Masters: Mizoguchi Kenji, The 142
Cinemaya (Osian's-Cinemaya) The Asian Film Quarterly ix
Collected Screenplays of Yoda Yoshikata, The 14
Collected Works of Japanese Film Directors 8
Collection of Japanese Classical Literature 124
Commercial College 9
'Complete Realisation of a Vow, The' 107

Confucianism 16, 19, 60
Contemporary Japanese Filmmakers 29
Conversations with the Demon Takahashi Oden 17
Cooper, Gary 60
Crime and Punishment 107
Crow in the Moonlight 65

Daiei 1, 5, 10, 12, 69, 110, 113, 127, 135
Daiichi Eiga 45, 48, 69
Dali, Salvador 12
Danzaimon 2
Dawn of Manchuria, The 41
Day Our Lives Brightened, The 92, 187
De Maupassant, Guy 4, 37, 46, 111–112
Doll's House, A 94
Dostoevsky, Fyodor 107
Downfall of Osen, The 13, 35, 36, 38, 41, 47, 55, 61, 70, 73–75, 80, 181, 185
Drops of Blood on the Snow 24, 187
Dumas Fils 24
Duty and Duty 24, 187

Edo Period 6, 15, 60, 94
Eisenstein, Sergei 42, 100, 143, 145
Elan Vitale 69

Far Eastern Communist University 6
Festival of Gion, The 45
Film and the Modern Spirit 97
Film Commissioner of the Cabinet 86–87, 181
Films are Difficult 159
Five Scouts 45, 187
Five Women Around Utamaro 94, 181, 184

Five Women who Loved Love 125, 127
Foggy Harbour 41, 186
Forsaken Mother, The 7, 187
Forty-Seven Ronin, The 74, 147–148, 184, 187
Fukuda Eiko 89
Fukuda Yoshiyuki 90
Futagawa Buntaro 9, 25

Gable, Clark 60
Gate of Hell 135, 187
Genealogy of the Cinematic Spirit, The 97
General Oyama Iwao 17
Gion Festival Music 131–134, 182–183
Godard, Jean-Luc 24
Gosho Heinosuke 9, 46, 65, 74
Great Kanto Earthquake 10, 22, 31
Griffith, D.W. 9

Hamada Yuriko 67
Hanada Kiyoteru 90
Hanayagi Kisho 74, 75, 121, 123
Hara Kensaku 38, 63
Hara Setsuko 91, 164
Harp of Burma 115, 187
Hasegawa Kazuo 22, 58, 127–128, 175–177, 182
Hatamoto Akiichi 39, 69
Hayakawa Sessyu 60-61
Hayasaka Fumio 114, 128
Hayashiya Tatsusaburo 118
Heizan 137
Hen in the Wind, The 92, 164, 187
Higuchi Ichiyo 2
Hirakata Park 151
Hirano Yoshimi 108, 145, 163
History of Film People: Mizoguchi Kenji, A 56
Hitchcock, Alfred 145, 147
Hori Yuji 169

Hosei University 53
Hototogisu 17, 19

I Was Awarded a Medal 111–112
Ibsen, Henrik 94
Ichijo Yuriko 57
Ichikawa Kon 34
Ichikawa Raizo 136, 137, 182
Ihara Saikaku 101–103, 107–108,
    124–129, 139, 141
Iida Shinbi 44
Ikebe Ryo 60
Ikenaga 4, 57, 144
Ikenaga Hirohisa 4, 57
Imai Tadashi 67, 91, 101
Imamura Shohei vii
Imperial Favour 41, 45, 185
Inagaki Hiroshi 8-9, 22, 46
Inn at the Ford, The 110–112, 115
Inoue Kintaro 65
Instigation 24, 187
'Investigation into What is Called a
    Human' 97
Irie Takako 13, 42, 167
Ishihama Primary School 1
Ishihara Yujiro 60
It's My Life 24, 187
Itami Mansaku 46, 65, 74
Ito Daisuke 9, 42, 47
Ito Kisaku 151
Itoya Hisao 65
Iwata Keiji 33
Izu Shimoda 37
Izumi Kyoka 4, 21, 36, 70, 74, 75, 76,
    81

Japan–China War 35, 41
*Japan Motion Pictures Limited
    Company* 7
Jien Deng Xin hua 111
Jinpu Gang, The 45, 151, 185
Juichiya Gisaburo 37, 39

Just Take it Out 65, 187

Kadokawa Pictures, Inc. 113, 118, 120,
    128, 132–134, 136, 140, 170,
    181–182
Kaeriyama Norimasa 24
Kafu 4
Kagawa Keiko 123
Kaigun Bakugekitai 45, 188
Kanagaki Robun 1, 17
Kanjincho 56
Katayama Akihiko 172, 182
Katsu Shintaro 58
Kawaguchi Matsutaro 1, 6, 14, 46,
    51–52, 86, 110, 121, 127
Kawakami Yasuko 141
Kawakatsu Kyoko 32, 142
Kawakita Nagamasa 5, 181
Kawarazaki Chojuro 154
Kawashima Yuzo 165
Kawazu Seizaburo 51
Keio University 9
Kikuchi Youho 39
Killing Sword, The 42, 187
Kimura Sotoji 45
Kinema Junpo 44
Kinoshita Keisuke 89, 91, 101
Kinugasa Teinosuke 7–9, 20–22, 25,
    119, 159
Kishi Keiko 92
Kishi Matsuo 7, 29, 56–58, 144
Kobayashi Takiji 53
Kobe Yuishin Journal 4
Koda Aya 34
Kogule Michiyo 70, 181
Koizumi Kasuke 29
Konjiki yasha 59
Koshoku Ichidai Onna 101
Kosugi Isamu 43, 181
Kuga Yoshiko 68, 72, 132–133,
    181–182
Kuko 2

Kuroda Kiyoteru 3
Kuroda Kyomi 163
Kurosawa Akira vii, 56, 89, 91–92, 101, 122, 149, 160
Kuwano Michiko 87–88, 181
Kyo Machiko 113, 134, 140, 166, 181-182
Kyoto Municipal Hospital 142
Kyoto Nikkatsu Studio 4–5, 7–10, 20–23, 25, 27–28, 30, 33, 57–58, 143, 181
Kyoto Senbon yakuza group 69

Lady Musashino 80, 164, 172–173, 182–183
Lady of the Camelias, The 24
Lady Yu 41, 66–67, 124, 151, 160, 169–170, 173, 182–183
Late Autumn 164, 187
Life of a Man, The 41, 187
Life of an Actor, The 78, 184
Life of Film, The 11
Life of Oharu, The vii, 10, 58, 74, 80–81, 101–102, 105, 107–108, 110, 114, 122, 138, 141, 144–145, 150–152, 157, 163–164, 166, 173, 176, 178, 181, 183
Little Cuckoo, The (Hototogisu) 19, 59
Living Dolls 42, 187
Look at This Mother 42, 45, 187
Love of Sumako the Actress 19, 93–94, 181, 184
Lump of Fat, The 46
Lupin, Morris 41
Lust of a Snake Character, The 110–111

Machan 5
Machida Hiroko 140
Man's Pain 8, 187
Manchurian Incident 37, 41
Manpontei 56

Masa 1
Matsuda Film Company 21
Matsudaira Suzu 142
Matsudaira Tadamasa 2, 31, 32, 70, 142
Matsudaira Tadanori 32, 53
Matsui Sumako 19, 30, 94
Matsumoto Kappei 88
Mayama Seika 147–148, 156
Meiji 9, 15–16, 18–21, 23, 28, 41–42, 46, 59, 74–76, 81, 89–90, 94, 98, 122, 159
Meiji University 9
Memories of the Explosion 90
Metropolitan Symphony 41–45, 138, 181, 185
Michiyo Kogure 68
Mifune Toshiro 58–59, 61, 108
Mikawaya Geisha House 1
Mimasu Aiko 141, 159
Mimasu Mantoya 153
Mistress of a Foreigner 37, 39, 185
Mito Mitsuko 89, 112
Miura Mitsuko 87–88, 181
Miyagawa Kazuo 123, 128, 145, 151, 157, 173, 176
Miyajima Katsuo 23
Miyake Kuniko 47, 90, 164, 181
Miyamoto Musashi 138, 184
Mizoguchi Kenji, The Man and the Art 5, 68
'Mizoguchi Theory of Actual Size-ism' 152
Mizoguchi Zentaro 1
Mizuno 2
Mizutani Hiroshi 151–152, 160
Modern Theatre 8, 9, 19, 20
Molière 37
Mori Kakuko 66, 79, 181
Mori Kiyoshi 29
Mori Masayuki 112–113, 134, 166, 181

Mori Ogai 116–123, 150
Morning for the Osone Family 89, 91–92, 187
Mother and Son-in-Law, The 19
Mother Caught in a Storm, The 92, 187
Murata Minoru 9
Murou Saisei 34
My Fault 19, 21, 39, 59, 186
My Little Neighbour 74
My Love Burns 11, 55, 81, 89–91, 93, 159, 181, 183, 188

Nagata Masakazu 5, 12, 14, 48, 69, 135
Naito Kojiro 144
Naito Konan 144
Nakadai Tatsuya 60–61
Nakamura Yoshiko 82
Nakano Eiji 69
Nakayama Utako 22–23
Naniwa Chieko 128, 131–132, 182
Narusawa Masashige 139
Natsukawa Daijiro 38, 61, 71, 73, 181
Natsukawa Shizue 43, 181
Natsume Shunji 138
Natsume Soseki 4, 47
New School Theatre 7, 9, 15, 19-20, 31
Night and Fog in Japan 90, 147, 188
Nihon Bridge, The 21, 33, 35–36, 38, 47, 74, 76, 80, 185
Nikkatsu 4–5, 7–10, 20–23, 25, 27–28, 30, 33, 57–58, 143, 181
No Money No Fight 41, 186
No Regrets for Our Youth 89, 91–92, 188
Number One Film 5

Occupation 59, 65, 87, 91
Ofuna Shochiku Studios 165
Oguchi Tadashi 7, 8
Oguma Hisakuni 152
'Oguri' 116

Oguri Takeo 21, 29
Ohama 1
Ohbora Gengo 7, 22
Ohinata Den 60
Ohkura Chiyoko 47, 181
Oishi Kuranosuke 55, 56, 122, 147, 148
Okabe of Sakanya 2
Okada Okihiko 167
Okada Tokihiko 38, 60–61
Okada Yoshiko 27–28
Okichi the Foreigner 144, 188
Okochi Denjiro 58, 176
Okura Chiyoko 48
Old Calendar Maker, The 124–125
Older Brother-Younger Sister 34
Onoe Matsunosuke 58
'Oppekepe' 90
Osaka Elegy 5, 10, 13, 26, 32, 35, 38, 39, 41, 47–48, 50, 55, 61, 63–65, 74, 81, 90, 97–98, 107, 114, 141, 145, 151, 164, 179, 181, 184
Osaka Story 139, 141, 188
Osanai, Kaoru 9
Oshima Nagisa 90, 147
Otani Tomoemon 133
Otowa Nobuko 169
Oya Ichijiro 137–138
Oyuki, the Madonna 45–46, 80, 181, 185
Ozaki 4
Ozawa Eitaro 112
Ozu Yasujiro vii, 35, 46, 50, 65, 74, 92, 145, 158, 163–164, 169, 182

Pacific War 35, 41
Page of Madness, A 25, 188
Paper Doll's Whisper of Spring, A 41, 186
Passion of a Woman Teacher, The 114, 188
Passionate Woman, A 101–102, 150

Personal History of Film, A 144
Philippines 17
Picture of Madame Yuki, A 41, 55, 66–67, 70, 107, 181, 183
Plays and the Artistic Life 19
Poppy 45, 47, 181, 185
Portrait of a Bride 21, 188
'Power of the Sister, The' 33
Predicament 24, 188
Princess Yang Kwei-fei 13, 32, 81, 134–135, 138–139, 151, 182–183
Pudovkin, Vsevolod Illarionovich 42

Quiet Two, The 21, 23–26, 188

Rain of Tears, The 7, 109, 188
'Random Memories' 159
Rashomon 135, 149, 188
Reflections on Japanese Film 97
Regarding Desire 24, 188
Resurrection 19, 21, 29–30, 51–53, 107, 185, 188
Resurrection of Love, The 29–30, 186, 188
Rickshaw Man, The 8, 188
Rope 145, 147, 188
Rossi couple, the 4
Run Run Shaw 135

Saburi Sin 60
Sada Keiji 92
Saegusa Genjiro 57
Saeki Kiyoshi 93
Saga Chieko 69–70, 141–142
Saikaku 101–103, 107–108, 124–129, 139, 141, 183
Saito Ichiro 114
Sakai Yoneko 5, 181
Sakane Tazuko 11
Salon Chie 70
Sankei 1
Sansho the Bailiff vii, 11, 22, 34–35, 55, 74–75, 81, 101, 110, 116–123, 150-151, 157, 164, 176, 183
Sanyabori (Tokyo Akasuka) primary school 2
Sanyukan 27, 29
Sata Keiji 60
Sato Koroku 7
Sawamura Sadako 140
Second World War 35, 67, 69, 87, 94, 97, 115, 119, 138
Seikichi Terakado 6, 12
Seven Samurai 122, 149, 188
Shibaki Yoshiko 139
Shibuya Minoru 122
Shiga 49
Shimamura Hogetsu 94
Shimazu Yasujiru 9, 74
Shimizu Hiroshi 46
Shimomura Chiaki 37
Shin Toho 10
Shindo Eitaro 50, 123, 131, 140
Shindo Kaneto 9, 64, 152
Shining in the Red Sunset 57, 186
Shinko Kinema studios 51
Shinpa (New School Theatre) group 7
Shinto Funeral Prayer for the Calendar-Maker Osan 124
Ship Shintoku, The 116
Shochiku 10, 165
Showa period 24, 36
Silver Lion 110
Simizu Masao 66, 181
Sisters of the Gion 5, 13, 41, 48–50, 55, 62, 74, 81, 97–98, 107, 114, 131, 141, 144, 151, 164, 181, 184
Skolimovski, Jerzy 147
Song of Failure, The 41, 186
Song of My Village, The 41, 188
Song of the Camp, The 41, 45, 77, 184
Story from Chikamatsu, A 10, 22, 55, 57, 60–61, 81, 101, 124, 128,

150–151, 164, 166, 174, 176, 182-183
Story of the Late Chrysanthemums, The 22, 35, 38, 41, 47, 55, 58, 65, 78–81, 97, 99, 121, 124, 138, 146, 151-152, 157, 164, 178, 181, 184
Straits of Love and Hate, The 10, 39, 51–53, 55, 58, 63, 66, 107, 140, 146, 151, 181, 184
Street of Shame 40, 55, 139, 140–141, 147, 151, 159, 182–183
Sugai Ichiro 105, 159–161
Sugimura Haruko 13
Sun, The 119, 188
Susaki Paradise, The 139
Suzu 1–3, 6, 31–33, 36, 38, 40, 68, 70, 142
Suzuki Denmei 60
Suzuki Kensaku 8–9, 28
Suzuki Shigeyoshi 42, 45
Sword, The 42, 86–87, 181, 184, 187

Tadanori 32, 53, 54
Taira Clan Saga 55, 122, 134–139, 151, 164, 166, 182–183
Tairano Kiyomori 55
Taisho 17, 20–21, 23, 28, 30, 36, 39, 52, 59, 94, 186
Tajima Kane 69
Takada Kokichi 82
Takahashi Oden 16–17
Takakura Ken 58
Takashima Tatsunosuke 70
Takasugi Sanae 95, 181
Takekawa Seiichi 32
'Takekurabe' 2
Takemitsu Toru 114
Tale of Genji, The 122, 188
Tales of Ugetsu 81
Tamai Masao 173
Tanaka 7–9, 11, 13, 28, 40, 68, 74–75, 82, 84, 87, 88–90, 93–95, 105,
108–110, 112–113, 115–116, 120–121, 123, 129, 132–133, 160, 163, 172, 178, 181–182
Tanaka Eizo 7-9, 28
Tanaka Haruo 129
Tanaka Kinuyo 11, 13, 40, 68, 74, 75, 82, 84, 87, 88, 89, 90, 93, 94, 95, 105, 108, 109, 110, 112, 113, 115, 116, 120, 121, 123, 132, 133, 160, 163, 172, 178, 181, 182
Tanizaki Junichiro 37
Tasaka Tomotaka 9, 42, 45
Terakado Seiken 6
'Thatching a Roof' 116
Three Great Films, The 33
Time of My Mother, The 19
To the Land of Snow Out of Desire and Duty 24, 25, 188
Together with Films 13
Toho 6, 10, 70, 105, 172, 181, 182
Tokudaiji Shin 88
Tokutomi Roka 17, 19
Tokyo Actors School 9
Tokyo Higher Teachers' College 9
Tokyo Hotel 65, 74, 188
Tokyo Imperial University 9
Tokyo March 143, 144, 182, 185
Tokyo Nichinichi Shinbun 16
Tolstoy, Leo 4, 19, 30, 51–53, 107
Tomioka Tadashi 4
Tomoda Junichiro 44–45
Tomu 9, 42, 50
Toshiba Corporation 53
Town with a Cupola, A 165, 188
Toyoda Shiro 139
Tree of Love 52, 188
Tsubosaka Reikenki 82-83
Tsuji Kyuichi 177
Tsukita Ichiro 48
Tsumakawa 2
Tsunoda Tomie 95
Tsuruta Koji 60

Uchida Tomu 9, 42, 50
Ueda Akinari 110, 116
Uehara Ken 60, 67–68
Ugetsu vii, 12, 81, 101, 110, 113–115, 150–151, 164, 166, 176, 181, 183
Umemura Yoko 33, 49, 82, 144
Urayama Kirio 165
Uryu Tadao 89, 97–101
Ushihara Kyohiko 9

Venice Film Festival 8, 110
Victory of Women, The 85, 87–89, 93, 101, 181, 184
Vidor, King 144
Village Tattooed Man, The 65
Von Stroheim, Eric 9

Wada Sanzo 4
Wakabayashi 2
Wakao Ayako 131, 132, 141
Wakayama Osamu 4, 8, 27–29
Walkover 147
Waltz at Noon 149, 188
Wang Zhao Ying 39
Warhol, Andy 147
Warner Brothers 34
Watanabe 3
Watanabe Untei 39
What Made Her Do It? 42, 45, 188
What's Your Name? 92, 188
Whirpool 19
Wild Goose 139, 188
Wilde, Oscar 76
Woman in the Rumour, The 81, 132–134, 139, 151, 182–183
Woman of Osaka, A 11, 78, 81, 82, 83, 84, 184
Woman of Pleasure, A 40, 186
Women of the Night 65, 81, 94, 95, 107, 108, 139, 151, 152, 164, 178, 181, 183
Wonderful Sunday 92, 188
Worrying about Mother 24, 188

Xihou Jiahua 111

Yae-chan, The Next Door Girl 74, 188
Yahiro Fuji 120
Yamada Isuzu 13, 38, 46, 48–49, 61–64, 71–73, 86, 181
Yamagishi Shizue 155
Yamaji Fumiko 39, 51, 63–64, 66, 181
Yamamoto Kaiji 29
Yamamoto Kajiro 9
Yamamura So 67, 93, 134, 181
Yamanaka Sadao 46, 65
Yanagawa Shunyo 21, 23, 39
Yanagi Eijiro 67
Yanagida Kunio 33–34, 115, 118
Yasumi Toshio 93
Yoda Yoshikata 4–6, 11–12, 14, 32, 37, 39, 45, 51–52, 65, 68, 103, 106–107, 110, 113, 120, 127, 129, 137, 139, 141–142, 145, 174, 177–180, 182, 187
Yosano Akiko 34
Yoshikata Yoda Collection of Scripts 103
Yoshikawa Eiji 135, 137
Yoshimura Kosaburo 92, 101
Yoshimura Tetsuo 29
Yoshio 1, 3, 53–54
Yoshiwara Hospital 65
Yoshizawa house 7
Youth Across the River 45, 188
Yuzen Dyes 178

Zentaro 1, 32